THE MENU, FOOD AND PROFIT

Other books by John Fuller published by Stanley Thornes:
Modern Restaurant Service
Essential Table Service

Some other books of interest published by Stanley Thornes:
Basic cookery: The Process Approach   David R Stevenson
Professional cookery: The Process Approach   David R Stevenson
The Prevention of Food Poisoning   Jill Trickett

The Menu, Food and Profit

John Fuller and Keith Waller

Stanley Thornes (Publishers) Ltd

First published in 1991 by:
Stanley Thornes (Publishers) Ltd
Old Station Drive
Leckhampton
CHELTENHAM GL53 ODN
England

British Library Cataloguing in Publication Data
Fuller, John
  The menu, food and profit.
  I. Title   II. Waller, Keith
  647.95

  ISBN 0-7487-1108-2

Typeset by Cambridge Composing (UK) Ltd
Printed and bound in Great Britain at The Bath Press, Avon

The Authors

John Fuller

An experienced author and editor, John Fuller is now an Honorary Visiting Fellow at Oxford Polytechnic. For many years Professor of Hotel Management and Director of the Scottish Hotel School in Strathclyde University he was also a visiting professor in Michigan State University, USA, and Surrey University, and a Chief Technical Adviser for the International Labour Office. His honorary posts included Catering Adviser to the RAF, first elected President of the Hotel, Catering and Institutional Management Association and Chairman of the City and Guilds of London Institute's Advisory Committee for Catering and Food (previously for many years he was one of their chief examiners in catering subjects).

He has advised many governments overseas and has lectured in all five continents.

His awards include the French Medaille du Merite Civique and Chevalier de la Courteoisie Francaise, the USA's Council on Hotel, Restaurant and Institutional Education's International Educator Award and their Howard B. Meek Fellowship. In the UK he is a Life Fellow of the HCIMA and an Honorary Fellow of the City and Guilds of London Institute.

Keith Waller

A Senior Lecturer in the Faculty of Business Food and Management at Blackpool and the Fylde College, Keith Waller has long experience in both craft (as a chef) and management, in both the hotel and institutional sectors of the catering industry. Since his full-time involvement in catering education he has graduated as a BA in Business Studies and has participated in a wide variety of hotel and catering courses up to and including degree-level.

As both an office-holder for the HCIMA in his region and as a Verifier for City and Guilds (NVQ IV) he is keenly aware of commercial realities. His experience is supported by regular returns to industry during academic vacations, and through research and consultancy.

His particular interests include the application of new technology (including computerised control and information processing) to food preparation, production and service. In addition, an interest in open-learning techniques has enabled him to contribute on principles of cooking to the Mastercraft series of publications.

Contents

Preface

There is continuing change in systems of preparation and provision of meals in professional catering. Principles and processes of cookery may endure but by moving their application, in many cases from caterer's premises to food processing plants, the activity and organisation of the professional kitchen is affected. This is reflected in new approaches to staffing, control and accounting, and even in the way in which the final product is marketed. Whatever the future may bring, this book assumes the need for a logical sequence of planning, development, application, control and analysis. The authors recognise the importance of clearly identifying targets, setting objectives and measuring performance as a continuous process in food management. This book's format seeks to conform to that pattern.

Because the catering industry seeks to satisfy many needs, at different cost and price levels, an infinite variety of operational opportunities exist. Consequently, this book recognises the impracticability of providing one simplistic answer to meet all circumstances. It does seek, however, to identify sound general principles and link them with appropriate practical suggestions for their application.

Some, in the catering industry, have long believed that if there are differences between profit and non-profit organisations then different principles and procedures must inevitably apply. *The Menu, Food and Profit* is, however, based on the view that there should be no significant differences in the successful management of any food operation. While some caterers may be subsidised or aim for zero profit (certainly not less), others will aim for wider profit margins. Ideas, and consequently advice, about profitability are directed toward the achievement of objectives and should, therefore, be applicable to all caterers regardless of profit targets.

During their course of study many, if not most, catering students are involved in the practical management of a food preparation and service activity (possibly an 'event'). Full-time students may undertake this as an assessed assignment; part-timers will experience it at work. This book's sequence, as indicated in the opening paragraph above, also seeks to parallel this practical aspect in its linkage of market identification, theme design, planning a menu, product development, company purchasing, materials control and analysis of costs and sales.

Despite its early preoccupation with traditional craft skills and classical dish preparation, catering education has, especially in more recent years, recognised the need to develop a wider business understanding whilst maintaining appropriately high professional standards. Colleges and the examining bodies have played a prominent part in ensuring the development of successful, profitable food operations. Thus, this book aims to meet the needs of students following both full-time and part-time courses of study, and especially those at NVQ Levels 3 and 4, including City and Guilds of London 7062 and 7063, Professional Cookery and Master Chef courses; BTEC National and Higher Diplomas, and National and Higher Certificates in Hotel, Catering and Institutional Management; HCIMA Certificate and Diploma courses; and Degrees.

John Fuller and **Keith Waller**

Acknowledgements

The authors are grateful for help and advice from colleagues in teaching and in industry, and particularly to: Mike Coyle, Principal Lecturer, Blackpool and the Fylde College; John Cousins, Head of Department of Hotel and Catering Management, Ealing College; Graham Hague, District Catering Manager, Blackpool, Wyre and Fylde Health Authority; and David Singleton, Commercial Director, Whitbread Restaurants.

Among firms and organisations which kindly responded to enquiries and requests for illustrative and/or textual material and to whom thanks are due are: HCIMA Library Services; the Department of Health and Social Security; the Ministry of Agriculture, Fisheries and Food; the British Nutrition Foundation; the Dairy Produce Advisory Service; the National Dairy Council; the Butter Information Council Ltd; Peerless Food Products; the Danish Dairy Board; the Sea Fish Industry Authority; the Shellfish Association of Great Britain; the Meat and Livestock Commission; the National Association of Catering Butchers; New Zealand Lamb Meat Producers Board, Catering Advisory Service; the Bacon and Meat Manufacturers Association; the British Chicken Information Service; the Potato Marketing Board; the Flour Advisory Bureau; the Coffee Information Centre; the Tea Council Information Service; Whitbread Plc (Retail Division); McDonalds; Booker Food Services; the Institute of Purchasing and Supply; CMB Foodcan Plc; the British Egg Information Service; the North West Regional Health Authority, Regional Purchasing Department – Hotel Services.

Also acknowledged is the use made of material from John Fuller's *Professional Kitchen Management* (Batsford, 1981, now out of print), especially Part 3 – Foods, Menus and Control, and consequently to colleagues from the Universities of Surrey and Strathclyde, and Oxford Polytechnic, in the UK and the Universities of Cornell and Michigan State in the USA, who gave help in that work.

CHAPTER 1

Markets and Policies

In order to be successful, caterers need to identify the market in which they are to compete, taking note of social issues, developments and trends. A necessary early step in the catering cycle (see Figure 1.1) is to draw a 'typical' customer profile, and identify interesting and imaginative menu items which appeal to that type of customer. Price will offer both value to the customer and profit opportunity to the caterer. Production systems, staff and resources must be suited to the needs of the menu. Continuous review and analysis of sales will provide the necessary information (about customer satisfaction and profitability) for the caterer to continue improving performance (see Chapter 10).

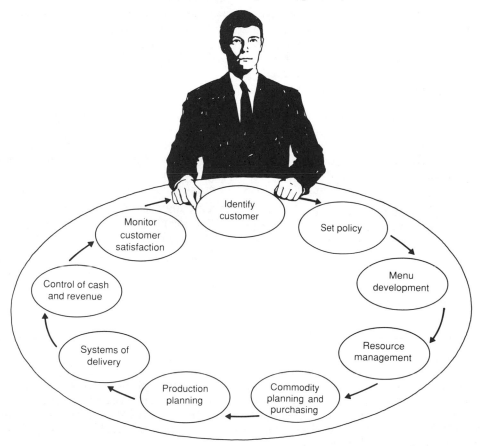

Figure 1.1 *The catering cycle: a continuous process for which the customer provides both the trigger and the target*

MARKETING

Each company will respond to market opportunities with different strategies. In many cases, for the larger organisations, market assessment will lead to diversification based on market identification and strong 'brand' images. For example, in Figure 1.2 the range of operations ensures that the widest possible variety of opportunities appeal to the maximum number of customers.

Whilst the benefits of a large organisation are retained each operation will have its own individual character and style aiming for high quality at each level, based on customer expectations drawn from the customer profile. Although the kitchen manager or chef may not be directly involved in the marketing process they should understand how the market they are serving is derived and defined.

SOCIAL ISSUES

A catering operation is influenced by its environment, consequently the menu-planner must be alert to current social issues. For example, caterers have been aware of the needs of ethnic customers and vegetarians for some time. With the growth of the 'green' movement in society, healthy eating will become a greater influence on the planning of menus. Caterers may not only have to provide dishes free of, or less dependent on, meat, but should also be conscious of the amount and type of fat present in food, whether or not their raw materials have been produced organically, as well as being able to identify a variety of flavours and colourings (the so-called E numbers).

Developments in food legislation are not only doing more to protect the consumer, but are also raising public awareness of possible dangers. Customers generally are becoming increasingly aware of healthy eating and food hygiene or, more precisely, the results of poor hygiene leading to the risk of food poisoning. Terms like 'salmonella' and 'lysteria' are known and understood by today's customer. A modern menu-writer should seek to ensure that the menu selection on offer does not place undue stress on the production system, such that the risk of contamination is increased by poor procedures.

All this must be done in such a way as to generate a reasonable profit. In the welfare sector, caterers will have to compete on an increasingly commercial basis. The menu-maker will have to respond to demands for value for money.

DEMAND AND CHANGE

All caterers are now more likely to respond to market demands, regardless of whether they are concerned with making a profit or not. As the industry has grown and become more competitive its customers have become more critical. In order to be successful, the caterer needs not only to cook and present food well but must also offer consistent quality at a reasonable price. This may be achieved through increased efficiency and cost reduction. Striving for greater efficiency leads to pressure for change.

Within the catering industry there are four main elements of change:

- Food – The search for low cost/high profit alternatives and the response to developing trends, like healthy eating and organic produce.
- Menu – Responding to customer needs. With the exception of formal dinners the menu should be short, cheerful, based around a theme and offer good value for money. The menu-writer should be ever-ready to respond to current issues and trends.
- Catering system – A reflection of the demands of the menu, products offered and type of raw material purchased (level of convenience).
- Technology – Developments in food processing and equipment place greater emphasis on the need to re-examine current production systems and menus.

Roasting, the oldest form of cookery, has changed considerably in relation to developments in technology. Wheels, pulleys and spits modified the open fire technique. Ovens, gas, electricity and thermostats meant further changes, not just in cooking technique but also to the type and size of meat joints used. Convection, microwaves, combination steamer/ovens and the use of probes to measure core temperature result in continuing modifications to cookery techniques. Roasting can now be automated and applied to a wider range of meat cuts, resulting in precise standards, less shrinkage and improved yield.

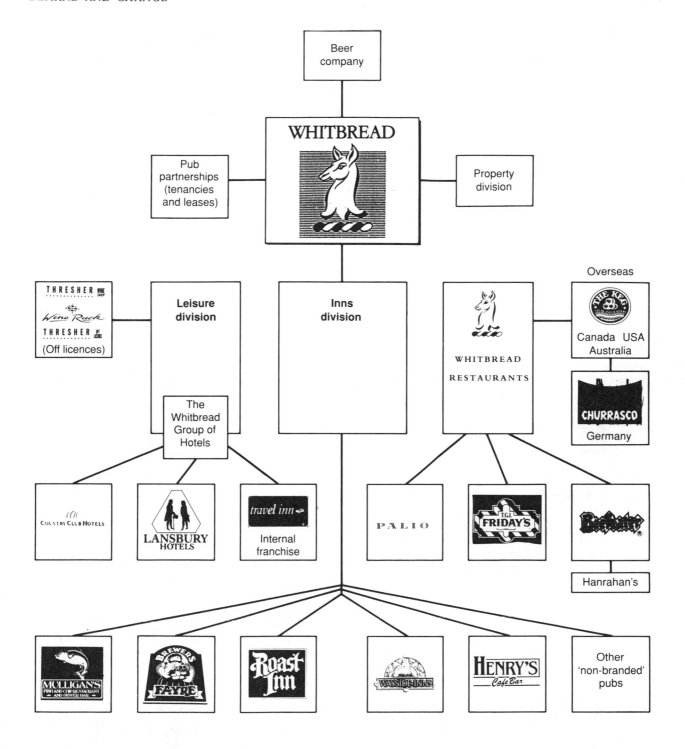

Figure 1.2   *Market opportunities: diversification; brand image; product differentiation*

More and more, today's customers are looking for greater variety and value for money as indicated by the growth in ethnic and budget restaurants. Customers are becoming increasingly more knowledgeable, influenced perhaps by the greater range of prepared 'classic' dishes to be found on the supermarket shelves, in their experience of foreign travel and the wealth of written and broadcast material on cooking, health and diet to be found in newspapers, magazines, bookshops, and on television and radio.

In order to be competitive, caterers will have to be more responsive to change and use the menu to market their products more effectively.

CUSTOMER PROFILE

Market surveys and research to determine customer needs and the operations potential to meet them are essential in determining the type of customer to be attracted and retained. Dividing a market into segments will enable the caterer to target menus more acurately. Segments may be based on such concepts as age, disposable income, leisure activity, social/political beliefs or any other factor which may enable individuals to be identified as belonging to a 'group'.

Menus may sometimes have to be sufficiently extensive to satisfy the needs of a clientele of almost all ages from children to senior citizens. They need to satisfy the finicky appetite of semi-invalids or the robust hunger of athletes and holidaymakers. Upmarket hotels for many years devised menus of wide enough appeal to cater for almost all clientele, whatever their nutritional requirements or appetite. In other professional kitchens, whether in restaurants, hotels, schools, canteens or hospitals, more particular knowledge of the type of customer to be catered for is of paramount importance. The immature palates and larger appetites of school children impose menu-making conditions different from those which confront the caterer responsible for the meals of a large office dining-room in which female staff might predominate.

> Some companies are clearly synonymous with a particular customer profile. For example, Happy Eater are equated with children (economical family meals on the move). Note the logo and positioning of restaurant sites.

Where there is considerable competition among caterers for a particular market segment they may encourage customers to discriminate through product differentiation, i.e. the special characteristics of one product that make it different from other similar products. For example, the burger in McDonalds will contain dill pickle, the bun in Wimpy may be wholemeal and the meat in Burger King will be flame-grilled.

Chefs' and caterers' taste for, and choice of, food does not always coincide with that of their guests. At least one famous chef-patron has registered public disaproval of those who require well-done steaks or seek to modify the garnish of a dish. Inevitably, caterers may want to cajole customers onto a more discriminating approach to food and menus. Discrete steps tend to work better than overt missionary zeal. Practical measures that usually work are:

- prepare, cook and serve as superbly as possible that which is known and liked by the customers;
- gradually introduce new items only as alternatives to proven favourites.

Violent assaults on customers' dining habits may seldom be successful in either commercial or welfare catering, but hyper-caution can be equally undesirable. Innovation should not inevitably be left to other caterers.

> A loss-making food operation in one large city-centre hotel prompted the Food and Beverage Manager to muse 'Why try to please everyone?' By offering a limited table d'hôte he lowered kitchen preparation costs, reduced service costs, and though tripling business volume, increased food costs by only 2 per cent.

A questioning approach should be adopted:
- Who are your customers?
- What do they eat?
- How much do they spend?
- Is lunch different to dinner? How? Why?

In many instances the lunch-time operation, particularly the menu, will be different to the evening business when research leads to a different customer being identified. Often this is the difference between a business lunch and a social evening. Where the menu remains the same for lunch and dinner, it is probable that popularity of individual items will differ as will the average spend.

Thus considering the customer involves giving thought to:
- nutritional considerations;
- meeting local tastes;
- responding to wider social issues;
- attracting custom and promoting business.

THE MENU AS A FOCUS OF ACTIVITY

It may be argued that our lives are governed by menus. Although not identified as such, the television page in the daily paper, a personal organiser of appointments, a list of treatments in a dentist's surgery and a brochure from a holiday company, are just a few examples of 'menus'. Each allows us to choose an activity or sequence of events. Each informs of likely outcomes and/or possible benefits. Some inform us of price. However, for most people, the term 'menu' remains synonymous with lists of food or bills of fare.

A familiar anecdote credits Henry, Duke of Brunswick as the originator of the written menu. In the mid-sixteenth century he required courses and dishes to be listed in order to regulate or plan his pattern of dining. To be aware of what was to come helped eliminate early over-indulgence and spread enjoyment throughout the meal. Whenever or however the written bill of fare orginated, for caterers and their clients alike the menu is now an established linchpin in meeting the needs of those eating away from home.

A menu indicates the limitations of a catering service, for as the French academic and writer Leo Dardarian observed (*Put Profit on the Menu*, Ahrens, 1959) 'the best of all possible restaurants would have no menu at all. Or, if it did, would probably have an infinite number of selections . . . to please every conceivable type of patron.'

To the customer today the purpose of a menu is unchanged from when it was first used by the medieval diner. It outlines the scope and order of the meal. To a gourmet, a menu may read like poetry; to a more down-to-earth eater it may be a mundane indicator of the price to be paid for the food served. But for both these extremes and between them, a menu must fulfil its function of accurately communicating or informing a diner about what is on offer. Indeed the menu can, and usually should, incorporate other sales messages about house wine, function facilities and so on.

The American academic and writer Seaberg reminded us (*Institutions Magazine*, USA) that the menu is an extremely common method of communication. Hence there is a danger of it being taken for granted by the compiler and the reader which demands constant vigilance from the caterer. As for food items, whatever language style is used the menu's terms should be precise and intended to illuminate rather than obscure.

Kitchen blueprint

For the caterer, a menu evolves from and expresses a particular catering policy. The menu also briefs the staff and determines the staffing level required to fulfil the catering intention. The menu will also determine the selection and layout of kitchen plant and equipment. 'Menu justification' has been cited on more than one occasion as a primary consideration in operational planning.

Steps in menu planning

The development of a menu after its marketing thrust has been determined normally starts with a first draft. Subsequent stages will lead to product planning, costing and pricing (considered in Chapter 3) and food-buying specifications (considered in Chapter 4). A final version of the menu considers all these factors. When the menu is completed, its effectiveness must be monitored. Actual costs and sales records constitute the raw material, as it were, for reviewing and revising the menu (considered in Chapter 10). As part of a basic food operations plan, factors about the menu must, where possible, be established ahead of any physical layout and equipment planning.

These factors include:

- style and quality of the menu;
- whether à la carte, table d'hôte or a blend of both;
- menu range related to number, variety and standard of dishes;
- preparation and cooking of each dish in terms of recipes, portions, quantities and service style;
- speciality items to be featured (for advance planning of appropriate equipment);
- extent of processed and convenience foods usage (i.e. kind and quantities of foods to be produced and served determined so that requirements, in terms of processes and equipment, can be efficiently planned);
- style/method of service.

The various kitchen sections (or parties) receiving advance copies of the menus will plan their work according to its requirements. From their point of view, as much as from the customers', it is disastrous if its language is ambiguous or lacking in meaning.

In many operations the chef is still the menu-maker. In such cases, menus should be composed according to a clear catering policy expressed by the proprietor or management. A chef's menu composing will have to take into account cost, pricing and profit constraints, plus other constraints relating to purchasing and dish merchandising.

The aim must always be for consistent, achievable quality, not just of the food but of the total meal experience. The caterer will seek to understand why people choose to eat away from home and what influences their meal preference. Once identified, the factors that contribute to the enjoyment of the meal can and should be promoted through the menu.

PROMOTING BUSINESS WITH THE MENU

Kitchen craftsmen and women can become over-concerned with the minutae of balance in organoleptic and gastronomic terms, but in professional catering balance must be put into context. Balance is one feature of the menu in its role as the great silent salesman fulfilling a whole complex of purposes. However, gastronomy and sales are not incompatible. A good menu is not only a piece of advertising or publicity, but by helping create appetite it can lure customers to the table. Occasionally a menu may have enough individuality to create a stir and achieve publicity outside the establishment, even if only in the catering trade press.

To do its job, a menu should have visual appeal. Attention to style, design, typography and printing is obviously a matter for the relevant experts, but this does not mean that practical people in catering should not seek to be closely involved in all possibilities of business promotion through an effective menu.

It is not uncommon for food and beverage managers to seek ideas, price comparisons and layout tips from the menu examples of their competitors. But simply to find out what the other caterer is charging or what size and style they have chosen for actual menu cards or display material are only the beginnings of menu consciousness.

Awareness of menu development nationally and internationally, at all levels, means intelligent appraisal of as many relevant menu examples as can be obtained, including monitoring the trade press. Critically looking at external menus involves far more than a quest for howlers in colour repetition or nit-picking over misplaced French accents. Try to make a total evaluation of the menu's effectiveness, not only in its gastronomic balance but in the context of show case, shop window or silent sales aspects.

Some features which the chef and others in the management team should think about include:

- House specialities – these should be rigidly specified and uniform in size and quality through the use of standardised recipes.
- Fresh local produce – be sure that the case for featuring local foods has been properly considered and that the product served is genuinely local in origin.
- Promoting desserts – consider having a separate menu for puddings and sweets. Customers might choose to miss the starter in order to reserve appetite for the sweet. Starters will appear more tempting if they do not have to compete with the sweet course.
- Novelty – tune the menu to modern trends. Search for something new. Balance innovations with old favourites.
- Family business – do not ignore the young as they are often an effective way of reaching the parents. Junior portions and special dishes are appropriate in many operations.
- Choice monitoring – use sales history and other market research techniques to learn what items are most frequently chosen and use this information to streamline the menu's range (see Chapter 10).
- Identifying 'dodos' – do not include items on the menu which are obsolete or do not sell well, no matter how attractive they may appear.

A LA CARTE

Hors d'oeuvre
Salade Niçoise	£1.80
Avocat Singapore	£2.00
Saumon fumé au pain bis	£2.50
Truite fumée, sauce raifort	£2.20
Crevettes Marie Rose	£2.10
Pot de crevettes au beurre	£1.80
Terrine de foies de volaille	£1.80
Foie gras de Strasbourg	£3.00
Assiette de saucisson	£2.00
Jambon de Parme et melon	£2.50

Potages
Crème de champignons	£1.80
Consommé Madrilène	£1.80
Tortue claire au paillettes	£2.00
Bisque de homard	£2.20

Oeufs, pâtés alimentaires et riz
Oeuf en cocotte forestiére	£1.20
Omelette au choix	£2.00
Spaghetti Bolognese	£1.80
Risotto au foies de volaille	£1.50

Poissons
Truite amandine	£8.50
Filet de sole Dugléré	£9.00
Sole de Douvre Colbert	£10.50
Goujons de plie, tartare	£9.00
Filet de plie meunière	£8.50
Scampi provençale	£10.00
Darne de saumon pochée	£11.00
Homard thermidor	£12.50

Entrées
Escalope de veau Cordon Bleu	£12.50
Suprême de volaille Lapérouse	£10.50
Tournedos Rossini	£12.50
Noisette de porc Normande	£10.00
Foie de veau Lyonnaise	£9.50
Entrecôte chasseur	£10.50
Filet de boeuf au poivre vert	£11.50
Rognons sautées Turbigo	£10.00
Entrecôte minute Diane	£12.00

Grillades et rôtis
Entrecôte maitre d'hotel	£10.00
Filet de boeuf, Bernaise	£12.00
Châteaubriande garni (2)	£20.00
Côte de porc verte-pré	£9.00
Côtelettes d'agnea grillée	£9.00
Poussin rôti à l'Anglaise	£8.00
Caneton rôti, sauce pommes	£9.50
Carré d'agneau persillé (2)	£17.50

Pommes et legumes
Pommes nature	£1.00	Petits pois	£1.00
Pommes purée	£1.00	Broccolis au beurre	£1.50
Pommes sautées	£1.20	Haricots vert	£1.20
Pommes croquette	£1.20	Chou-fleur mornay	£1.50
Pommes frites	£1.00	Courgettes glacées	£1.20

Desserts et fromage
Salade des fruits	£1.00	Vacherin au fraises	£1.50
Poire belle Hélène	£2.00	Cerises jubilée	£2.20
Crèpes Suzette	£2.50	Baba au rhum	£2.20
	Fromage au choix	£1.50	

Café
Viennois	£1.20
Décaféiné	£1.20
Espresso	£1.50
Liqueur coffee	£2.20
Tea (various)	£1.00

Figure 1.3 *A la carte menu*

MENU CONSTRUCTION – TRENDS AND DEVELOPMENTS

Two types of menu are readily recognised – 'à la carte' and 'table d'hôte'. An à la carte menu (shown in Figure 1.3 on the previous page) offers a selection of independently-priced dishes from which customers, by exercising choice, construct their own menu pattern. A la carte may involve delay in service, for example grills and sautés may take up to 20 minutes to be cooked. Table d'hôte (shown in Figure 1.4) is today's version of the 'ordinary' and is derived from the long-standing 'host's table' of the old-time inn. It is a set menu at a fixed price, with much less choice. As these dishes have all been prepared for the host's table there should be no need to wait while they are cooked.

Menu styles

Traditional ideas remain, but today menu-planners aim to limit the number of items on the menu and to co-ordinate different menus used in any one operation, in order to minimise production procedures and problems. Thus, today's menu can be one of several types. In addition to à la carte (short or extensive) and table d'hôte, there may be variants such as:

- a selective menu plan (see Figure 1.5)
- a static menu; (see Figure 1.6 on pages 10 and 11)
- a cyclical menu; (see Figure 1.7 on page 13)
- a market menu.

Doubtless, other terms than those listed above will enter catering jargon to describe menu variants.

Figure 1.4   *Table d'hôte menu*

STARTERS

Chilled melon
Half a charentais melon, served on a bed of ice, with ginger and/or sugar if you wish

Stuffed mushrooms
Local mushrooms stuffed with onion, garlic, herbs and breadcrumbs before being coated and fried

Soup of the day
Our soups are produced from fresh ingredients. Our staff will be happy to describe today's speciality to you

Vegetable satay
Aubergine, courgette, pepper, mushrooms and onion, marinated with herbs and spices and then lightly grilled and served garnish with salad and a sauce of sour cream and chives

MAIN COURSE

The main course price includes your choice of starter and sweet

Fried scampi   £10.00
*Whole fresh scampi tails, crumbed and fried until golden,
served with your coice of sauce – tartare, sweet and sour or tomato*

Grilled lamb chops £11.00
Choice English lamb chops, grilled and presented with a garnish of grilled tomato and watercress

Entrecôte steak £12.50
Prime Scotch beef, cut from the loin, grilled to your choice, served with fried onion rings and mushrooms

Southern fried chicken £10.00
Crumbed and crisply fried, this dish is served with bacon, sweetcorn fritters and tomato chutney

Grilled gammon £10.50
Prime, lightly smoked gammon, cooked and presented with pineapple

All of the above are served with chips or jacket potatoes, peas, green beans or a selection from the salad bar.

DESSERT

Triple sorbet
Orange, lemon and raspberry sorbet

Swiss apple flan
Apples cooked with sultanas in a sweet, crumbly, pastry

Blackforest gâteau
Chocolate gâteau with cherries and cream, and just a hint of kirsch

Cheeseboard
Various British and Continental cheeses, served with biscuits

Coffee or tea

Figure 1.5   *Selective menu*

MAIN COURSES

All main courses except those marked with ★ are served with: Peas plus a choice of jacket potato (with butter or sour cream and chives) or buttered new potatoes (in their skins) or french fries; or you may choose a Continental or Mixed Salad.

For main courses marked ★ accompaniments are as stated in the menu description.

Summer Selection

Each season at Beefeater you'll discover a range of dishes highlighted as seasonal selections. These dishes have been specially chosen either for their seasonal flavour or to offer something a little different.

GREEK CHICKEN WITH LAMB KEBAB £7.65

A tender chicken breast in a Greek style marinade of yogurt, cucumber and mint accompanied by a very tasty kebab of 3 tender lamb pieces marinated in yogurt and mint skewered with courgettes and red peppers. Served with mushrooms and a dipper pot of yogurt and cucumber dressing.

SUMMER SALMON £7.85

A real Summer classic – delicately poached fillet of salmon served cold with a Lollo Rosso salad and a sauce boat of delicious mayonnaise style dill dip. Served with buttered new potatoes in their skins and garnished with a lemon wedge.

STEAKS

All our prime quality steaks are grilled to your liking and garnished with mushrooms, watercress and tomato. All weights are approximate before cooking.

RUMP STEAK 8oz £8.35
12oz £10.75

Offered to you as a standard 8oz steak or 12oz for the larger appetite.

PEPPERED STEAK £9.25

For those who like steak with a difference we offer an 8oz rump steak dusted with crushed peppercorns, and served with a boat of our special creamy peppercorn sauce.

SIRLOIN STEAK 6oz £7.65
8oz £9.25

Succulent top quality sirloin for you to enjoy as a standard 8oz steak or 6oz for the smaller appetite.

T-BONE STEAK 14oz £11.50

You'll need a healthy appetite to handle our T-Bone – 14ozs of prime steak!

FILLET STEAK 8oz £11.25

Our finest quality steak for you to enjoy

CHICKEN

MARINATED CHICKEN £7.20

A tender chicken breast is marinated in carefully chosen spices, then grilled and garnished with mushrooms.

CHICKEN OSCAR℠ £8.45

A Beefeater speciality and a firm favourite. A double chicken breast, grilled and topped with Hollandaise sauce containing broccoli florets, prawns, smoked salmon and snowcrab. Garnished with mushrooms.

CHICKEN KIEV £7.40

We take a succulent chicken breast, fill it with tangy garlic butter, coat it with breadcrumbs and deep fry until golden brown. Garnished with mushrooms.

FISH

FILLET OF PLAICE £6.25

A choice fillet of plaice, freshly battered and deep fried until golden brown. Garnished with a lemon wedge.

FRIED SCAMPI £7.25

A generous portion of succulent scampi breadcrumbed and deep fried. Garnished with a lemon wedge.

SALMON TROUT WITH WHITE WINE AND BASIL SAUCE £8.45

A grilled 7oz Salmon Trout fillet, served with a boat of creamy white wine and basil sauce, garnished with a lemon wedge.

VEGETARIAN

★VEGETABLE TIKKA MASALA £5.99

For this special Indian dish, we take a selection of vegetables and combine them with a sauce made with tomato, cream and yogurt, flavoured with herbs and mildly spiced. Served with delicately flavoured basmati rice and a spicy poppadom.

★PASTA LUCANA £6.15

A must for pasta lovers. A combination of pasta twists in a tomato and vegetable sauce, smothered in a vegetarian cheese sauce and topped with a crispy crumb. Served with salad and two slices of garlic bread.

OTHER DISHES

BEEFEATER MIXED GRILL £8.65

A traditional mixed grill containing rump steak, lamb cutlet, sausage and a gammon steak garnished with mushrooms.

GAMMON STEAK £6.65

A tasty 8oz gammon steak garnished with a pineapple ring.

RACK OF LAMB £8.15

A lean and succulent 6 rib rack of lamb grilled as you wish, served with mushrooms and your choice of cranberry and redcurrant jelly or mint sauce.

Figure 1.6 *Static menu – Beefeater Summer Menu (Courtesy of Whitbread Restaurants)*

SIDE ORDERS

CONTINENTAL SALAD £1.00
Iceberg lettuce, white and red cabbage, cucumber, endive and radicchio.

MIXED SALAD £1.25
Iceberg lettuce, white and red cabbage, cucumber, endive, radicchio, celery, tomato, sweetcorn, kidney beans and croutons.

Continental and Mixed salads are served with a CHOICE of DRESSINGS: French; Thousand Island; Blue Cheese; Green Goddess; Ranch or Honey and Tomato.

CAESAR SALAD £1.35
A delicious salad combining iceberg lettuce, white and red cabbage, endive and radicchio. All tossed in a smooth creamy garlic dressing topped with croutons and a sprinkling of parmesan cheese.

MUSHROOMS £1.00
GOLDEN ONION RINGS £1.00
A dish of crisp breaded onion rings.

GARLIC BREAD £1.10
3 slices of crisp french bread topped with garlic and herb flavoured butter

FOR OUR YOUNGER GUESTS

For our young guests up to the age of 14, we have this special menu selection which is of the same quality as our main menu – but in slightly smaller portions – all served with peas and a choice of jacket potato, or french fries; or with a Continental or Mixed salad; a choice of roll and butter or crispbread; soft vanilla ice cream† topped with raspberry, butterscotch or chocolate sauce with nuts.

RUMP STEAK (5oz) £5.60

FRIED SCAMPI (Half Portion) £4.35

CRUNCHY CHICKEN FINGERS £3.99
Served with a barbecue sauce.

HAPPY DAYS BURGER £3.99
A 4oz beefburger in a bun, with lettuce and tomato relish.

Mr Men Meals £1.99
This special meal is available for the very young. Mr Men meals are served at lunchtime and until 7.30 in the evening to children who are accompanied by an adult taking a main meal in the restaurant. Please, no more than 3 children for each adult restaurant diner unless a prior arrangement has been agreed with the manager.

Mr Men meals are completely free from artificial colours and flavourings.

Weights shown are approximate before cooking.
†*Our ice cream contains non-milk fat.*

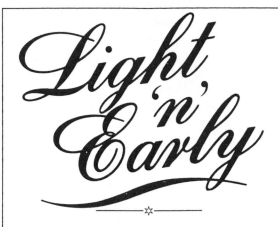

This menu is available Monday to Saturday at lunchtime and until 7.30 in the evening.

All Light 'n' Early Selections are served with a choice of french fries, jacket potato, buttered new potatoes (in their skins) or garlic and herb bread.

Also included in the price is a soft vanilla ice cream† topped with raspberry, butterscotch or chocolate sauce with nuts.

SALAD BOWLS
Our salad bowls are made from a selection of Lollo Rosso, iceberg lettuce, white and red cabbage, cucumber, endive, radicchio, celery, tomato, sweetcorn, and kidney beans dressed in a light mayonnaise.

Topped with either:-

HOT FILLET £5.15
Strips of spicy marinated fillet steak, grilled and combined with sliced mushrooms
or

HOT CHICKEN FILLET £4.95
Succulent and tasty strips of grilled chicken fillet, garnished with a twist of orange
or

KING PRAWN SALAD ROYALE £5.35
A stunning combination of tuna, prawns, smoked mackerel and smoked trout topped with five King Prawns and our special seafood sauce. Garnished with tomatoes and a lemon wedge.

STEAK & KIDNEY PIE £4.25
A traditional British favourite. Tender steak and kidney in a rich gravy, topped with light puff pastry in a deep earthenware dish. Served with peas.

ROAST CHICKEN £4.25
A quarter of succulent roast chicken accompanied by a boat of rich gravy and served with peas.

FILLET OF COD £4.15
5oz of prime cod, deep fried in batter and served with peas and a dipper pot of tangy tartare sauce.

Figure 1.6 *Static menu – Beefeater Summer Menu (cont.)*

The chief modification, as observed before, is reduction in menu choice on all types of menu. This may be linked with attempts to interpret customer demand more accurately. Such menus concentrate on most-frequently chosen dishes.

The selective menu compromise

A compromise between table d'hôte and à la carte involves pricing the meal by reference to the main menu item. In selling, menu price may be determined by the main course item that is chosen. A selective menu plan (see Figure 1.5) could take the following form:

- five or six appetizers;
- seven or eight entrées (the main item to determine price), with a selection of vegetables and/or salads in addition;
- seven or eight puddings/desserts, or cheese and biscuits;
- coffees or other beverages.

Although no price is identified for appetizers and puddings these are not given away. Care must be taken to ensure that their cost is taken into account when pricing the main item. Ideally there should be little difference between the cost of each unpriced item. This method requires a careful approach to costing which may restrict other menu objectives, such as artistry and creativity. Suplementary pricing is often used to allow the caterer to include items (appetizers and puddings) which do not easily fit into the pricing structure.

Static menu suitablility

Many caterers, especially those operating steak houses, themed operations, carveries and other speciality restaurants, may adopt a static menu (see Figure 1.6). Although unchanging, such menus achieve public acceptance through their predictability. For caterers, they facilitate an accurate forecast of demand and the restricted range of dishes enables kitchen and service staff to gain expertise quickly. Moreover, costs can be more easily monitored and controlled. Although less frequent, however, adjustments and alterations need to be effected from time to time even on static menus. Menu monitoring involving sales history, cost and price appraisal must be just as actively applied as to any other kind of menu.

Care should be taken to identify evidence of 'menu fatigue' – items which are no longer popular – and any consequent reduction in the attractiveness of the menu as a whole.

The cyclical approach

Cyclical menus (see Figure 1.7) are those whose pre-determined form is repeated or rotated. Style (and items chosen for inclusion) is most frequently influenced by season, but the number of changes per year will be decided by each caterer according to the needs of customers and the length of each cycle (two, three or four weeks). Thus various patterns emerge, the aim being to simplify menu writing and control whilst maintaining customer interest and appreciation.

Caterers must decide for themselves how long each cycle should be and the number of times each cycle is run for. It is advisable, however, not to create too long a cycle. As a rough guide, each cycle should run three of four times. After repetition of a two-week cycle, three or four times, the season will be over and a new set of menus will be needed. For clear identification, menus may be numbered, for example, Winter Cycle 1, Lunch Menu 10. After careful analysis to identify menu fatigue, changes in cost and profitability, the cycle may be used again, perhaps with minor adjustments, when that particular season returns.

This type of menu is most common in the welfare sector where numbers are fairly static and reasonably accurate forecasts may be made, thus facilitating the benefits of large-scale contract purchasing (considered in Chapter 4).

Cyclical menus require careful planning. The repetition of each dish or menu item in the same context with other dishes enables better conclusions to be reached regarding dish popularity. A menu-maker can thus more accurately forecast how much of each item to prepare for the day's business.

As a prime purpose of cyclical menus is to gauge dish popularity, they must be supported by a sales record. Sales history enables best-selling items to be used more often and poor-selling ones to be eliminated.

Market responsiveness in menus

Market menus are those particularly responsive to season and availability. Many chefs believe in the personal appraisal of fresh produce and base their menus on daily visits to the markets, in order to make their selection, before completing their menus. Market menus were especially associated with the

VICTORIA HOSPITAL	WEEK A MON.		WARD	Name

COOKED BREAKFAST

SELECT ONE

1. Chilled Orange Juice DRF (10)
2. Grapefruit Segments DRF (10)
3. Porridge DRF * (15)
4. Cornflakes DRF (15)
5. Branflakes DRF * (15)
6.

COOKED – PLEASE SELECT

7. Grilled Pork Sausage D (5)
8. Baked Beans DR (10)

BREAD

9. Wholemeal DRF * OR (15)
10. White DRF (15)

Butter DRF   Jam F   Marmalade F

PORTION:–
NORMAL
SMALL

D = DIABETIC
R = REDUCING
F = LOW FAT
* = HIGH FIBRE

OR CHOOSE FROM A LIGHT BREAKFAST CHOICE

SELECT ONE

11. Chilled Orange Juice DRF (10)
12. Grapefruit Segments DRF (10)
13. Porridge DRF * (15)
14. Cornflakes DRF (15)
15. Branflakes DRF * (15)

SELECT ONE

16. Wholemeal Roll DRF * (15)
17. Croissant

Butter DRF   Jam F   Marmalade F

VICTORIA HOSPITAL	WEEK A MON.		WARD	Name

STARTER

Chilled Grapefruit Juice DRF   OR (10)
1. Homemade Vegetable Soup DRF (10)

MAIN COURSE – SELECT ONE

2. Homemade Pork & Apple Casserole DRF
3. Baked Salmon Fishcake with Parsley Suace DRF (20)
4. Country Vegetable Pie made with Flaky Pastry D (20)
5.

WITH

6. Chipped Potatoes
7. Creamed Potatoes DRF (10)
8. Sliced Green Beans DRF
9.

ALTERNATIVE MAIN COURSE

10. Homemade Vegetable Soup with Crusty Roll DRF (30)
11. Corned Beef Salad with Beetroot D   WITH
12. Wholemeal Bread and Butter DRF * (15)

PORTION:–
NORMAL
SMALL

D = DIABETIC
R = REDUCING
F = LOW FAT
* = HIGH FIBRE

SWEETS – SELECT ONE

Gooseberry Pie made with Wholemeal
13. Pastry   WITH
14. Custard Sauce DRF (10)
15. Rice Pudding DRF (20)
16. Ice Cream D (10)
17. Fresh Fruit (Dessert Apple) DRF (10)

SAUCES

Salad Cream Portion
Brown Sauce Portion
Tomato Sauce Portion

NOW YOU HAVE FINISHED WITH YOUR MEAL WAS IT?

Excellent   Fair
Good   Poor

VICTORIA HOSPITAL	WEEK A MON.		WARD	Name

STARTER

1. Chicken Soup DRF (10)

MAIN COURSE – SELECT ONE

2. Cottage Pie with Potato & Carrot Topping with Gravy DRF (20)
3. Mushroom & Courgette Vol–au–Vent D (20)
4. Mushroom & Courgette in Sauce (Diets Only)

WITH

5. Creamed Potatoes (Diets Only) DRF (10)
6. Mixed Peas and Corn DRF

ALTERNATIVE MAIN COURSE

7. Egg & Cress Sandwich on white bread DRF (30)
8. Gala Pie with Side Salad & Pickled Onions D (10)
9.
10. Wholemeal Bread and Butter DRF * (15)

PORTION:–
NORMAL
SMALL

D = DIABETIC
R = REDUCING
F = LOW FAT
* = HIGH FIBRE

SWEETS – SELECT ONE

11. Rhubarb Fool DRF (10)
12. Fruit Scone with Jam
13. Ice Cream D (10)
14. Fruit Yoghurt DRF (10)
15. Cheese and Biscuits DRF (10)

SAUCES

Salad Cream Portion
Brown Sauce Portion
Tomato Sauce Portion

NOW YOU HAVE FINISHED WITH YOUR MEAL WAS IT?

Excellent   Fair
Good   Poor

Figure 1.7   *Part of a cyclical menu – Blackpool Health District*

philosophy of Bocuse and other practitioners of the now less-recent (and less-popular) nouvelle cuisine. Consequently, such menus have been particularly linked with chef-patrons running their own establishments and aiming to appeal to the gastronome (or would be gastronome) though extending from

modest, through middle to higher price levels. However, the market principle may be effectively applied, in conjuction with other types of menu, to the benefit of both caterer and consumer. The well-chosen plat du jour or 'blue plate special' can demonstrate this principle.

The growth of country house hotels has seen a revival of the kitchen garden and in particular the inclusion of fresh garden vegetables and fresh herbs on the menu.

PLANNING CONSIDERATIONS

The menu is the focal point around which all other planning activity revolves. Figure 1.8 identifies those elements of the catering system that, if planned and controlled properly, are likely to result in a successful operation.

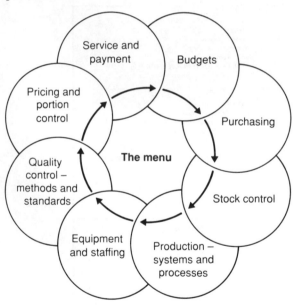

Budgets – set cost and price policy, identify control centres.
Purchasing – set specifications, reveiving and control procedures.
Stock control – security, prevention of waste, loss and fraud.
Production – planned, measurable performance; consistent standards.
Equipment and staffing – tailored to menu and production needs.
Quality control – standardisation of recipes, methods and yields.
Pricing – accurate calculation of real costs plus gross profit.
Service (revenue) – analysis of sales, contribution and profit (% and £).

Figure 1.8   *The menu as a focal point for planning*

Budgets, cost and price

The caterer will endeavour to offer products at a price which will both attract customers and offer a pre-determined level of profit. There are three main influences on price:

- the price charged by competitors;
- the price the customer is prepared to pay;
- the cost of production.

The cost of production is the only element over which the caterer has direct control. If the true cost is known then decisions about pricing are made easier.

It was once thought that food cost was almost the sole factor in the pricing of a meal and certainly the most important. Most caterers today, however, decisively link food cost with labour cost. Because of concern with labour costs, management may make decisions about using processed and pre-portioned foods or be influenced by the advantages of restricted menus. Here it need only be stressed that modern menu-makers will be concerned with devising a menu to produce a desired profit.

Whilst management may set budgets for labour and overheads, define food cost limits and set profit targets, it would be a naive chef who did not recognise that food is only part of the menu cost.

Purchasing

Effective purchasing will have a significant effect on costing, pricing and profitability, and is therefore worthy of detailed consideration (see Chapter 4). Suffice to say at this stage that the following points should be considered when planning the menu.

Availability and season

Ideas about using up foods held in store first and incorporating left-over foods into the menu in, for example, composite (made-up) dishes may have relevance in some operations, but generally food orders and purchases should result from specifications for particular purposes.

Seasonal gluts, particularly of vegetables, are now less important from a control aspect because of new modes of production, marketing, distribution and processing of foods from around the world. Consideration must also be given to the improved quality of convenience products and the associated predictability of price and quality.

Nevertheless, there will be some operations where market menus will be applied to gain cost advantage from what is abundant and fresh. Over and above this consideration, however, is that of gastronomic appeal. Living patterns will determine the need for light, cool fruit desserts in hot weather and substantial stews in bleak weather. Thus it may make sense to recognise seasonal change in menu-making, for gastronomic and nutritional reasons, even when matters of cost and availability are less relevant.

Seasonal relevance in menu-making does not merely involve exploiting available and cheap foods, but of reflecting in the year's menus seasonable rhythm and variety with foods that appeal because they match weather, other current conditions, human moods and desire for variety. Caterers' buying know-how must embrace local knowledge of regional food products, but must also take account of the seasons in countries from which we import. Modern chefs must pay heed to the fruit crops of Africa and Asia, the vegetable crops of the Americas and the Antipodes as well as to the orchards of Kent and the potato fields of Cyprus.

There is nothing complex about designing a menu in sympathy with season, but simple though this is it demands a knowledge of food and an instinct for balance.

Processed food

An important catering aim is to reduce the number of commodities to be purchased, received and stored. Such an aim is best achieved when a commodity has a variety of applications and can fulfil a variety of purposes on a menu.

The principal effects of using processed foods is on the allocation of labour, space, storage facilities and equipment. Less space is needed for handling convenience products. This can concentrate certain kitchen activities, particularly in the larder. When vegetables, fish, meat and poultry are supplied in processed form, the chef's need to allocate work to different sections diminishes. The work of kitchen staff can become increasingly concerned with the final cooking and presentation.

Chefs who at first deplored certain products because they believed them to be artificial or that they reduced the chef's role now recognise that usually only basic chores have been eliminated and that the skills of cooking, finishing and garnishing can remain in their hands. Indeed, they allow even greater care and concentration on the finer points and can help widen the scope of menus.

Stock control

Having purchased raw materials, based on the requirements of the menu, it is important that they are controlled. The level of waste, loss or fraud that exists will influence the profitability of an operation. The menu must be written with stock-holding in mind.

Production systems

The menu and its production system are inextricably linked. Both influence, and are influenced by, staffing, equipment and raw material usage. The objectives of a production system must be to provide the desired product, as and when required by the customer, in the most efficient and effective manner. Consequently, the choice of production system will be determined by answers to two questions:

- What is it that my customers want?
- How can I best provide it?'

If the customer wants a cheap, economical, meal in comfortable surroundings then other considerations like seasonal availability and levels of service may have to take secondary place. The caterer may decide to spend a greater proportion of capital on furnishing the restaurant and reduce the salary bill by employing unskilled staff. As a result of reduced investment in kitchen equipment and the use of unskilled labour the caterer will be influenced toward a 'convenience' system of catering.

This is but one example. The permutations of customer wants and caterer's response are innumerable and it is not possible to offer definitive solutions. However, it is possible to identify basic systems, together with the main elements within each system. The reader may then draw conclusions about how each system may be adapted and elements manipulated, to aid efficiency and effectiveness in any given situation.

The systems approach
(See Figure 1.9.)

System aims are:
- to anticipate operational effectiveness;
- to anticipate likely situations and provide routines for them.

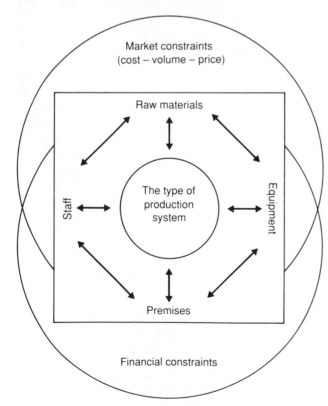

Figure 1.9   *The systems approach*

The work load involves:
- each task to be defined;
- tasks to be grouped to form jobs;
- 'best' methods to be devised, then the regular performance of these methods and a re-examination of their effectiveness;
- the elimination of variables

The ideal system requires:
- that any dish be ready when required;
- consistent quality;
- acceptable costs;
- minimum skill and labour;
- easy-to-operate service arrangements;
- minimal equipment and space requirements;
- quick and simple operational control;
- a high level of customer appeal;
- flexible design providing for ease of adaptation;
- a good profit return on capital in commercial catering, and minimum cost for maximum productivity and customer satisfaction in non-commercial catering.

The formula for a commercial system
The following steps are essential:
- take a familiar food;
- devise a fast, streamlined but sophisticated service;
- offer 'carbon copy' products of high quality at low price;
- provide a simple but attractive setting;
- choose a first-class location (site selection);
- provide support with extensive merchandising;
- ensure that tight controls provide for quick answers.

(Most of the above points are also applicable to non-commercial operations.)

Such a system should result in:
- a high turnover;
- low overheads;
- a good return on the capital invested.

A production system may be thought of as a cycle, the operational cycle, of a catering enterprise. There is a definite cycle which applies to all types of catering; it encompasses the flow of work and the path or progress of raw material through to finished product (see Figure 1.10). The traditional partie system was dependent on high staffing levels. Emphasis on preparation and cooking demanded a high degree of demarcation and specialisation, supported by a ready supply of cheap labour. Labour, even unskilled, has now become an expensive commodity. At the same time high-level technology has been greatly under-utilised in the catering industry. New cooking methods, techniques and equipment have emerged.

Although the elements of the production cycle still remain, emphasis has shifted from preparation and cooking to purchasing and service. For operations based on using cook-chill or cook-freeze products, where the emphasis will be on holding food in a chilled or frozen state, methods of production and service will be determined by the needs of the holding system.

Unlike most other industries, catering usually combines production and retailing under one roof, with production being the direct result of a customer placing an order. The traditional kitchen is basically a manufacturing unit with the disadvantage that the majority of raw materials involved are highly perishable and the finished product has little or no shelf life; once produced it must be sold. Labour and raw materials must be available to meet demand, whenever it may arise, and there are often long spells of non-productive activity. The cost of the operation is increased as a result of the high levels of waste both of labour and raw materials.

One of the major problems that caterers face is matching staffing levels to customer demand. As can be seen in Figure 1.11 customer demand fluctuates through the day, peaking briefly during the main meal times.

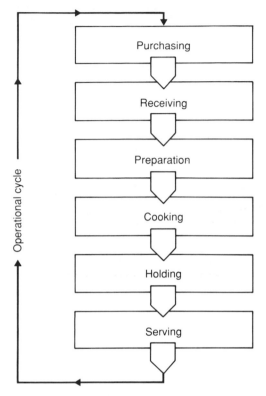

Figure 1.10   *Elements of a traditional production system*

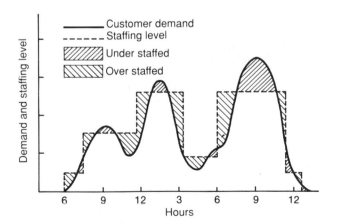

Traditional system

Production linked to peaks and troughs of customer demand, making it difficult to match employment levels.
Staff on a variety of shifts over an 18-hour day.

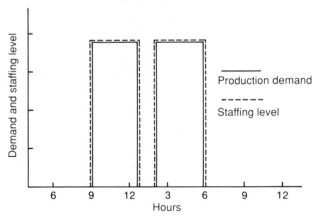

Centralised production

Production and service separated so that production and staffing levels can be matched.
All staff on a straight 9 to 6 shift, Monday to Friday.

Figure 1.11   *Comparison of working hours, productivity and customer demand*

Staffing levels cannot be matched exactly to these peaks and troughs, consequently there are periods of under- and over-staffing. If we take the customer away from the production decision then production and manning levels can be more closely matched.

For the caterer with several units the problems of control are multiplied. One solution is to adjust the system so that all or most of the production takes place in one central unit where finished products can be stored, chilled or frozen, before being transported to the end units for final cooking or reheating, and service.

Centralised production

Manufacturing industries are aware that it is cheaper to produce products, in quantity, on an assembly line, and separated from the purchase decision, than it is to produce them individually, as each customer places an order. The same can be true for food production.

Greater control and standardisation will be achieved if caterers centralise major steps in food production.

Centralised production systems benefit a variety of catering operations:
- in-flight catering;
- hospitals;
- pubs;
- banqueting;
- universities and colleges (summer schools etc.).
- transport;
- school meals;
- restaurant chains;
- industrial, on-site catering;

Centralising production necessarily requires methods of holding and storing the prepared dishes in suitable containers which, together with the additional costs of chilling, freezing and transportation, must be measured against cost savings.

Comparison of processes

Current developments in centralised production tend to be based on the application of one of three processes. Cook-freeze, cook-chill and sous-vide are all processes designed to prolong storage life by the control of food deterioration which may result from growth of micro-organisms, enzymic and chemical reactions and/or loss of water. Each process facilitates benefits from labour-saving techniques without compromising the skill or talent of the craftsmen and women concerned. In each case the essentials are high-quality raw materials, good hygienic practices and strict adherence to system guidelines, particularly time and temperature control.

Cook-freeze

A cook-freeze system would normally have the following advantages:
- increased output per man-hour (reduction in peaks and troughs);

- long production runs and economies of scale;
- bulk purchasing, cheaper, more quality control;
- use of seasonal produce;
- reduction in wastage;
- standardised end products;
- standardised yield and portion control;
- price/cost control – accurate, identifiable and accountable;
- prolonged storage allowing product availability throughout the year.

Cook-freeze requires a high capital investment in equipment and may not be adaptable to all systems. In addition, only a limited range of dishes will freeze successfully.

Cook-chill

A cook-chill system, whilst not having all the advantages of cook-freeze, can be tailored to meet most applications, regardless of scale. Capital costs are less, and with one or two exceptions there is less need for specialised equipment. Storage of finished products is limited to five to seven days and there is, therefore, less advantage to be gained from bulk purchase and long production runs. However, cook-chill is applicable to the full menu range.

Sous-vide

Sous-vide tends to be seen as a development of the cook-chill system which is more appropriate to quality restaurants than to large-scale catering.

The system enhances the benefits of chilling by inducing a vacuum or controlled atmosphere (combination of gases), the absence of air further retarding the growth of micro-organisms. A longer shelf life than the cook-chill system is possible. The major advantage is that flavour, juices and nutrients are 'sealed in' and weight loss during cooking can be reduced.

The system has proved beneficial for busy à la carte restaurants and can be used in banqueting and outside functions.

Staffing and equipment

When great establishments operated a full partie system they were seldom limited by the considerations of craft skills. In such cases, it was usually the maitre chef exploiting the talents of the team stars and highlighting the specialities perfected by them.

Most modern chefs plan menus requiring smaller but more efficient kitchen brigades. They must be prepared to give thought to the demands of the actual meal service as much as to the preparation of the food in the kitchen. Menu items must always be within the ability of the staff employed. The caterer may receive raw materials in unprocessed or highly-processed form. The degree of processing will determine the number and skill level of the staff that the caterer employs.

In many operations, available space and kitchen equipment limitations will become a major factor when planning a menu. Thought will have to be given to avoiding over-heavy loads on the oven at any one time and balancing the methods of cooking so that facilities for steaming, boiling, frying, roasting and so on, are all used equally.

Ideally, the menu style and food and beverage policy need to be determined before equipment is installed. Equipment purchased should be justified by the real needs of the menu. Existing equipment provision should be reviewed in the light of actual menu requirements with consideration given to the possibilities of eliminating redundant machinery, re-siting present equipment, and replacing with equipment better adapted to the menu needs.

Quality control

This depends upon clearly-defined standards, based on customer expectations, that are monitored and controlled during production. Chapter 3 considers quality control in more detail.

Pricing

In creating and pricing a bill of fare the menu-maker will consider food cost in relation to the size of portions which are to be served. The weight of cuts of fish, meat and poultry must be clearly established (even if subject to regular review) and the portion size of even the least-costly elements must not only be determined but also carefully controlled.

One aspect in the composition of a menu is maintenance of price stability over a period. Prices will be set for a given period during which cost, and consequently profit, may vary. The temptation to compensate for an increase in raw material prices by changing portion size or the combination of ingredients must be avoided if the caterer wishes to retain the confidence of the customer. The menu must be priced to allow for expected increases in raw material prices. The caterer will have to balance the need for competitive pricing with the likely customer resistance to frequent price changes.

Booking policy and service

Method and style of service will be a matter of company policy, but just as menu content will have been influenced by customer expectations so too will the system of delivery. There is a direct relationship between the production system and the method of service. Style of service will also influence price and profitability. In traditional restaurants, tables often stand empty, awaiting the customer who has made a reservation. Many restaurants have successfully moved away from the traditional reservation system. Customers are encouraged to arrive without booking at the restaurant where a comfortable waiting area is provided, more efficient use is made of the available tables and the caterer has the added benefit of generating profitable drink sales to waiting customers.

Seats at tables are often occupied by people who are not actually eating, often as a result of the delay between ordering and receiving their meal. Part of the planning process should include the identification of those menu items which might cause delay between ordering and receiving, and concequently which should be avoided.

In most cases, the service of food will also involve the collection and control of revenue. Whatever the sytem employed it should provide the opportunity for analysis of sales and revenue, and subsequent development of the menu.

THE RELATIONSHIP BETWEEN PRODUCTION SYSTEMS AND MENUS

Ideally, the caterer must:

a) identify the customer/consumer;

b) assess customer wants – define the product/menu;

c) develop a system suited to the most effective achievement of a) and b);

d) install plant and machinery, employ staff and purchase raw materials, based on the chosen system.

By way of making some evaluation and comparison it may be useful to consider three distinct systems: traditional; centralised production; and fast food.

Traditional systems

Caterers in the traditional sector will be responding to fairly conservative demands from the customer. There might be both a table d'hôte and an à la carte menu, with the table d'hôte changing daily. Dishes will often be from the classic repetoire with staffing, equipment and kitchen organised accordingly.

Typically, the systems are based on retaining a high level of dry and grocery stores. Fresh goods, such as diary produce, meat and poultry, and fruit and vegetables, tend to be ordered daily, as required. Use of convenience foods will be limited, normally in direct relation to the price of the meal. The menu-maker is likely to have a wide knowledge of raw material availability and quality. Purchasing will be based mainly on personal expertise and the demands of a frequently-changing menu.

Labour costs and overheads and, therefore, the mark-up and final price will be high in comparison to the original food cost. Pricing will also be influenced by the customers who are likely to be selective and prepared to pay for the added benefits that traditional systems offer. In some cases, customers will be prepared to pay a great deal, often at a high percentage mark-up from the original cost of the raw materials used.

Centralised production

Caterers working in a central production unit are usually constrained by working within strict cost budgets. The eventual customer, whether commercial or welfare, is likely to be seeking value and/or economy.

Centralised production units can take greater advantage of purchasing benefits, particularly bulk-purchase discounts and seasonal reductions in price. Purchasing will be based on the use of detailed raw material specifications. The cost of stock-holding can be reduced, as only those materials associated with the dishes currently in production need be purchased.

As centralised production is based on manufacturing principles, the dishes coming off the production line are likely to have similar characteristics, for example, frozen entrées (curry, chilli, goulash, pies) with all the same shape, size and texture. Because of savings in production cost there will be a smaller mark-up and prices will be competitive. Menus are likely to be static or cyclical, in order to benefit from large-scale production.

Fast food

There are many definitions of fast food, but the essential elements are:

a high-volume, retail trade, based on the use of a limited range of raw materials and minimum processing, with a concentration on merchandising and disposable packaging.

The menu range is necessarily limited, based on themed specialities with the emphasis on signature dishes like the 'Quarterpounder'. Standardisation will be based on the use of convenience raw materials with strict purchase specifications and high levels of recipe, portion and quality control. Purchase costs of raw materials would be comparatively high. On-site production costs will be low; normally limited to assembly and service of the product. Pricing will be competitive, based on narrow margins for each product. Profit will be reliant on high turnover.

Summary

Catering is a diverse industry and it is tempting to assume that each sector is unique. It is especially common to divide the industry into commercial and non-commercial operations as if they were totally incompatible. Although every operation will have its own unique attributes, there are many elements which are common to all caterers. Customer orientation, in particular, concerns all caterers.

Through the menu the caterer seeks to meet the wants and needs of the customer or consumer (previously identified through market research and/or previous menu monitoring). The menu expresses catering intention, i.e. policy. It also builds in such merchandising means as will help achieve this. In modern catering operations the customer will not need to enter the restaurant to read the menu. Legislation requires that the menu be displayed in such a way that the customer may read it before entering. A menu thus observed will convey more than just the type of food available, it can, and ought to, suggest the concept and style of operation, and level of service.

Despite the caterer's view of their concept, customers develop their own perception of what it is that the caterer is offering. The menu transmits messages, both tangible and intangible, to the customer. The caterer must ensure that these messages are clearly understood.

A properly-prepared menu informs the customer of the foods available and how much either each item or the meal in total will cost. The menu need not be a dull piece of cardboard. A visually-attractive, well-written menu can help to build a positive mood in the customer before the meal and increase the desire to return in the future.

Check list

1. Has a market been identified?
2. Does the menu reflect social issues, trends and developments?
3. Has a customer profile been drawn up?
4. Is the menu interesting and imaginative, appealing to the consumer?
5. Does the menu contain sufficient variety?
6. Does the menu assist with merchandising and selling?
7. Is the menu accurately priced and profitable?
8. Does the production system meet the demands of the menu efficiently and effectively?
9. Do resources, staff and equipment, reflect the demands of the menu and its production system?
10. Have review and analysis procedures been considered?

Menu Compilation and Design

Once company policy has been formulated it is then necessary to relate the company's intention to the customer. A balanced selection of dishes should be displayed in a sequence and form that both attracts and informs customers. Menu compilation and design significantly influence sales and hence profitability.

MENU STRUCTURE

Business and gastronomic balance

Menu balance is not simply a matter of food aesthetics. There may also be social and nutritional considerations, in addition to the more obvious business challenges of cost, price and marketing considerations. Yet despite financial pressures there is still potential for gastromomic artistry in menu-making.

Thus the chef's approach is mindful of cost and nutrition, but gastronomic balance and appeal to taste are also challenges. Gastronomic balance in menu-making demands from the chef a wide knowledge of foods in their raw state and a wide repertoire of dishes in their prepared and cooked form. It also calls for flair in putting food components together which can only be compared with the instinct intrinsic in other forms of creative art. Composing an essay, a song, a picture or a letter depends on craft skill, but also on a vital interest in, and sympathy with, the subject. So it is with menu composition. Nevertheless, a number of tangible factors are involved. These include colour, texture and flavour.

Colour: An inexperienced menu-maker can spoil a bill of fare by including too much of any one colour.

In a set menu, the frequent appearance in a sequence of dishes of one colour is to be avoided. For example, if white or brown occur in the main dish and then also predominante or recur in a sauce, vegetables or other accompaniments, this will have an adverse effect on diners, even though individually the dishes may be tasty. Agreeable colour contrast is not, however, solely a question of having one course varying from another, but of achieving appropriate colour composition within the principal courses of the meal.

Many classic garnishes automatically take care of such problems, yet at the same time there is often a failure to develop the visual virtues of food in appetite creation. Nouvelle cuisine exploited this aspect of meal presentation to the full, although (some might argue) at the expense of portion size.

Texture and flavour: Considerations of these might be dealt with separately because each factor has its own value. However, most people with a practical involvement with food, regard the texture and flavour as being inextricably linked. Just as the gelatinous body of a good soup stock is a necessary vehicle for the effective carrying of flavour, so generally is the texture and consistency of food linked with its taste and seasoning. In writing a menu it is, therefore, vital to provide not only changes of taste and colour within each course and from course to course, but also to provide variations of consistency and texture within each of the various preparations.

Flavour contrasts may again be regarded as a matter too obvious to dwell on, yet there are many pitfalls awaiting even flavour-conscious chefs. Whilst few would deny mulligatawny soup a place on luncheon menus, its strong flavours mean that thought must be given to what follows. There is little doubt that delicately poached fish, for example, could hardly hope to make much of an impact when it follows the curry-stuff of such a first course.

Within the courses traditional accompaniments and classic compositions (whether they are as simple as apple sauce and roast pork or as refined as lamb cutlets Reform) often solve, or partially solve, the flavour-contrast problem. Emollient sauces with fatless white fish or sharp sauces with fatty meats, poultry and game are elementary flavour designs, but the exercise becomes more complex when several courses need to be woven together.

Generally, the menu-creator seeks to awaken appetite in the opening courses and, if the menu is extensive, to progress gradually from milder flavours of pasta, egg and fish items to the more robust impact of meat entrées, relevées and roasts.

Type of menu

The menu as the whole basis of the kitchen operation is a subject of almost inexhaustible possibility. Hermann Senn, like many others, devoted a substantial work to the subject. It is significant that his *Menu Book and Register of Dishes* was originally called *Practical Gastronomy* in its first edition. The chef and the caterer must have recourse to culinary and gastronomic textbooks generally to nudge their memory and stimulate their thinking when preparing menus. There is no disgrace in using works of reference, on the contrary the skill with which an experienced chef can exploit reference material will often be a measure of success.

Menus, like meal times and cookery itself, are subject to constant change due to social and economic pressures. Fashions and vogues come and go so that studying past practices may often offer little reward other than appreciation of the constancy of change and give scholarly satisfaction.

Breakfast

The British breakfast has, according to many surveys, steadily lost support. When a cooked breakfast is packaged as bed and breakfast within an hotel's overnight charges it is still taken, but otherwise it is eaten less, both in the home and outside.

In considering the origins of the British breakfast and whether it is apposite today, it should not be forgotten that the historical breakfast of cold meats and chops taken at a later hour was as much an early luncheon as a breakfast, as we now know it, and that changing menus once again merely reflect changing meal times linked with changing social customs.

1. Fruits

Fresh	– grapefruit, melon, juices
Poached	– (compôte) figs, prunes, apples, mixed fruit (often dried)
Baked	– apples

2. Cereals served with cream or milk (hot or cold)

Cold	– Cornflakes, Weetabix, Shredded Wheat, All Bran, muesli
Hot	– porridge

3. Fish

Grilled	– mackerel, kipper, herring, bloater
Shallow fried	– white fish, fish cakes
Poached	– white fish or smoked haddock
Kedgeree	

Most of the above served plain or with a little butter, a little of the cooking liquor or a simple sauce (the exception being the kedgeree, which ought to be accompanied by a light curry sauce).

4. Eggs

Poached	– Most egg dishes may be served with accompaniments, usually selected from the meat range below
Boiled	
Fried	
En cocotte	
Sur plat	
Mollet	
Scrambled	
Omelette	

5. Meat

Hot	– grilled (or griddle fried) bacon, ham or gammon, sausage, lambs' kidney or calves' liver. Hot meats may be accompanied/garnished by a selection from the egg range above, together with sauté potatoes, potato fritters, bubble and squeak, fried bread, mushrooms and/or grilled tomato
Cold	– ham or pressed meats, tongue or salt beef. Cold meats may be accompanied by potato and/or sliced tomato, but not salad

(A combination of mixed hot meats, egg, tomato and/or mushroom, potato and/or fried bread constitutes the traditional English breakfast. In its true form these items would be arranged in chafing dishes on a sideboard for guests to make their own selection. The emergence of self-service buffets at breakfast constitutes, in some respects, a return to the traditional English breakfast.)

6. Bread	**7. Preserves**
Rolls	Marmalade
Toast	Jam
Melba toast	Honey
Croissant	Syrup
Brioche	

8. Beverages	**9. Dessert fruits (fresh)**
Tea	Apple
Coffee	Apricot
Chocolate	Pear
	Peach
	Grapes

Figure 2.1 *Breakfast items (sequence)*

Figure 2.1 on the previous page indicates the scope of items from which a breakfast menu can be composed. Today, only three courses are normally taken at breakfast, for example:

- fruit or cereal;
- fish, eggs or meat with an appropriate accompaniment;
- beverages, bread and preserves.

Tourist hotels may enhance breakfast menus with appropriate regional specialities, for example:

- fruit pudding and haggis in Scotland;
- black pudding in Northern England;
- lava bread in Wales;
- potato bread in Ireland.

> Other items that may be offered in addition to the items mentioned above, particularly when a self-service buffet is used and where the caterer might reasonably expect customers from Europe or Scandanavia, include a selection of thinly-sliced continental sausages, thinly-sliced continental cheeses and yoghurt. Waffles and/or pancakes served with maple syrup and doughnuts are suitable for the American/Canadian market.

Luncheon and dinner – a comparison

Normally luncheon as a meal is lighter than dinner in the sense that it has fewer courses and takes a shorter time. Nevertheless, actual dishes considered suitable for luncheon are often more substantial than any classical dinner dish. For example, luncheon features cheaper meat cuts, made-up dishes and offal which traditionally were not judged correct for dinner. Figure 2.2. compares a luncheon and dinner menu sequence.

Although the traditional sequence of lunch and dinner items (as identified in Figure 2.2.) continues to be used by most caterers, strict adherence to good examples of suitable dishes is now far less important, so that pasta and grills are now commonly included in the dinner menu. It is more important to hit the menu target with dishes that appeal than to worry about how classically appropriate the choice may be.

It is, in the main, the hotel sector which is likely to discriminate between those dishes suitable for presentation on luncheon menus and those that are more suited to dinner.

Luncheon

Today, for many customers, starters are omitted from their selection and the meal consists of only a main course and sweet. Whereas the end of luncheon was often the signal for the appearance of the cheeseboard, it is now more likely to be offered as an alternative to sweet or dessert. For some customers, where cheese is offered in addition to the sweet, there is a growing preference to take the cheese first followed by the sweet, following the continental fashion. Such changes in sequence of this and other items initially disturbed traditionalists, but there is little doubt that the greatest chefs and successful caterers have been those who were quick to note the hint of changes and fully exploit them.

The style and pattern of luncheon is by no means as formal as dinner, though differences between these two meals continue to narrow. There are usually fewer courses, but normally a wider choice of dishes at each stage of the meal.

Modern chefs need to be prepared to compose luncheon menus briefly and imaginatively and take into account some present patterns while being aware of more traditional concepts.

Afternoon tea

High labour costs and low profit margins on food, linked with decreased demand, have reduced the frequency with which afternoon tea is served.

This typically British institution seldom involves menu composition. Its collection of sandwiches, scones and pastries, do, however, involve the chef and caterer in some planning (colour, taste, texture) and must also affect the day's food costs and the solidity of subsequent meals.

Dinner

In many hotels and restaurants, evening dinner is generally regarded as more important, and therefore commands a higher price, than luncheon.

Hors d'oeuvres are appearing more frequently on formal, composed, dinner menus in response to customer demands. The development of nouvelle cuisine, in particular, stimulated the growth in the use of single item hors d'oeuvre as a tasteful and visually appealing appetiser.

	Luncheon	Dinner
Hors d'oeuvres	Fresh fruit, juice of cocktail, shellfish cocktail, hors d'oeuvres variés including simple and complex salads	Hors d'oeuvres variés or single item, caviar, oysters, avocado, smoked salmon, trout and ham
Soup	Broth, velouté, purée, chowder	Consommé (hot or cold), creams and bisques
Farinaceous	Pasta (all varieties), rice, gnocchi	
Egg	Poached, mollet, sur plat, en cocotte or omelettes	
Fish	Steamed, grilled, fried in batter, à l'anglaise, à la française, cod, haddock, plaice	Poached – salmon, turbot, sole Meunière – sole, trout Shellfish – lobster, crab, scampi
Entrée	Stews – ragoût, navarin, blanquette Fricassé, hot pot, goulash, curry, pies and steamed puddings	Sauté – tournedos, noisettes, chicken Vol au vent – various
Relevée		Poêlé – chicken, carré of lamb Braise – ham, tongue, duck
Sorbet		Various, including champagne
Roast	All butcher's meats, sometimes poultry, but not game	Feathered and furred game – grouse, partridge, pheasant, venison, hare Poultry – chicken, turkey, duck
Grill	Chops, cutlets, steaks, noisettes – beef, veal, lamb, pork, gammon, poussin	
Cold meat	Carved meats – buffet style	Individual items in aspic, mousse, mousseline, terrine
Potato	Boiled, creamed, roast, boulangère	Noisette, parisienne, fondant
Vegetable	Roots, pulses and leaves	Asparagus, broccoli, endive
Sweet	Hot and cold milk puddings and soufflés, fruit pies, flans and tarts, gâteaux, ices and coupes	**No** 'puddings', hot and cold soufflés, bavaroise, cream caramel, bombes and biscuit ices
Savoury		Croûte, canapé, tartlets (all served hot)
Cheese	All varieties – served with celery, apples and grapes	Soft and blue cheeses – served with grapes
Dessert	All fresh fruits	Fresh fruit and nuts
Coffee	Including decaffeinated; tea may also be served	Specialist and liqueur coffees – served with petits fours or mints

Note: Many popular restaurants no longer differentiate between lunch and dinner. Pasta, egg dishes and grill items now appear on many evening menus. However, the traditional sequencing of courses on offer is still widely used.

Figure 2.2 *Traditional concept of lunch and dinner sequence*

The chef Escoffier was reputed to believe that a fine soup was the most appropriate appetiser at dinner, especially if it was one of the consommés or lighter cream soups.

The general pattern of dinner has altered little though there is, perhaps, a tendency to dispense with the relevée as a distinctive course. A number of popular-priced restaurants have successfully dispensed with relevées and roasts to concentrate almost entirely on the entrée and grill selection.

When the meal is of great length sorbet may be introduced between the relevée and the roast, as it was traditionally thought to provide an interlude, a time to pause, relax the digestive system and refresh the palate.

At dinner there is a greater inclination to offer wines and for the customer to take time to savour both the food and wine. Consequently, the dinner menu has not been foreshortened as drastically as the luncheon menu. Dinner is still envisaged as a partnership of food and wine and an occasion in which these elements have social as well as gastronomic value. Dinner still, therefore, offers to the chef a major challenge in menu composition. Within its scope the chef is able to weave interesting gastronomic patterns and the food provided is often aided by the social importance of the occasion and the emphasis of fine wine.

Suppers

Suppers are, perhaps, less easily definable than dinners or luncheons. Theatre suppers were often intimate little affairs after the show, in which a simple assembly of courses, similar to those offered on a dinner menu, made the meal. To most people, supper implies a kind of early or late dinner of somewhat reduced scope. It often offers to the chef or menu-composer an interesting exercise in the creation of a subtle as well as simple meal (see Figure 2.3).

Menus for special occasions

This chapter will not attempt to deal at length with menus for functions and special occasions. The extent and variety is such that even chefs of the longest experience may be taxed when asked to create a menu along lines which demand a new approach. A special occasion may call for the featuring of one or more special foods, highlighting dishes or courses of some particular nationality, or assembling courses to compliment or offset a particular range of wines. What-

Supper would normally be limited to four courses as follows:

1. Appetiser
Single item hors d'oeuvre
Consommé

2. Main course
Grilled or fried fish or shellfish
Cold salmon, trout or lobster
Entrée, sauté, paêlé or braised meat
Grilled meat (roasts are seldom served)

All of the foregoing would be appropriately garnished and accompanied by vegetables. Cold meat, poultry, timbales and terrines accompanied by salad and possibly potatoes.

3. Dessert or **savoury course**
Hot soufflés, pancakes or fritters
Iced soufflés, bombes or coupes
Savouries or cheese
Dessert fruits

4. Coffee
Served with petits fours

Figure 2.3   *Supper sequence*

ever the function or occasion, the basic aspects of menu composing remain constant and the chef who is successful in menu selection from day to day requires only application of a little flair and, possibly, reference book research to rise to the special occasion.

Luncheon functions

Normal lunch dishes are featured subject to their suitability for function service; thus it is not usual to include farinaceous (for example, pasta) or egg dishes. Some stews and savouries are avoided for similar reasons. Service as a rule is designed for speed and this will influence the selection of items for inclusion on the luncheon function menu.

Dinner functions

The chef or caterer may compose menus from the full repertoire, but with service considerations and numbers in mind.

Buffet menus

Light buffets may be required for all kinds of catering, including tea and supper dances. Menus should include items easily eaten with a fork or even the fingers.

Full supper buffets, though they are not served course by course, require items to be arranged in the printed menu in appropriate groups.

An interesting addition to a buffet is the inclusion of hot dishes capable of being eaten with a fork, for example, curry, strogonoff and scampi provençale.

Sometimes hot consommé or turtle soup may be served at the end of a party.

MENU LANGUAGE

A menu must sell itself and so its most effective language is the native one. Unfortunately, catering's history is entwined with French cuisine, and its present and future linked with ethnic cookery of various kinds. Thus, today, several influences are brought to bear upon professional menus. Tourist boards in many countries have fostered the development of menus of a national character. In the UK, for example, campaigns like 'Taste of England, Scotland and Wales' resulted in menus not only in English but in jargon which incorporates words unearthed from folk history. Old Scots terms like 'cullen skink' or a Cornish dish like star gazy pie have to be interpreted to the consumer just as much as French terms. Additionally, increased travel and other factors have popularised ethnic dishes not only from Europe but also from the East and the Americas.

One advantage of using French (when used properly) on menus is its precision, related to a codified repertoire. When French is abandoned as a menu language, considerable care needs to be taken to ensure that the menu language is explicit and informative.

Jargon or special language on menus seems inescapable. This book does not attempt to examine the language of all countries but recognises France's special significance in the menus of the Western world. The grammar of professional cookery, i.e. its discipline and procedures, owes much to tradition. Thus, although the following text considers how French menu language has been applied, there is no merit in composing menus in traditional French jargon unless it can be seen to fit accurately and effectively into an appropriate marketing and merchandising pattern.

If the menu is composed in classic style and in French, thought should be given to the desirability of supplying succinct menu notes in English; these owuld at once define the dishes and also help to create interest and develop the appetite. If the menu is to be composed in English then the food and beverage management team must collaborate in providing suitable designations which go further than

'roast beef and two veg.'. Some menus have tended, perhaps, to go too far in flowery descriptions, but certainly there can be no fault in indicating precisely the cut, origin and method of cooking and serving meat, as in a menu item like 'roast shoulder of Southdown lamb served with redcurrant jelly and watercress'.

In anglicising menus there is always the problem of dealing with straightforward cookery processes, like meuniere or sauté. Many consider it reasonable to maintain well-known descriptive designations of this kind on a British bill of fare and find nothing incongruous in, for example, terms like 'hors d'oeuvre' and 'entrée'.

One rule regarding British dishes on the menu should be that when they are distinctively British, for example, Scotch broth, Lancashire hot pot or roast sirloin of beef with Yorkshire pudding, they are rendered in their own language in preference to translations into French. This is consistent with featuring specialities of other countries, for example, Osso buco (Ossi buchi), in the languages of their countries of origin.

Controversy will obviously continue over what method is best and it can only be urged that within the policy determined by the management the approach should be consistent.

Menus in French

Modest establishments in any country other than France itself should be reluctant to follow old-fashioned French menu writing. Yet operations of the chef-proprietor type still aim for the gourmet market by catering in the French style. French menu language may puzzle customers but it can be interpreted through the restaurant sales staff. It remains meaningful to the trained chef and may continue to be of value and convenience. French was not imposed on the menu for pretension. Because of the part that French practitioners played in developing professional cookery, it conveniently codifies dishes.

Menu writing in French must conform to French grammatical codes, including the correct use of plurals and gender. Care should be taken with spellings. If the menu is in French then the dish should use the French spelling; if the menu is in English the dish should be spelt as it would be in its country of origin or its accepted English equivalent.

Menu jargon

The making of dishes and the language of menus are, if not the same thing, inextricably linked together. Professional cookery in Western civilisation, though developed largely under French influence, derives items from its repertoire from a variety of sources.

In creating dishes to a high and uniform standard, serious craftsmen and women know the advantage of dishes being recognisable by name, content and appearance, wherever they are served. Hence the evolution of menu language which, though apparently French, is both more than and less than French in that it is a technical and artistic jargon. Names of dishes do not merely describe the central item but indicate to the knowledgeable the method of cooking and the accompanying sauces and garnishes.

FRENCH MENU VOCABULARY

The central factor of traditional French menu writing or menu understanding is a good vocabulary of French words for food and cookery processes. Without learning a comprehensive range of French words, the menu is bound to remain a mystery. Of course, no one, not even the most eminent of chefs, is expected to memorise the meaning of all the thousands of French dishes. A competent chef would aim to recognise the more commonly-met items and to interpret these reasonably using the reference works and repertoires at hand.

Describing cookery processes

Descriptive terms such as rôti, sauté, poêlé and the like are phrases which indicate not an elaborate garnish and sauce, but a simple mode of dressing or serving. In pommes sautées, to sauté the potatoes describes the process of jumping or tossing them in shallow fat. In rognons sautés (kidney sauté) or boeuf sauté the word takes on an added significance because when meat is sauté it is invariably finished by cohering it with sauce, cream, butter, wines or a combination of these items, so that the final dish is not at

all similar to the dry, shallow-fried sauté potatoes. Differences of this kind, where the same word appears to describe a somewhat different end product, can cause scepticism in the uninitiated, but serve to emphasise that an understanding of cookery processes is needed for menu interpretation, especially by service staff to help customers.

National descriptions

Not only are cooking processes described straightforwardly but they are sometimes linked with the country in which a particular style of cooking predominates. 'A l'anglaise' inevitably means extremely simple cooking, but according to the context might apply to plain boiling or the traditional English way of dressing roast meat. In other cases, too, styles of cooking or dressing vary according to the food with which the designation is linked. Thus, 'à la française' used in conjunction with peas denotes how they are stewed with lettuce and onion. One will obviously not expect to find these vegetable ingredients in a pouding de riz à la française (French style rice pudding) in which the French touch is achieved by the addition of beaten eggs. 'Hongroise' indicates the use of paprika and Hungarian methods. 'Italienne' suggests pasta or the use of garlic and/or tomatoes. Other national designations include, among many, 'Americaine', 'à la Russe', 'Japonnaise', 'Indienne' and 'Portugaise'.

Association words

A second category of dishes are less simple to interpret without the key to the convention. These are the kind which though not simply a descriptive French version of a cooking process still yield clues to those with knowledge of French and who have knowledge of commodities and their places of origin. One of the simplest examples applies to those dishes where association words indicate a mixture of vegetables as an ingredient to, or accompaniment for, a dish. Thus 'potage cultivateur' or 'potage santé' with soups readily disclose their meanings. In entrées of, say, lamb cutlets or other small cuts the words 'aux primeurs' indicate the presence of spring vegetables. Jardinière and similar words show where an assortment of trimmed vegetables, irrespective of season, will provide the garnish.

Indicating shape and cut of garnish

Less easy to the uninitiated are ways of describing vegetable garnishes by virtue of their cut. 'Paysanne', indicating a rough slicing of vegetables has now lost its original peasant roughness to become as neat and precise as any other. It may nowadays be forgotten that little cubes (macedoine), whether of fruit or vegetables, were named after the cluster of small islands comprising Macedonia. Similarly, other terms like 'julienne' and 'brunoise' have a commonly-accepted definition, though their origin may be forgotten.

Geographical clues

Some association words seem less straightforward because they require some geographical or horticultural knowledge. Of this sort, 'potage Argenteuil' is an example. This soup and other dishes with the Argenteuil designation involve asparagus, strictly speaking the especially luscious asparagus originally developed in the Argenteuil area. Similarly 'Périgord' indicates the presence of truffle, 'Florentine' an accompaniment of spinach, and 'Chantilly' the addition of whipped cream, all because of the association of a commodity with a town or geographical area.

The chef and menu names

Whatever the origin of the dish and however it came to be named, the chef has a great deal to do with the dish and its place on the menu. There are two categories of dish which chefs are directly involved in naming. First, there are the dishes which they invent or perfect and which may be named after them, and secondly there are dishes which because they have been derived and perfected by a chef are named by that chef.

Dishes named after chefs, however, form a small group of their own and it is, perhaps, an indication of surprising modesty that this is a relatively small group. Typical of this kind of dish is filet de sole Dugléré in which the name of the master chef is permanently associated with the dish of his creation. Examples of other dishes named after chefs, either because they invented them or to honour them, are Faisan Carême, Tournedos Vatel and cold paupiettes de sole Escoffier.

Chefs inventions are often stimulated by either a special occasion, a special customer or by a combination of the two.

Historic occasions

Poulet sauté Marengo is often cited as typical of a dish both honouring and arising from an historic occasion. Shortage of ingredients on the eve of battle prompted some inspired improvisation on the part of Napoleon's chef and earned the dish a lasting place in classic cookery. Another battle, Creçy, is linked with carrots which apparently abounded near the scene of the fighting.

Naming dishes after patrons

Having created or distinctly adapted a dish sufficiently to give it a new individuality, the chef and restaurateur may give it a name which they hope will not only distinguish it on menus of their own establishment, but ultimately earn a lasting place in the culinary repetoire.

Honouring gourmets

In the Middle Ages and well into the nineteenth century it was, perhaps, the male gourmet who inspired the creativeness of chefs and consequently prompted the naming of dishes. Note the association between rich and prosperous men of affairs and richness and prosperity at the table. Many dishes à la financiere cloak with anonimity the financier whose gastronomic interest had influenced the chef. In other cases, the financier emerges by name immortalised in dishes such as sole Colbert. Here the dish derives its name from Jean Baptiste Colbert, the father of France's financial system.

Artists, men of letters and composers

As there is an affinity between the arts it is not uncommon to find painters who write well or writers who paint well and this mélange of talent not infrequently also embraces cookery and dining. It was not merely to honour his musical compositions that dishes such as Tournedos Rossini were named after the great Italian man of music.

Sole Colbert was amongst the recipes listed in the works of Antonin Carême, chef to the Prince Regent, and the recipe is annotated 'Sole, from the inventor'. This indicates that Carême does not claim the credit for this dish but whether one may further assume that Colbert himself had done more than inspire it is less certain.

Alexandre Dumas, père, essayed to enter the ranks of professional cookery writers with his *Dictionnaire de la Cuisine*, but like the English journalist, Sala, whose book *The Thorough Good Cook* has more literary than practical merit, he would have been better advised to have remained the influence behind the scenes rather than a would-be chef.

Not only are individuals linked with dishes but categories of individuals (sometimes where one particular person had been originally in mind) also provide and still provide dish-designation inspiration for chefs. Hence the many dishes à la Royale, à la Princessè, Marechal and Cardinal, most of which were brought into being on occasions or functions when an eminent royal, soldier or churchman were to be present or honoured.

Feminine influences on the menu

One of the significant parts played by Escoffier, and the hotelier, Ritz, was their contribution in persuading respectable women to dine in the restaurants of hotels. Social and economic factors prompted the emergence of women into public dining, but Ritz created settings which facilitated this social culinary change and Escoffier led the movement which acknowledged women as having taste, discernment and a right to be catered for at intimate dinners and on more formal public occasions. During those early days of the twentieth century and even after the death of Edward VII, women became steadily more heard in menu matters and exerted an ever-increasing influence.

This influence was typified by women of the theatre, opera house and concert platform who became personal friends of Escoffier and his more eminent colleagues in the kitchen. Sarah Bernhardt and Nelly Melba not only gave their names to dishes created as a testimony to their artistry, but also actively concerned themselves with food. Many leading feminine personalities of the Escoffier era may be credited with some gastronomic knowledge over and above their power as artists to inspire chefs.

However, feminine influence prevailed earlier in the Victorian era, for though there was a distinctive and almost spectacular emergence of women into gastronomy at the turn of the century and after, there were other periods when women managed to make their mark. They were not always considered quite respectable by society for it was a mistress of Louis XV of France, Du Barry, who not only gave her name to food but who is also credited with promoting the standing of women cooks through the creation of the now invisible culinary order, the Cordon Bleu. It is perhaps ironic that the dish with which her name is chiefly associated, Crême Dubarry, is believed to have been linked with the whimsical concept of cauliflower sprigs being comparable with the powdered, white wigs of the Du Barry epoch.

A la maison

Chefs and the general public alike no longer favour menu designations which refer vaguely to the style of the house or to the fashion of the chef. Furthermore, there is a lingering suspicion that such designations permit an elasticity of execution that may mislead. However justified this suspicion may be, the fashion of the house has caused the permanent inclusion of several famous dishes in the culinary repertoire.

Even before the days of hotels, in London's Reform Club, the chef Soyer devised a mode of cooking and garnishing breadcrumbed lamb cutlets which now have enduring fame as Côtelettes d'agneau à la Reform. Where the à la maison has become a specific maison and method, all valid objections can be overruled. Pommes Delmonico, Salad Waldorf Astoria and Pommes Voisin are all dishes named after famous establishments in which they reached perfection and comprise a respectable and distinctive section in our catalogue of dishes.

Moreover, inventiveness continues, for example, Tasse de consommé truffé sous croûte (cup of truffle-flavoured consommé under puff pastry cap) was devised and named Consommé Valery Giscard D'Estaing (or Consomme V.G.D'E) by Paul Bocuse (a chef and writer) during Valery Giscard D'Estaing's presidency of France.

The above explains something of how menus and dish naming evolved in the Western tradition. This aids understanding of the codification of the past and possibly predicts the future, but no menu maker should be hidebound by such evolution. At best, the body of knowledge helps us from reinventing the wheel, as it were, and may provide stimulus for modern menu building.

MENU WRITING AND LAYOUT

Menu complication involves not just the selection of dishes but also consideration of how they should be displayed in order to both enhance the presentation and promote sales of individual dishes in harmony with the total meal experience.

The value of constant appraisal and reappraisal of one's own and others' menus cannot be over-estimated. Those who manage kitchens are not responsible for all elements in menu production but they can still help appraise a menu's design, including the artwork, typeface (style of lettering) and its marketing and merchandising qualities. Above all they have a significant role in ensuring continuing creativity and orginality.

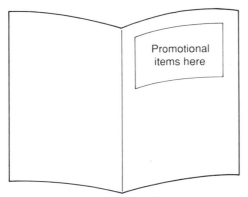

On an open double page, the eye moves to the top right-hand corner first.

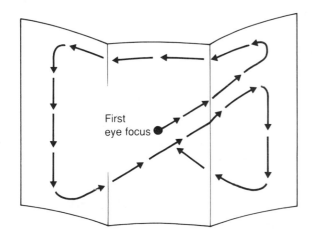

The direction of eye movement across a three-fold menu.

Source: Menu Pricing and Strategy, Miller.

Figure 2.4   *Direction of eye movement across menus*

Without going into great detail about layout it may be observed that on an open double page, the eye tends to gravitate first to the top right-hand side (see Figure 2.4). In buying magazine space, advertisers will often pay more for the top right-hand page position. On a three-fold menu it is the centre that gains most attention. Consideration should be given, therefore, to good selling spots on a menu card, for example, where best to affix clip-on or clip-in cards for the day's/meal's specialities or plats du jour.

Otherwise menus should follow a logical course sequence. In some operations there may be a case for a separate menu card for puddings and desserts. Wine lists are a separate matter but a menu can, and often should, help sell wine, especially house wine in bottles or carafes.

MERCHANDISING

As the menu is an integral part of the merchandising process, both the positioning of menu items and the technical and descriptive language used may enhance sales. Similarly photographs may be introduced into the display, or customers' attention drawn to other display material, speciality boards or sweet trolleys.

THE LAW AND CONSUMER PROTECTION

Whilst the menu-maker may be concerned with business and gastronomic balance the legal implications of providing food for the public must not be forgotten.

Broadly speaking, the consumer requires protection on two fronts. First, their health and well-being, which requires protection from risk as a result of careless food handling. Secondly, their rights as an individual in relation to the exchange of goods or services for money. Some legislation is aimed at the food industry in particular; other laws relate to trading in general.

Trading standards officers, environmental health officers and the Health and Safety Executive (HSE) 'police' the industry on behalf of the local authorities who act for the benefit of the public in general. These public officials may have right of entry to catering premises or may alternatively make test purchases in order to obtain evidence. It should be stressed at this point that these organisations would much prefer to act as advisers rather than prosecutors. Prosecutions normally only take place when caterers fail or refuse to respond to good advice.

The following is a list of legislation relevant to advertising and selling:

- The Food Safety Act 1990;
- The Consumer Protection Act 1989;
- The Trades Description Act 1968;
- The Fair Trading Act 1973;
- The Sale of Goods Act 1979;
- The Price Marking (Food and Drink on Premises) Order 1979.

As of 1 March 1989, Part 3 of the Consumer Protection Act has made the following a criminal offence:

- giving a misleading price during the course of business;
- failing to correct the misleading price.

This reinforces the Price Marking (Food and Drink on Premises) Order 1979 and covers such elements as the amount, the circumstances and what is included in the price, and applies to both employer and employees even if errors are unintentional. A Code of Practice (see Figure 2.5) has been provided, giving examples of possible offences. Like the Highway Code this code does not have the force of law, but a breach of the Code would be assumed to have been a breach of the intention of the law.

- Prices should be inclusive of VAT.
- Prices should be inclusive of any non-optional service charge.
- The amount of optional service charge should not be included or suggested in the total bill.
- Cover charge or minimum charge should be shown prominently on the menu or price list.
- Additional charges should be made clear on the menu or price list.

Figure 2.5 *Code of Practice for Traders on price indications*

The Food Safety Bill 1990, although primarily concerned with the safety and hygiene of food, food premises and food workers, offers similar protection to the Consumer Protection Act in relation to vague and misleading terms, such as 'homemade' and 'fresh'.

Descriptions in advertisements and on menus are conditioned by the Trade Descriptions Act 1968. Care must be exercised when offering a range of dishes that terms are used correctly and truly reflect the contents of the meal. The Act is concerned with

any form of communication which describes the product on offer. The following sections are the most relevant:

- Section 1 states that it will be a criminal offence to make misleading statements about goods or services.
- Section 2 identifies the different elements of description, of which the following are most applicable to food:
- quantity or size;
- method of manufacture or production;
- composition;
- fitness for purpose;
- physical characteristics (free from additives, etc.).
- Section 11 states that it will be an offence to make false or misleading statements about price.
- Section 14 states that it will be an offence to knowingly or recklessly make a statement in the course of business which falsely describes goods or services (in particular, quality, quantity and price).

It is an offence if one price is indicated on a menu outside an establishment and another is shown inside.

The Fair Trading Act, 1973 has extended consumer protection to include various aspects of promotion of goods and selling. An offence will be committed if information that is false or misleading is given in respect of goods offered. Caterers must take care when compiling menus that descriptions applied and other information given, in order to promote custom, conform also to this Act.

The Sale of Goods Act 1979

This Act recognises the existence of a contract between the caterer and customer. In particular, it emphasises the significance of fitness for purpose. The product must be fit for the purpose for which it is intended and the assumption will be that in a catering situation the customer intends to eat the product. It must, therefore, be fit for human consumption.

Price Marking (Food and Drink on Premises) Order 1979

Anyone who advertises, by any means, that they are, or may be, selling food or drink for human consumption must give an indication of the price of that food and/or drink and any additional charge which is payable. Where the item is sold by reference to quantity or unit of measurement then the price indicated must be the price per unit or measure.

If there are less than 30 items on the menu then all prices must be displayed. If there are more, then at least 30 must be displayed. If menu items are listed in categories then at least five from each category should be displayed. If the menu is table d'hôte then individual items need not be priced. All prices quoted must be inclusive of value added tax (VAT).

All prices must be displayed at or near the entrance to the eating area. Any service charge or minimum order must be displayed with equal prominence.

The Order extends to all caterers with the exception of bona fide clubs, canteens and/or educational canteens or residential establishments where food is only served to customers who have engaged sleeping accommodation. The Order does not extend to situations where food and drink is prepared by special request and price has been agreed in advance, for example, outside catering.

VAT – service is subject to VAT so must be added to the rest of the bill and the total amount will be calculated for VAT.

Summary

Compilation of good menus clearly requires a great deal of thought and reference to a variety of talents and skills. It is unlikely that any single individual would be able to respond and adapt to all the requirements. It may well be necessary to seek the advice of experts before finalising the menu. In particular, the menu-planner should be aware of the need of expert advice in relation to:

- the law;
- marketing and market research;
- art, design and printing.

Whether bound by traditional concepts of sequence and presentation, responding to trends or being innovative, consistency and reference to accepted practice is important.

The art of composing menus may best be perfected by practice and by studying others. To the craftsman or woman aware of cookery methods and garnishes, the reading of a menu can be full of interest and meaning. Critical appraisal of the menus of others and particularly the study of those created by modern masters can be stimulating as well as instructive. For the special occasion, cookery skills alone are not enough. No one thing makes a chef a person of discernment, but breadth of reading, width of interest and social contact can help towards creating the whole person as well as the professional chef. Such a person will more readily capture the importance and drama of the big occasion, in culinary terms, on his menu.

On ordinary days, the most routine meal will gain from the planning of the cultured as well as the skilled chef. Though the early-nineteenth century gastronome and writer Brillat Savarin's aphorisms tend to have been done to death, there is one so succinct, so apt and so true, that it must be quoted in order to underscore the importance of the art of selecting dishes to complete a good meal. Savarin used five words only to express the importance of his kitchen blueprint: 'Menu mal fait, diner perdu' which translates as 'Menu badly done, dinner lost'.

Fine chefs and caterers gain similar satisfaction from composing a balanced menu as they do in creating a splendid dish, but they must not be satisfied by meeting aesthetic criteria alone. They must reconcile personal creative satisfaction with any food operation's aim that a properly constructed menu should help to sell and achieve cost and profit objectives.

Check list

1. Does the menu reflect company policy?
2. Does it achieve a suitable balance?
3. Is it in the correct sequence?
4. Is the language appropriate?
5. Has it been checked for spelling and grammatical errors?
6. Does it advertise/merchandise products successfully?
7. Have all the legal implications been fully considered?
8. Have suitable instructions been given to the printer?

CHAPTER 3

Products and Dishes

The preparation of an effective menu requires not just the compiling of an harmonious list of dishes, but also careful product planning and dish development.

PRODUCT PLANNING

Product planning is a continuous process, a constant response to changes in demand, eating habits, competition, technology and economic conditions. The objective will be to match the product to market expectations and produce a saleable product based on the needs and wants of the customer. Effective product planning is dependent on accurate forecasting.

Forecasting

The objectives of forecasting are to predict the number of customers and the choice of menu items. Forecasting will aid purchasing and maintenance of stock levels leading to a tighter control of costs, a reduction of food waste through over-production, and loss from inefficient storage, processing and portioning of ingredients. Accurate forecasting will avoid customer dissatisfaction through non-availability of popular items.

All too often in the catering industry forecasting is based on intuition or guesswork. Although personal opinion and informed judgement can be useful it will be more efficient to apply an objective approach towards predicting level of demand. Forecasting techniques must be consistent, accurate and reliable.

Production planning relating to the kitchen

This is an activity specifically related to the kitchen and involves volume forecasting, standard yields, standardised recipes and standard portion sizes (yield).

Volume forecasting

This is prediction of future requirements, based on historical evidence, broken down into sales per item. It involves a comparison of actual and potential business activity to form decisions for the future. Volume forecasting allows the caterer to formulate budgets and project sales mix.

Required
Past records (sales history), popularity index, advance bookings, current events and current trends.

Popularity index

This involves the use of a notional base (100) to identify average sales figures. The following is an example of how the popularity index is calculated for a number of items.

For a menu with a choice of seven main course items, selling 80 covers:

$80 \div 7 = 11.43$
(11.43 is the average number of dishes sold).

To find the index for each menu item, divide actual sales by the average (11.43) and multiply by 100 (see Figure 3.1 overleaf).

In addition to analysing actual results (discussed in Chapter 10), the popularity index may be used to forecast future sales. For example, turnover is expected to increase from 80 to 125 covers. Based on the same seven menu items the average would now be 17.85. Assuming that the popularity of items remains the same, by applying the new average to the index anticipated sales can be identified.

```
Average of 11.43
Menu    Number
item    sold        Average              Index
A       16    ÷     11.43   ×   100  =   140
B       20    ÷     11.43   ×   100  =   175
C       23    ÷     11.43   ×   100  =   201
D        4    ÷     11.43   ×   100  =    36
E        8    ÷     11.43   ×   100  =    70
F        8    ÷     11.43   ×   100  =    70
G        1    ÷     11.43   ×   100  =     8
```

Menu item D is less than half as popular as the average; item C is just over twice as popular as the average.

```
Average of 17.85
Menu                            Forecast
item    Index       Average     sales
A       140   ×     17.85   ÷   100  =   25
B       175   ×     17.85   ÷   100  =   31
C       201   ×     17.85   ÷   100  =   36
D        36   ×     17.85   ÷   100  =    6
E        70   ×     17.85   ÷   100  =   13
F        70   ×     17.85   ÷   100  =   13
G         8   ×     17.85   ÷   100  =    1
```

Figure 3.1 *Popularity index (forecasting)*

Clearly the process is not an exact science, customers are fickle and apt to change their habits, but the method does have some advantage over the wild guess.

Standard yields

This is number of portions available from each particular food item, for example, the number of steaks on a sirloin, the number of tomatoes in a box and the weight of fruit in a tin. Yield will be different and specific to each commodity.

Required

Raw material product specifications and product testing.

Standardised recipes

The specific quality and quantity of ingredients, together with precise measurements and instructions for the method of manufacture are intrinsic to the idea of standardised recipes (see Figure 3.2).

Item: Rognons sautés Turbigo

Number of portions: 10   Portion size: 8oz

Ingredient	Quantity	Weight	Unit cost	Per	Ingredient cost
Lamb kidney	16	2lb	0.65	lb	1.30
Diced onion		4oz	0.20	lb	0.05
Mushroom		8oz	0.80	lb	0.40
Chipolata	8	8oz	0.84	lb	0.42
Butter		4oz	0.80	lb	0.40
Demi-glace	1pt	20oz	0.40		0.40
Parsley					0.02
Croûton	10	5oz	0.20		0.20
Seasoning					0.01
Total cost					3.20
Cost per portion					0.32
Gross profit @ 80%					12.80
Total selling price					16.00
Price per portion					1.60

Method:
1. Clean, trim and dice the kidneys.
2. Saute the seasoned kidney in hot clarified butter.
3. Add lightly cooked onion and continue to sauté.
4. Add quartered mushrooms and continue cooking.
5. Add grilled and sliced chipolatas.
6. Bind with demi-glace.
7. Correct the seasoning.
8. Present for service, decorated with heart-shaped croûton fried in butter and dipped in parsley.

Figure 3.2 *Standardised recipe card*

Required
A standard recipe manual, possibly stored on a computer file (in many sectors of the industry this would be supported by pictoral representation of the desired end product).

Standard portion size/yield

This is defined as the number of items or weight per portion, together with the number of portions obtainable from the end product or a given recipe.

Required
Accurate instructions, diagrams, a portion guide (for example, 20 portions from roast leg lamb or 12 portions from gâteau) and sufficient portioning equipment (measures, scoops, ladles and scales), recipe testing and adherence to standardised recipes.

Although dividing foodstuffs into equal-sized, profit-able portions involves practical skills it also depends on marketing, merchandising and cost calculations.

Portion size is decided after considering the type of customer, how much will be spent and the amount of profit required. Portion control does not necessarily mean reducing size nor penny pinching which can swiftly lead to dissatisfied customers.

The term 'portion size' is used only in catering but portion principles operate in every business. Nobody expects to get 19 or 21 cigarettes in a packet of 20 or a varying amount for each litre of petrol pumped into the car. Similarly, in food and beverage operations, portion control means providing an exact, predeter-mined helping to each customer.

A selling price needs to be set carefully, in advance, and this must assume that costed portions are neither exceeded nor reduced. Either form of inexactness may have detrimental effects on the business. By standardising the portion size food costings can be effective and there may be greater certainty of achiev-ing gross profit targets.

Portion size

An average stomach is said to accommodate about 1 kg (2.25 lb) of food, both liquid and solid. This may give some guide to portioning (see Figure 3.3).

Today, portion control is increasingly effected out-side the kitchen through the purchase of pre-portioned items such as sliced bacon, steaks and fish fillets, as well as the more easily-recognised butter, milk and cream portions.

On this stomach-capacity basis a typical main meal might include:		
	g	*oz*
Appetiser	100	4
Main item plus sauces, etc.	150	6
Salad	50	2
Vegetables	100	4
Potato	150	6
Bread and butter	50	2
Dessert	150	6
Beverage	100	4
	850	34

Figure 3.3   *Portion size and stomach capacity*

Yield testing

Linked with purchasing specifications and standard recipes is the need to test commodities, which have been prepared and cooked, for their yield. Such tests help to identify appropriate portion sizes. Entered on to a standard recipe card, portion sizes may be varied for different outlets and service styles.

The examples of percentage losses in commodities of various kinds (see Table 3.1) are quoted as a pointer to the importance of regular yield testing. This is applicable not only to high-priced, luxury items, but also to foods of more modest cost, such as vegetables, which may have large volume of sales. It must be remembered that even the minutest detail of variance, if repeated, will become a significant cash amount at the end of the year.

Table 3.1   Food loss in preparation

		Loss (%)	*Edible (%)*
Beef	entrecôte (on the bone)	40	60
Beef	fillet (untrimmed)	10	90
Beef	rump (on the bone)	30	70
Crab	⎫	70	30
Duck	⎬ eviscerated	30	70
Poultry	⎭	25	75
Fruit	*	3–50	
Gammon	(on the bone)	15	85
Lobster		65	35
Round fish	(average)	60	40
Salmon		25	75
Flat fish	(average)	50	50
Vegetables	*	6–60	

Note: * Loss varies according to quality. Apparently cheap fruit and vegetables can have a high 'real cost' when trimming and waste is evaluated. Similarly, peeling and trimming need careful supervision.

Consideration must also be given to current developments in technology and new equipment, together with the resulting changes to traditional principles of cookery. For instance, the development of the sous-vide system and the use of combi-ovens have both resulted in changes to methods of cookery, but significantly also demonstrate valuable savings by reducing losses during cooking.

The use of forecasting, together with standardised production techniques, will enable predictions to be made in relation to levels of profitability. However, it is essential that a programme of careful monitoring is developed in order to compare predicted and actual performance. Differences will occur for a variety of reasons. Early action on these differences is essential.

Standardised production output is affected by the quality of preparation, cooking and serving equipment as well as by the quality and nature of raw materials and the skill of the staff.

Standardised recipes, methods and portion yield are not only a basis for costing and pricing, but also provide the foundation for quality control, cost control and analysis.

QUALITY MANAGEMENT

Can the caterer offer a guarantee or assurance of both food safety and quality?

Quality management is the means by which products achieve high reputation. The aim of quality management is to ensure that problems do not occur, this is achieved through system design which identifies standards and control points for the whole operation.

Quality and price

It is not true to say that as a product becomes more expensive so its quality increases; some expensive products are of relatively poor quality. However, it is true to say that quality has its price. The cost of quality arises from the control, monitoring and supervision, of raw materials, equipment and staff, and the setting and maintenance of standards. Whilst identifying the cost of controlling quality remember that there is also a cost to poor quality. The steak that is not cooked to the customer's satisfaction will need replacing. The true cost of poor quality is not the cost of the raw materials wasted, but the selling price of the steak that cannot now be sold.

Control and assurance

In developing a quality management system a caterer is faced with the choice between quality control and quality assurance. Quality control is that activity which attempts to ensure quality by testing the product, random sampling if quantities are large and rejecting defects. Quality assurance is a method of predetermining quality by setting clear raw material and product specifications, following standardised recipes, working methods and yields, and employing suitable equipment design.

There are problems involved in developing a reliable system of quality assurance in food production. The caterer must be constantly on guard against changing standards in both raw material and staff input. Quality cannot be improved at any stage, it can only be maintained.

DISH DEVELOPMENT

As was discussed in Chapter 1, there is a strong link between menu composition and methods of production/production systems. This link is further related to dish development in that dishes will only be developed in line with current policy, the needs of the menu and the capabilities of the system.

Much current activity has been by way of product standardisation in order to ensure consistency in

The origins of quality assurance in food production can be traced to manned space flight. Despite all the technology available to propel man and machine through space, scientists were still left with the problem of man's digestive system and bodily functions, and its propensity to remove any substance that could be harmful to the body, for example, bacteria, by the quickest route possible. NASA worked in conjunction with the US Army and the Pilsbury Corporation to develop a system that could provide a 100 per cent guarantee of safety from contamination. A system sustaining that level of quality assurance is only attainable by building quality in rather than testing for quality at the end.

relation to customer expectations. All organisations will participate, to some degree, in dish development. For the small operation it may be an *ad hoc* activity in response to requests from customers, new products or equipment, or even an article in a magazine.

For large organisations dish development is likely to be part of a formal, planned process, often in response to the need for product differentiation. In many cases, dish development will take place in a specialist, experimental kitchen. The end product is likely to be influenced, not just by aesthetic considerations (colour, flavour and texture), but also by manufacturing criteria and specifically the capability of the product to be reproduced consistently on a national scale.

> For some organisations, dish development may involve the selection and testing of convenience products. Testing of products may range from simple, sample tastings by the management team to a detailed analysis of the product. For example, the following points may be analysed for frozen, breaded scampi:
>
> 1. uniform shape and size;
> 2. raw weight/colour/texture;
> 3. raw weight/colour/texture (bread coating removed);
> 4. cooked weight/colour/texture;
> 5. graded comparison of points 2, 3 and 4 above;
> 6. flavour;
> 7. quality of crumb (colour, fresh bread, rusk);
> 8. use of additives;
> 9. deterioration/holding time once cooked;
> 10. cooking time/temperature;
> 11. oil absorption (cost and effect on quality, flavour etc.);
> 12. price and discounts.

Co-operation during development

On some menus offering a wide selection, chefs and managers may face new dish design or development with more reluctance than in operations with limited choice where customer appeal is achieved by a few accurately-aimed choices.

Smaller catering businesses may have to rely on a single member of staff to develop new dishes. In larger operations, developing and producing specifications for a dish should involve not only a food and beverage manager or chef, but also include co-operation with accounts, control and marketing elements.

Questions to be determined include:

- Is there a potential market for this product?
- What should be the selling price of the product or what price can the market (consumer) be expected to pay?
- What are its unique or special qualities?

- What ingredients need to be specified?
- What will be the cost of raw materials?
- What procedures will be involved in preparation and cooking?
- What equipment will be required (especially important if new and/or additional items are needed)?
- What labour costs are involved?
- What portion size will be appropriate in relation to the selling price?
- What is the best method of finishing (garnish, sauce and such elements) and packaging (presentation procedures) the product?

Whatever the size of the business, the more staff (kitchen, service and others) that are involved in resolving the above questions the more committed will be their involvement and interest, leading to an enthusiasm in perfecting a dish and helping to promote its sales.

METHODS OF PRODUCTION

Comparison has been made in Chapter 1 between the cook-freeze and cook-chill systems. A great deal of the work relating to dish development is influenced by the application of these systems.

The cook-freeze system, in particular, will require adjustments to be made to traditional recipes. This is particularly true in regard to the type and amount of starch thickening used. Traditional, roux-based sauces do not freeze well. Recipes need to be modified by the use of a specialist stabiliser.

Like cook-freeze and cook-chill, sous-vide aims at both standardised production techniques and reduction in waste. It has the added advantage that there is less loss through shrinkage during cooking, and flavour and nutrients are retained. Cooking loss could be as little as 10 per cent as compared with a cooking loss of between 20–30 per cent with traditional methods.

Systems like sous-vide provide an indication of how dish development contributes to the ever-closer link between catering and food manufacture.

Dish development and production should be based on specifications, i.e. short, simple descriptions of recipe, production method, portion size, garnish, presentation and service style. This ensures that management's decisions on portions and service are known to kitchen and waiting staff alike. Menu specifications are effective tools in maintaining standards and are also essential for staff training purposes.

When Wimpy opened their first high street restaurants it was suggested that the large picture of menu items that adorned the walls of the restaurants (a unique phenomenon in those days) were as much for the education of the staff as they were for the customers.

Many caterers, particularly in on-site event catering where use of casual labour is high, now consider the use of colour photographs essential to the maintenance of standards.

FOOD VALUES

Chefs and others concerned in catering for hotels and restaurants sometimes question the necessity of concerning themselves with food values. Some of those engaged in cooking and catering in hotels often make, two inaccurate points regarding the acquisition of simple facts about nutrition. These points are:

- De luxe restaurants offer such a wide range of top-class foods that the prospects of malnutrition are non-existent.
- Hotels and restaurants, as distinct from the welfare sector, cannot compel their clientele to select and eat certain foods.

Such reasoning, superficial though it is, is attractive to those too lazy or too lacking in social conscience to recognise the real responsibilities borne by all those involved in the provision of food for the public.

The great chefs, throughout history, have been enquiring invididuals, constantly alert to know more about the commodities that they use, the best way to use them and the dietary effects they have.

Men like Alexis Soyer, who organised soup kitchens for the poor of London, improved catering for British soldiers in the Crimea. They remain concerned about nutritive matters, not only for reasons which affect humbler social groups. Soyer knew, as do all intelligent practising chefs, that the food values of the finest raw materials may be impaired by bad cooking and use of incorrect methods as well as poor selection by the customer, whether rich or poor. True, the chef or caterer cannot compel customers to eat what is good for them, but customer choice can be influenced by the way in which the menu is set and the way in which the dishes featured in it are cooked and presented.

The caterer is confronted with two types of dining philosophy; on the one hand that of eating to live and on the other of living to eat. Chefs and gourmets are alive to the attractions of the table as one of the means by which civilised man heightens his appreciation of the pleasures of living. The caterer must, nevertheless, be conscious that whatever its pleasurable aspects, eating satisfies a primary need. The caterer cannot ignore the fundamental aspect of eating; that of maintaining life and health. The process of nourishing the body through food and drink in a developed society can, and indeed should, be linked with refined enjoyment as distinct from gross indulgence.

The modern caterer will also be mindful of current social trends and legislation, both of which place greater reliance on the caterer being more aware of the nutritional content of food and the effect that the dishes on offer may have on the health of the consumer.

> The 1983 NACNE (National Advisory Committee on Nutritional Education) and 1984 COMA (Committee on Medical Aspects of Food) reports have emphasised the need to reduce the intake of salt, sugar and fats whilst increasing the use of fibre in the diet.

Nutritive knowledge

The science of nutrition is relatively young. Biochemists, medical men and other research workers are still discovering new facts about food and discarding or amending old ideas and theories about diet or about the cooking methods. Yet there is a good deal of basic knowledge about food values which it is quite simple to understand and which must be learned and appreciated by the competent caterer.

The assessment of food values is largely a matter of common sense. If the menu is based on the use of fresh foods with a wide variety of dishes, blends and contrasts of flavour, colour and texture, and which are cooked efficiently and served when newly-cooked, then most of the important rules of nutrition will have been followed. Obviously, the modern trend toward centralised production and food manufacture must be of concern to the caterer. The nutritional effect of systems like cook-chill, cook-freeze and sous-vide must be evaluated during system planning and dish development.

The nutrients

Food is composed of several different substances (nutrients), each of which plays a part in meeting the needs of the body and enabling it to function. A good diet should maintain a balance between nutrients while varying for different individuals. Often occupational groups are used as guidelines for energy requirements as this is an essential factor in the development of a balanced diet (see Tables 3.2 and 3.3). An excess of all or any one of the three main nutrients can result in a build up of body fat.

Carbohydrates are a major component of almost all diets and normally meet most of our energy require-

Table 3.2 Daily energy needs

It has been calculated (*Manual of Nutrition*, HMSO) that daily requirements, based on varying but average activities, are as follows:

Occupation	Age range	Total daily need	Activity example
Female doctor	18–54	2 200	Moderately active
Male clerk	18–34	2 700	Sedentary
Male supervisor	35–64	2 900	Moderately active
Male mechanic	18–34	3 000	Moderately active
Male miner	18–34	3 600	Very active

ments. Sugars and starches belong to this group (see Table 3.4).

Fats (or lipids) have a dual role. They provide the most concentrated source of energy and in addition provide essential fatty acids which are needed for maintaining health; they are particularly important for babies and young children. Fats are a source of the fat-soluble vitamins A, D and E, they provide an essential part of the bodies cell structure and are necessary for the production of certain hormones. Apart from animal fat (suet, lard, dripping and fat contained in meats), plant oils, fish oils and diary products are the main source of fats (see Table 3.5 on page 42).

Proteins supply nitrogen, an element essential for both growth and repair of body tissues. Proteins also function as enzymes and as hormones in regulating body functions. They may also contribute to the supply of energy, but only if the body does not have a sufficient supply from other sources. While in general carbohydrates and fats are interchangeable as

Table 3.3   100 calorie portions of various foods

Commodity	Weight of edible portion (g)	(oz)	Approx. measure
Dairy foods, fats and oil			
Butter	13.5	(0.5)	1 tablespoon
Cheese, Cheddar	24.6	(0.9)	1 small cube
Cream, double	22.4	(0.8)	1.7 tablespoons
Eggs	68.0	(2.4)	1 very large egg
Lard	11.2	(0.4)	0.8 tablespoon
Margarine	13.6	(0.5)	1 tablespoon
Milk (whole)	153.8	(5.4)	1 teacup
Olive oil	11.1	(0.4)	0.8 tablespoon
Cereals			
Bread, white	42.9	(1.5)	1 thick slice
Biscuits, sweet	21.3	(0.8)	2 small biscuits
Biscuits, cream cracker	22.7	(0.8)	3–4 biscuits
Cornflakes	27.2	(1.0)	0.5 of a cup
Cornflour	28.2	(1.0)	2 tablespoons
Flour (white)	28.6	(1.0)	2 tablespoons
Spaghetti	26.5	(0.9)	15 (250mm) strands
Oatmeal	24.9	(0.9)	1.6 tablespoons
Rice	27.7	(1.0)	2 tablespoons
Meat and fish (raw)			
Bacon (middle)	23.5	(0.8)	1 rasher
Cod (fillet)	131.6	(4.6)	1 small steak
Herring	42.7	(1.5)	1 small fillet
Beef (sirloin)	36.8	(1.3)	0.2 of a portion
Lamb (leg)	41.7	(1.5)	1 slice
Pork (chop)	30.4	(1.1)	0.2 of a portion
Chicken (whole)	43.5	(1.5)	1 small drumstick
Vegetables			
Cabbage, Savoy	384.6	(13.6)	0.5 of a cabbage
Carrots (old)	434.8	(15.3)	5–6 medium carrots
Lettuce	833.3	(29.4)	12–16 lettuces
Onions	434.8	(15.3)	4 small onions
Potatoes (old)	114.9	(4.1)	1 small potato
Tomatoes	714.3	(25.2)	10 medium tomatoes
Turnips	500.0	(17.7)	4 small turnips
Pulses			
Peas (fresh)	149.3	(5.3)	0.5 of a cup
Haricot beans	36.9	(1.3)	2 tablespoons
Fruit and nuts			
Almonds (shelled)	17.7	(0.6)	1 tablespoon
Apples, cooking	270.3	(9.5)	2 medium apples
Apples, eating	217.4	(8.2)	3 small apples
Apricots, dried	54.9	(1.9)	4 halves
Bananas	126.6	(4.5)	1 large banana
Chestnuts (skinned)	58.8	(2.1)	6–8 chestnuts

Table 3.3   *(Continued)*

Commodity	Weight of edible portion (g)	(oz)	Approx. measure
Coconut (shelled)	28.5	(1.0)	1.5 tablespoons
Oranges	285.7	(10.1)	2 large oranges
Peanuts, roasted	17.5	(0.6)	1 tablespoon
Prunes (dried)	62.1	(2.2)	5 prunes
Sugars and preserves			
Jam/marmalade	38.3	(1.4)	2 tablespoons
Milk chocolate	18.9	(0.7)	1 small slab
Sugar, white	25.4	(0.9)	1.5 tablespoons
Honey	34.7	(1.2)	2 tablespoons
Beverages			
Beer (bitter)	312.5	(11.0)	0.5 of a pint
Spirits (70° Proof)	45.0	(1.6)	50ml
Wine, red	147.1	(5.2)	1 glass
Wine, sweet white	106.4	(3.8)	1 small glass
Coca-cola	256.4	(9.0)	1 large glass
Lemonade	476.2	(16.8)	2 glasses
Cocoa (powder)	32.0	(1.3)	2 tablespoons
Coffee (ground)	34.8	(1.2)	2 tablespoons
Tea (leaf)	92.6	(3.3)	5 tablespoons

far as their nutritional value is concerned, no other nutrient can substitute for protein (see Tables 3.6 and 3.7 on pages 42 and 43).

Mineral substances build and repair body tissues and regulate the body process. Calcium is well-known as being important for strong bones and teeth.

Vitamins regulate the body process. Vitamins are divided into groups and identified by letters (A, B, C, D, E etc.). Some vitamins are fat-soluble and some dissolve in water.

Table 3.4   Percentage carbohydrate in various foods

Commodity	Carbohydrate (%)
Bread, wholemeal	54.3
Cornflakes	85.4
Flour, white	80.0
Oatmeal	72.8
Rice	86.8
Peas (frozen)	10.6
Potatoes (raw)	18.0
Honey	76.4
Jam	69.2
Sugar	105.0

Table 3.5 Percentage fat in various foods

Commodity	Fat (%)
Butter	82.0
Dripping	99.1
Lard	99.1
Margarine	81.0
Bacon (raw)	40.5
Beef (raw)	22.0
Ham (cooked)	18.9
Lamb (raw)	30.2
Pork (raw)	29.0
Herring	18.5
Salmon (canned)	8.2
Sardines (in oil)	13.6
Cheese, Cheddar	33.5
Eggs (fresh)	10.9
Almonds	53.5
Coconut (desiccated)	62.0
Peanuts (roasted)	49.0
Flour, white	1.2
Oatmeal	8.7

Table 3.6 Amounts of various foods containing approximately one-third of the daily protein requirement of a moderately-active adult male

Commodity	Weight (g)	(oz)	Approx. portion/measure
Meat and fish group (raw)			
Bacon (middle)	175	(6.2)	5 rashers
Cod (fillet)	144	(5.1)	1 portion
Lamb (leg)	140	(4.9)	1 portion
Beef (stewing steak)	124	(4.3)	1 portion
Liver (ox)	118	(4.2)	1 portion
Dairy group			
Cheese, Cheddar	96	(3.4)	6 cubes, 25mm (1 in)
Eggs (fresh)	203	(7.2)	4 small eggs
Milk (whole)	758	(26.8)	3 glasses
Cereal group			
Bread, wholemeal	284	(10.0)	5 thick slices
Bread, white	321	(11.3)	6 thick slices
Oatmeal	202	(7.1)	1.5 cups
Rice, polished	385	(13.6)	3 cups
Biscuits, sweet	403	(14.2)	40 biscuits
Biscuits, cream cracker	263	(9.3)	30 biscuits
Vegetable group			
Cabbage, Savoy	758	(26.8)	1 medium cabbage
Carrots (old)	3571	(126.1)	36 medium carrots
Cauliflower	1316	(46.5)	2 small cauliflowers
Potatoes (old)	1190	(42.0)	10 small potatoes
Fruit group			
Apples (eating)	8333	(294.2)	60–80 apples
Apricots (dried)	521	(18.4)	40–50 halves
Bananas	2273	(80.2)	30–40 bananas
Oranges	3125	(110.3)	20–30 oranges

Water, although not strictly a nutrient, is included as it also builds body tissues and is essential for life.

Fibre, like water, is strictly speaking not a nutrient, but it is believed to play an important function in maintaining health. Although fibre consists of indigestible material, roughage, found particularly in whole cereals, fruits and vegetables, it is essential to the digestive system. Roughage provides bulk which aids peristalsis, that is helps the body push food through the small intestine where most nutrients are absorbed.

Besides the major nutrients, food contains a multitude of other chemicals which perform various important roles, such as giving flavour, colour and other desirable qualities. These substances include pigments, food acids, esters and other organic compounds.

Nutritive loss in cooking

Cooking causes many chemical and physical changes in food which usually make it more acceptable to the customer by making it more digestible and palatable, and by improving its flavour. Keeping quality is also improved and, if thoroughly cooked, food will be rendered safe as far as any bacteria, which might have been present, are concerned.

However, there is a risk of decrease in food value if due care is not observed during the cooking process. For protein, fat and carbohydrate foods, there is little danger of loss during cooking. There will, however, be some loss of vitamins and minerals. Emphasis should, therefore, be directed toward care in the cooking of fruits and vegetables where vitamins, particularly vitamin C, are most easily lost.

The nutritive value of foods is not only dependent on their specific content but also on the quantity consumed. Hence, for the British consumer, potatoes, although containing far less vitamin C than, for example, blackcurrants, are a more important source by virtue of the comparative amounts we eat.

Table 3.7 Percentage protein in various foods

Commodity	Protein (%)
Meat group (raw)	
Bacon	14.4
Beef	17.1
Chicken (meat and skin)	17.6
Chicken (meat only)	20.5
Gammon (lean only)	29.4
Lamb	15.9
Pork	16.0
Dairy and farm group	
Cheese, Cheddar	26.0
Fresh eggs	12.3
Fresh milk	3.3
Fish group	
Cod	17.4
Herring	16.8
Salmon (canned)	20.3
Sardines (in oil)	23.7
Pulses	
Peas (frozen)	5.7
Lentils (dry)	23.8
Peanuts (roasted)	24.3
Cereals	
Flour, white	9.8
Oatmeal	12.4

Further discussion of sources of nutrients and particular food values may be found in the relevant chapters on commodities. Suffice to say at this point that nutritional content is an important consideration of dish development and the caterer should study consumer tastes and endeavour to satisfy these demands, whilst at the same time reconciling them with the demands of good nutrition.

GROUPING FOOD

In planning menus and developing dishes from a nutritive aspect a simple grouping of food into three main categories should suffice to aid the chef. These divisions are body builders, energy and heat producers, and protectors.

Body builders

This group of food, having as its function the building and renewing of body tissues, comprises proteins and minerals.

Proteins are the very basis of life. They are obviously important during pregnancy, childhood and growth, and can be significant in surgical cases, particularly the treatment of burns. All proteins are composed of chemical elements known as amino acids. Animal proteins (meat, fish, milk, cheese and eggs) have a high biological value, which means that they contain all of the essential amino acids. Vegetable proteins (peas, beans and lentils) and also cereals and nuts are said to have a low biological value since they do not contain all the essential amino acids. But this does not mean that their importance in the diet is diminished, since each plant protein contains a different group of the essential amino acids a mix of two or three such foods can provide all the necessary requirements.

Animal protein foods are usually the most expensive but often the most appetising. It is important to mix both animal and vegetable protein in the diet. Protein foods normally contain the necessary minerals.

Energy and heat producers

Foods within this group are those which provide fuel for the work and warmth of the body. The two kinds of foods which fulfil this function are:

- fats;
- carbohydrates (sugar and starch).

The bodily requirements of food vary; energy requirements in particular will be dependent on the weight, size, age and occupation of the individual. Children, in particular, require special consideration when planning the menu. They must obviously be adequately provided with body-building materials and protective elements. For adults, once basic needs are satisfied, the main consideration is likely to be the level of carbohydrate intake in relation to particular energy requirements. Energy is required from food even when the human body is at rest because it is needed simply to keep the body living – to maintain warmth, to keep the heart beating and blood circulating, and to continue the action of breathing. The basic energy requirement for this is known as the body's basal metabolism.

Foods sometimes fulfil more than one function and pulses, like peas and beans, whilst having a function as body builders, contain an appreciable amount of heat and energy value. Food taken in by the body, and capable of producing heat and energy, may be converted by the body into body fat if taken in excess of requirements. When intake falls below the level required then conversly, body fat is used as fuel and weight is lost. Calorific value refers to a food's capacity to produce heat and energy for the body.

Food would be unappetising and monotonous without a certain amount of fat. Fortunately, adequate amounts are present in the average diet. Because fats digest more slowly than other foods, meals containing a good proportion of fat are more satisfying and lasting. However, since some forms of heart disease are known to be associated with increased levels of cholesterol in the blood (which may be influenced by the amount and type of fat in the diet) it would be unwise for people susceptible to heart disease to consume certain types of fat, especially that of animal origin, in excess.

Recent guidelines have suggested limiting saturated fat in the diet and this advice has sometimes been translated as a requirement for a dramatic reduction in the consumption of red meat and diary produce in favour of poultry and fish. However, lean meat, trimmed of visible fat, has a low residual fat content and remains a valuable and nutritious food.

Protectors

These are foods which maintain health and guard against disease. They may be found amongst the two preceding groups. Especially valuable are diary foods, eggs, fruits, vegetables and salads, oily fish, liver and goods produced from wholemeal flour.

These foods are valued because of their vitamin and/ or mineral content; the elements in foods which, though present in relatively tiny amounts, perform some specially valuable function. Their relevance is most apparent when they are absent or drastically reduced in the diet. Vitamin C illustrates this aspect. A traditional ailment among sailors in the past was scurvy, an almost inevitable consequence of the restrictions placed on the diet by spending many months at sea. The antidote to scurvy was found to lie in citrus fruits (oranges, lemons and limes), which all contain vitamin C. This was discovered even before the study and naming of vitamins got under way. In Western cultures, deficiency diseases are now rare, but unfortunately this is not the case in less-developed countries.

The four main vitamins

Vitamin A – necessary for the promotion of growth and the health and efficiency of the eyes; fat-soluble.

Vitamin B – a group of vitamins of which deficiency leads to loss of appetite, stomach disorders and digestive problems, general weakness and lassitude; water-soluble.

Vitamin C – (ascorbic acid) beneficial to growth and healing; water-soluble.

Vitamin D – beneficial to growth and repair, absorption of calcium for bones and teeth; fat-soluble.

COSTING AND PRICING

Whereas menu pricing will be a matter of catering policy its foundation must lie in accurate costing of dishes and recipes.

Objectives and strategies

Initially a business will determine an overall profit target; the desired level of return on capital employed. Based on forecast sales and projected sales mix, estimates may be drawn on probable cost of sales in terms of raw materials, labour and overheads. Traditionally, the catering industry has measured performance (the relationship between cost of goods sold and selling price) as a percentage of the selling price, the gross profit percentage (GP%). The level of gross profit will vary according to the level of service offered. Based on a given GP% assumptions may be made about probable net profit on sales. However, this type of pricing policy is fraught with problems and assumptions about profit are quite likely to prove false.

The price must reflect customer expectations. Despite the accuracy of GP% calculations a quality product which the customer perceives as being under- or over-priced is likely to meet with some resistance. Gross profit percentages may prove a useful starting point for the pricing decision, but should not be the determinant of price.

Identification of operational cost elements

In order for a food operation to be profitable other, non-food costs have to be identified and built into the pricing structure. For the purpose of analysis, costs can be divided into three specific groups, fixed, managed (semi-variable) and variable costs. An example is shown in Figure 3.4.

Some confusion can arise from these definitions, especially in regard to which costs are fixed and which vary. It is important to remember that we are measuring the costs over a period of time or in relation to a specified level of production.

Variable costs are set (the same) for each item, but vary in total in direct relation to the number of items produced.

Fixed costs remain the same no matter how many items are produced, but as fixed costs are divided between the items produced, as the number of items increases each bears a smaller proportion of the cost.

Managed (semi-variable) cost can be modified by management decisions.

Further confusion may arise from costs which do not neatly fit into any of the above categories. Take for instance labour costs which are neither fixed nor variable. It might seem logical to identify these costs as managed. However, more careful analysis will reveal that it is possible to classify labour costs under each of the three categories as follows:

- Full-time employees = fixed cost (does not vary with the number of meals served).
- Part-time employees = managed cost (does not vary in direct relation to the number of meals, but is controlled in anticipation of expected demand).
- Casual labour = variable cost (hired for the express purpose and in direct relation to confirmed business, the number of customers; for example, for banquets calculate one waiter to ten customers).

For many caterers the conventional costs (elements of price) will be identified as: raw materials (food); labour; and overheads. Elements of price are illustrated in Figure 3.5 (overleaf).

Pricing methods

Several approaches to pricing are possible in relation to food sales:

- cost plus percentage – food cost (40 per cent) plus gross profit (60 per cent);
- ratio mark-up – for example, 4:1 indicates that price equals four times cost;
- fixed-sum addition – £1.00 per item, regardless of basic cost;
- differential gross percentage – promoting particular products;
- incremental pricing – for example, party bookings which are cheaper per head as numbers increase;
- backward pricing – cost tailored to meet acceptable price;
- market pricing – determined by the customer and the competition.

Number of covers	50 £	200 £
Fixed cost – rent and rates	50	50
Variable cost (total) – raw materials (food)	25	100
Managed cost – heat and light	5	8
Total cost	80	158

If we run a take-away pizza house then rent and rates remain the same (£50) regardless of whether we sell 50 or 200 pizzas. Raw material costs, at 50p per head, will vary in direct proportion to the number of pizzas sold. We can choose whether to have heat and light on or off but it is less likely to be in direct relation to output. Using the figures above, if we sell 50 pizzas the cost of each will be £1.60 (£80 ÷ 50), whereas if we sell 200 pizzas the cost of each would be 79p (£158 ÷ 200). If the selling price had been set at £1.50 the implications are obvious.

Figure 3.4 *Cost, volume and pricing decision*

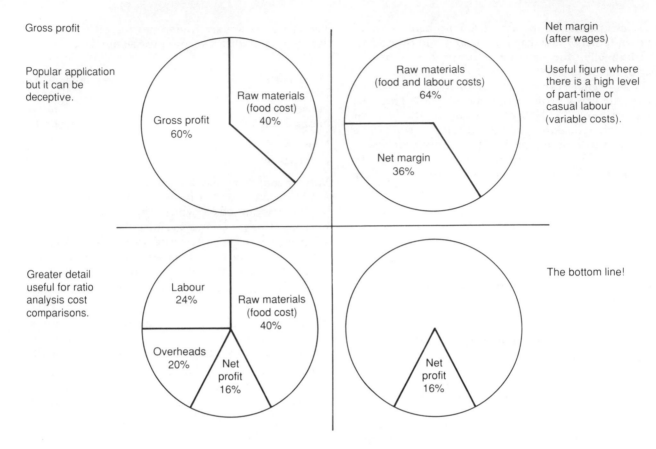

Different operations place greater emphasis on different elements of price when assessing performance.

Figure 3.5   *Elements of price (selling price = 100 per cent)*

Pricing method may be applied to each dish, each group (starters, main course, sweets) or the whole meal.

Caterers may aim for an overall gross profit target by setting different GP margins for various items (differential GP). This creates some interesting business incentives, particularly in relation to improving profit levels (see Figure 3.6).

It may not be immediately apparent in the example in Figure 3.6 that there is an important distinction to be drawn between GP% and actual cash GP (£GP). This distinction is shown in Figure 3.7.

Over-reliance on GP% is fraught with problems. Each item on the menu should be assessed for its contribution to the overall success of the operation. It may be argued that providing the soup is an essential pre-requisite to selling the steak. Judgements

about profitability should be based on comparitive calculations not assumptions. To that end the following figures can provide useful guidelines:

- average spend per customer;
- average £GP (total cash GP divided by the number of covers).

Price discretion

The fact that catering, because it is a service industry with a high proportion of fixed overheads and labour costs, generally works on a comparatively high level of gross profit means that a fairly wide range of price discretion is possible. The caterer will have the opportunity to choose from a wide variety of price options for each product or service offered (see Figure 3.8).

Before: GP = 60.50% 100 covers	GP (%)	Take-up (%)	Price (£)	GP in the £
Soup and starters	80.0	50	2.00	80.00
Main courses	58.0	100	5.00	290.00
Sweet	55.0	70	2.00	77.00
Total GP	60.5			447.00

After: GP = 61.8% 100 covers	GP (%)	Take-up (%)	Price (£)	GP in the £
Soup and starters	80.0	70	2.00	112.00
Main courses	58.0	100	5.00	290.00
Sweet	55.0	50	2.00	55.00
Total GP	61.8			457.00

Many customers do not take all three courses. The sweet, often being visually more attractive, tends to be the more popular. Note the effect if customers' allegiance could be transferred from sweet, with a relatively low GP%, to starters with a relatively high GP%. Overall GP% and GP in the £ will be improved from 60.5% (£440) to 61.8% (£457) without increasing the number of covers or customer spend.

Figure 3.6 *The results of encouraging a switch in customer preference*

Price and volume

The caterer will have the opportunity to modify prices in order to increase total volume of sales and overall net profit. There is often an assumed relationship between selling price, volume of sales and net profit; as price decreases so sales will increase. Even if this is so how will it affect net profit? Once again the answer is not always obvious, as may be seen in Figure 3.9.

Take the following figures:

£1.00 soup   @ £0.20 food cost = 80% GP or £0.80 GP
£10.00 rump steak @ £4.00 food cost = 60% GP or £6.00 GP
£12.00 fillet steak @ £5.04 food cost = 58% GP or £6.96 GP

The amount of labour required to generate GP cannot be ignored. Assume that the labour charge for producing and presenting each of the three dishes mentioned above was £1.00. This is not an unreasonable figure if the soup is fresh and requires accompaniments to be served. Even if we only use food and labour costs we are clearly losing money on each portion of soup we sell, despite the fact that it apparently has the superior GP%.

Note also that despite the fact that rump steak has the higher GP% it also generates a lower cash GP than fillet, yet there is unlikely to be any difference in the cost of labour or overheads required for these two dishes.

Figure 3.7 *Distinction between £GP and GP%*

Example	Raw material cost (£)	Selling price (£)
Hotel sells film for camera, from reception	1.30	1.50
Hotel sells cheese sandwich, from bar counter	0.30	1.50
Hotel sells smoked salmon sandwich, from bar counter	0.80	1.80
Hotel sells smoked salmon sandwich, room service	0.80	1.80

In the case of the film, little additional labour is required and the product is available in many other outlets at a similar price. It would be pointless to charge any more or any less; there is little or no price discretion. In the case of the smoked salmon sandwich served in the room it is unlikely, considering the high element of labour involved, that all costs have been recovered. However, the caterer is aware that a reasonable profit has been made on the smoked salmon sandwich sold in the bar where less labour (service) was required. It may also be noted that a large profit has been made on the cheese sandwich. The caterer could choose to make room service more expensive and the cheese sandwich a lot cheaper or, as is the case here, maintain a more uniform pricing structure. There is overall greater price discretion.

Figure 3.8 *Price discretion*

The numbers in Figure 3.9 appear to offer contradictory evidence. The best total sales will be achieved if the price is low and 300 covers are sold. Conversely, if only 20 covers are sold at the highest price a superior NP% will be achieved.

Since cash in the bank is the only tangible measure of success there might be some value in using £NP as the yardstick by which to measure performance, making the mid-range price the most effective.

Despite all the permutations, the eventual selling price must ultimately be influenced by the customer. However, numbers provide the essential picture of

Assuming a correlation between the price of the product and the number of items sold, sales will decrease as the price increases.			
Selling price (£)	0.10	0.30	0.50
Number of covers	300	80	20
Total sales	30.00	24.00	10.00
Unit production cost	0.09	0.09	0.09
Cost of goods sold	27.00	7.20	1.80
Total cash net profit	3.00	16.80	8.20
Unit cash NP (£NP)	0.01	0.21	0.41
Unit percentage (NP%)	10%	70%	82%

Figure 3.9 *The effect of volume on sales and net profit*

how well we are performing, provide the basis by which to measure results and are essential for the purpose of control and analysis (discussed in Chapters 9 and 10).

FOOD PRODUCTION LEGISLATION

Although concerned with satisfying customer demand, nutritional balance and pricing objectives, through the use of the most effective production system, the caterer must always be conscious of legislation and the health and welfare of the customer.

Current legislation is formulated in the following acts:

- The Food and Drugs Act 1955;
- The Food Hygiene (General) Regulations 1970;
- The Food Hygiene (Amendment) Regulations 1990;
- The Food and Drugs (Control of Food Premises) Act 1976;
- The Food Act 1984;
- The Food Safety Act 1990.

The Food and Drugs Act 1955

Section 8 prohibits the sale of food which is 'unfit for human consumption'. Food does not necessarily have to be injurious to health in order to be considered unfit, for example, mould on bread would be unfit, although it might not cause illness.

Section 2 prohibits the sale of food which is 'not of the nature, substance or quality demanded'. If the menu states fresh fruit then tinned fruit would be unacceptable (i.e. not of the 'nature' required). If the menu states 'bread and butter' then margarine would not be acceptable (i.e. not of the 'substance' required). If there were foreign bodies in salad it would be of inferior 'quality'.

Section 7 enables the Minstry of Agriculture, Fisheries and Food (MAFF) and the Secretary of State for Health and Social Services to issue regulations concerning labelling, marking or advertising of food intended for human consumption.

Section 4 permits the appropriate Ministry to make regulations in regard to the composition of certain foods, for example, the fat content of cream and butter (see the relevant chapters for detail).

Section 13 gives power to the appropriate Secretary of State to make regulations in respect of hygiene in food premises (the Food Hygiene (General) Regulations 1970).

The Food Hygiene (General) Regulations 1970

These Regulations define 'food', 'food premises', 'food rooms' and 'food handlers'. Although there are some exceptions (covered by separate legislation) it is safest to assume that any premises, rooms, staff or products associated with the sale of food are covered by the Regulations. They form a basic re-enforcement of a commonsense approach to hygiene and highlight the various elements (premises, plant, equipment, clothing and personnel). The Regulations mention sanitary provision and adequate supplies of cleaning material, lighting and ventilation, the accumulation of refuse as well as recommendations for the covering, storage and temperature control of food intended for sale to the public.

The Food Hygiene (Amendment) Regulations 1990

These Regulations contain a new regulation, regulation 27, specifying minimum and maximum storage temperatures for a wide variety of foods. They form the basis of any inspection that may be carried out by environmental health officers. Caterers are advised to contact the local environmental health officer (EHO) for advice, as precise requirements will vary. For instance, the number of wash-hand basins necessary would depend not just on the size of the kitchen, but also design layout and the number of staff employed. Each kitchen would be judged on the accessibility of cleaning facilities to each member of staff.

The Food and Drugs (Control of Food Premises) Act 1976

This Act further reinforces the Food Hygiene Regulations so that where a person has been convicted of an offence under this Act the court may apply to the local authority to have the premises closed.

The Food Act 1984

This Act updates and reinforces the Food and Drugs Act 1955.

Section 1 states that it is an offence to sell, advertise or have possession of food which is injurious to health.

Section 2 prohibits the sale of any food not of the nature, substance or quality demanded by the purchaser.

Section 6 refers to false or misleading descriptions regarding nature, substance or quality, including nutritional and dietary value.

Section 8 makes it an offence to sell food which is unfit for human consumption.

Sections 9,10,14,16,19 and 21 deal with authorisation and methods of enforcement, including closure of premises and disqualification of the offending caterer.

The Food Safety Act 1990

This Act seeks to consolidate and update previous food legislation. Like previous legislation, the Act 'enables' the creation of regulations. Such regulations are likely to include the registration of food premises and certification of food handlers. The Act creates new powers of inspection and seizure by the EHOs, who will be empowered to issue Improvement Notices (setting a time limit for action) and, with the support of the courts, Prohibition Orders preventing further business activity. The caterer may be able to use 'due diligence' as a defence but would have to prove that all possible precautions were taken. This would normally require reliable documentary evidence that procedures, processes and controls have taken place.

Summary

Good menu planning is founded on the development of a suitable range of dishes which reflect consumer demand. Product planning and dish development require the use of forecasting techniques, and the standardisation of recipes and methods, in order to assure consistent quality. Profitability can only be maintained through the use, not only of standardisation and control procedures, but also by applying book-keeping and accounting principles.

In developing new and interesting dishes the caterer will be aware of nutritional values in the foods used and the effect of both traditional and modern cooking methods. Even so, the menu-planner will be required to respond to developments in production systems and processes.

If menu fatigue is to be avoided the choice of dishes offered must be the subject of a continuous programme of development – creating new dishes and responding to changes in food processing and supply, equipment technology and methods of cookery. Such development will involve not only reference to food values and nutritional content but also the combination of textures, flavours and colours, as well as the identification of cost and the control of quality.

Check list

1. Has demand been accurately forecast?
2. Has the nutritional value of the dish been assessed?
3. Have dishes been tested/tasted?
4. Have recipes and methods been standardised?
5. Is dish method/recipe consistent with the system of production?
6. Are equipment and staffing allocations consistent with the needs of dishes which have been developed?
7. What quality assurance/control techniques have been applied?
8. Has yield been calculated?
9. Are accurate costings available and up-to-date?
10. Does the dish/system of production comply with the requirements of current legislation?

Purchasing

Harsher economics of catering linked with techno-logical changes and new consumer tastes have altered, and continue to alter, the nature of purchasing in the catering industry. Escalating manpower and food costs have fostered the development of less-expansive menus. Shorter menus tend to reduce the need for a number of highly-specialised buyers.

AN APPROACH TO BUYING

Increasing food cost engenders ever-increasing con-cern with tight specifications and ease of portion control. Seeking uniform-size fish or pre-cut meat portions is now the rule rather than the exception. Professional buyers' or managements' concern with standards of quality and size and the new sources of supply may limit a chef's role in the buying pro-cedures in some operations. The chef may have less direct responsibility for initiating specifications and purchasing which are increasingly determined by top management adopting firm menu and food and bev-erage policies. Kitchen responsibilities in relation to buying are increasingly those of ensuring that the standards set through specifications are met.

It is important that everyone involved in the purchase activity, regardless of levels of authority, clearly understands the total philosophy and the purchasing policy of the organisation, and has received suitable training and instructions.

Any system involved with the creation of an end product may be divided into three distinct parts, input – process – output. In order to achieve the desired standard of output it is essential that both input and process are carefully controlled. Purchasing is concerned with the control of raw material (the input part).

Catering is a diverse industry, for this reason it is not possible to offer a single, definitive solution to the purchasing problem. However it is possible to ident-ify those elements within the purchasing process which have a significant effect on the ultimate success and profitability of an operation, regardless of its size or the market in which it operates.

> In many operations the opportunity to make a 2 per cent saving in costs is overlooked while a great deal of time and effort might be spent trying to increase revenue (sales) by a similar amount. Those organisations that are able to do both are going to be highly successful.

Wise purchasing can lead to both cost savings and revenue increases. If chefs take advantage of their knowledge of meat they may not only be able to negotiate a better price but by careful specification of quality, shape and size of cut they may also be able to obtain less trim and waste, and hence more por-tions per pound.

AIMS OF PURCHASING

The three specific aims of an efficient purchasing department may be grouped as follows.

Select and purchase

The aims are to obtain the most appropriate materials, in terms of quality and quantity, for a specified purpose, at the most appropriate time and at the best price. In short, to secure value for money, consistent with the company's quality standards and image.

Procedures

The aims are to apply the correct procedures, documents and controls necessary in the control cycle, as defined by the size, type and structure of the establishment. In short, to ensure that the goods are used for the purpose for which they were originally bought.

Accounting

The aims are to enable accurate accounting for goods and services bought, handled and/or sold; to make payment for goods received in accordance with terms and conditions as agreed with the supplier; to ensure that the organisation actually receives goods ordered and paid for; and to utilise, where possible, the technological aids which can assist efficient/effective control.

PURCHASING POLICY

Purchasing policy varies between different organisations with different corporate objectives, but it should always be based on the optimisation of purchase costs. This will be governed by levels of stockholding, methods of purchasing, type and quality of raw material, quality of end-product, type of supplier and method of payment. The efficient organisation of the purchasing function is based on a clearly-defined structure and span of control which identify levels of responsibility and delegate authority as necessary.

Physical control will determine method and authority for placing orders with suppliers. It will identify who checks deliveries, who authorises requisitions, who has access to store areas and what documentation is used. The extent to which purchasing is carried out at unit level depends on the nature of the operation and its corporate structure.

Major chains are generally committed to a system of centralised buying based on pre-defined menus and using specialised/standardised products and strict cost control. Unit managers often have little discretionary control over price, brand or supplier.

> The largest hotel company in the UK, Forte, has its own supplies division which is, in effect, a wholesaler.

Institutional caterers normally rely on centralised buying, contracting to nominated regional suppliers after raw material specifications have been put out to tender. There may well be a national/regional department responsible for tendering and testing procedures prior to agreeing a supply contract.

Independently-owned operations run by owner-managers will do all of their own buying. These smaller units may recognise the advantages of buying in bulk and some have formed consortia in order to negotiate discounts with suppliers.

Franchise units, although individually-owned and operated, are usually supplied by the franchiser or from nationally-approved sources. Consequently, they usually have little option concerning their purchases.

RESPONSIBILITY

Responsibilities for buying both perishable goods and commodities for the dry stores still vary considerably in the catering industry. In larger hotels, hotel and restaurant groups and larger institutions, buying is a highly-specialised function. In many establishments the duties of a buyer may be spread over a wide range of commodities.

The prime requisite in buying for catering establishments is complete personal integrity plus grasping the concept of getting the best bargain in terms of quality and price that is compatible with the establishment's catering policy. Buying should not be a matter of 'automatic' re-ordering on the basis of past experience with repetition of regular orders. Rather, it should follow thoughtful estimating based on intelligent forecasting, prevailing prices, specifications, stock held and other related factors.

The chef and, indeed, the catering officer or catering manager may not, therefore, have sole responsibility for purchasing goods and nominating suppliers. There are, however, many instances, particularly in smaller kitchens, where cooking and catering are of necessity combined with purchasing. In any event, chefs will invariably be carrying a major responsibility for the acceptance of goods delivered. It is obvious that they must have sound knowledge of the raw materials and commodities that they and their staff are to use. Their technical advice is likely to be of value in preparing specifications.

In order to identify more carefully various responsibilities it may be useful to identify two distinct elements within the purchase procedure: selection and buying.

Selection

This involves obtaining information on products and suppliers; making comparisons between quotations, prices and services; approving or appointing a supplier; determining the required quality standard; choosing the state of each commodity (fresh/tinned/frozen); selecting brands; and authorising payments based on agreed payment methods and frequency.

Buying

This involves determining quantity and frequency of supply; negotiating the best price (which may not necessarily be the cheapest as quality should play a part in the decision); placing orders; and receiving and acknowledging receipt.

For the larger organisations, both public and private, these two elements are frequently separated. A centralised purchasing department is often responsible for selection, and usually price negotiation, with individual units being responsible for placing orders.

THE PURCHASE CONTRACT

There is a saying that 'possession is nine-tenths of the law' and it is true that much of the British legal system is related to the law of contract which governs the exchange of goods, services and/or money. The caterer must, therefore, be aware of his legal rights, obligations and liabilities in all business activities related to buying and selling.

The law will assume a contract to exist in any situation where goods are exchanged, whether there is a written document or not. All that has to be proved is that an offer was made and accepted. The problem with a verbal contract is proving precisely what the offer was, for there will be no physical evidence.

It is a good idea to involve company solicitors when negotiating a contract with a supplier. Although the person responsible for purchasing should have the technical knowledge to ensure that the supplier meets the requirements of the organisation, there may well be some legal jargon, fine print or implied terms that require specialist advice.

There are two important parts to a purchase contract:

- the general conditions;
- the product specifications.

General conditions cover such things as the period of contract, delivery point/dates/times, invoicing address, method of payment, discounts, refunds, inspection rights, non-availability and alternatively-acceptable products. The general conditions are normally the subject of negotiation between caterer and supplier. The caterer is well-advised to accept some of the suppliers' recommendations, as being difficult may well add to cost (for example, stipulating unusual delivery times or small minimum drops).

The product specifications, however, must be determined and controlled by the caterer who should be prepared to accept the advice of the supplier with regard to quality and availability of products, prior to setting the actual specification, but should not be persuaded to accept vague specifications or terms within the contract which allow the supplier to vary the specification without previous express consent. Product specifications must, by definition, be specific and they must be adhered to.

There are two common forms of contract entered into by the caterer:

- Contract A, specified period (usually three to six months) – This form of contractual arrangement ensures consistency of supply by confirming the source. Cost savings are derived from reduced administration time. This method is most suited to products where little change in price is expected. It enables more accurate budgeting and pricing.
- Contract B, specified quantity – This ensures continuity of supply for an essential item at an agreed price. It avoids the risk of fluctuation in price.

METHODS OF PURCHASING

Caterers can purchase commodities in a variety of ways. The ultimate choice of method will depend upon the type of commodity being purchased and the size and type of catering operation.

Nominated supplier purchasing

This gives a supplier the exclusive right to supply certain goods. This method is used in the health service, armed services and education authorities. The advantage of the system is that by assuring the supplier of their exclusive rights the caterer expects to receive excellent service and consistency in the quality of goods supplied, together with a substantial discount.

Tendering

This is used by organisations that can purchase large quantities of an item. Suppliers are asked to submit quotations (which may be in the form of a sealed or open bid) for the supply of specified commodities. It is normal for the supplier to return a product sample with the quotation and the supplier that is seen to offer the best value for money is selected. The edible yield, as tested by the prospective purchaser, is then used to determine the real price of the product. Reputation of the supplier may also influence choice.

Paid reserve

This occurs where the availability of specialist menu items is considered on a global scale and particularly where there may be limited supply or shortages as a result of a poor harvest, for example, specialist blends of tea. Caterers may anticipate their requirements and endeavour to ensure uninterrupted supply. Paid reserve involves the purchase, in advance, of a quantity (usually large) – of a particular commodity required to cover forecasted needs over a fairly long period (six to 12 months). The supplier would normally agree to hold stock and provide deliveries as required.

Total supply

Most of the leading suppliers now offer to supply the total needs of the caterer. Although there may be some restriction in product/brand choice and price competition the caterer benefits from fewer negotiations and a reduction in administration and paperwork. The number of deliveries is considerably reduced and the caterer's entire inventory can be delivered in one drop. Suppliers are more inclined to see their contribution as a service to the caterer. Developments in the one-drop method of supply have been greatly enhanced with the advent of the multi-temperature vehicle which allows products to be carried at ambient, chilled and frozen temperatures simultaneously. The modern vehicle is likely to have moveable bulkheads and sides as well as rear access, allowing it to carry every type of product in any proportion. This system can work for any caterer so long as the drop size is reasonable and the delivery cycle regular.

Cost plus

This method is used by institutions/hospitals who agree to pay the daily market price plus a percentage (10–12 per cent or higher depending on level of service required and the size/scale of the contract) to cover handling, transportation, administration and of course profit for the supplier. The caterer relies a great deal on the integrity of the supplier. Product specifications must be clear to everyone, particularly those responsible for checking deliveries. The manager must check invoice charges against market prices. In these circumstances, the supplier has no reason to over-estimate quotations in order to allow for unpredicted rises in market price during the period of the contract. Additionally, the caterer will obtain any benefit, should there be a fall in market price.

Centralised buying

This method is used by larger organisations responsible for many units. The units place orders with head office, the total order is then given to the supplier who delivers to central stores. The organisation is then responsible for deliveries to each of its units. Transportation costs must be offset against any savings made on bulk purchase. The negotiating power of a sizeable organisation buying in bulk can have a significant effect on prices quoted. Some of the largest organisations may be in a position to buy direct from the manufacturer, thus reducing costs still further. Buying direct from the manufacturer may also enable the caterers to specify production methods and have caterers' own-brand goods.

Daily market list

This is used for fresh produce where daily delivery is essential, for example, for fruit, vegetables and fish. The manager or chef will phone for quotations from approved suppliers. Quotations are entered against a list (see Figure 4.1). The manager or chef must then decide whether to split the list (share the order between several suppliers) or go to the supplier offering the best total price.

It is wise to record the actual price for the total quantity of each item required, rather than the price per unit, as the effect of differing methods of pricing and discounting may not be immediately apparent.

For example:

4 doz. lettuce @ £2.40 per doz.		= £9.60
4 doz. lettuce @ £2.50 per doz.		
	less 5% discount	= £9.50

Item	Quantity required	Supplier			
		A (£)	B (£)	C (£)	D (£)
Lettuce	4 doz.	9.60	9.50	9.80	9.30
Tomatoes	2 kg (5lb)	2.80	2.60	3.00	2.80
Cress	6 punnet	0.60	0.60	0.30	0.45
Carrots	25 kg (62.5lb)	4.80	6.00	9.00	9.00
Onions	12 kg (30 lb)	4.50	5.00	6.00	7.50
Celery	10 head	3.50	3.20	4.00	3.80
Total cost		25.80	26.90	32.10	32.85

Figure 4.1   *Market lists – comparing suppliers' prices*

Weekly/fortnightly quotation list

This method follows a similar process to the daily list described above and is used for grocery items where a weekly delivery is adequate.

Cash-and-carry

In this situation, the supplier acts as a warehouse/ supermarket which gives the small caterer greater access to wholesalers and manufacturers. The caterer obtains the benefit of competitive prices but carries the burden of transportation costs which add to the true cost of purchases.

Larger caterers may use the cash-and-carry for emergency supplies or unusual, non-stock items. The caterer has relatively easy access to warehouses which are usually situated in built-up areas, and can examine produce and compare price and value. By definition, a caterer would normally be expected to produce cash immediately although with the growth in credit cards and computers we are now in the age of EPOSFT (Electronic Point of Sale Funds Transfer). EPOSFT enables the supplier to be credited immediately with funds from the caterer's bank account, the caterer does not have to carry large amounts of cash or write out large cheques.

With the decline in the number of small, independent grocers many cash-and-carry outlets now see the caterer as a major market and, therefore, provide an excellent service.

BUYING KNOWLEDGE

Practical caterers may question the need for technical and commercial knowledge, but it is clear that someone in the catering operation should have an appreciation of the fundamentals of both. The range of professional knowledge is summarised in Figure 4.2. Training, research and past experience should all be harnessed to identify quality and fitness for purpose of food materials, in terms of preparation and presentation. These are usually expressed in a specification. The effectiveness and accuracy of the specification and resultant purchase must be gauged by yield and actually tested in the kitchen.

Buying has to be concerned with preventing waste and loss. Buying commodities that are on the one hand not good enough or, on the other hand, better than needed for their purpose, represents potential loss.

Whether the menu is short or extensive, the caterer will, initially at least, have a vast array of commodities to choose from. Perishable items like meat, game, fish

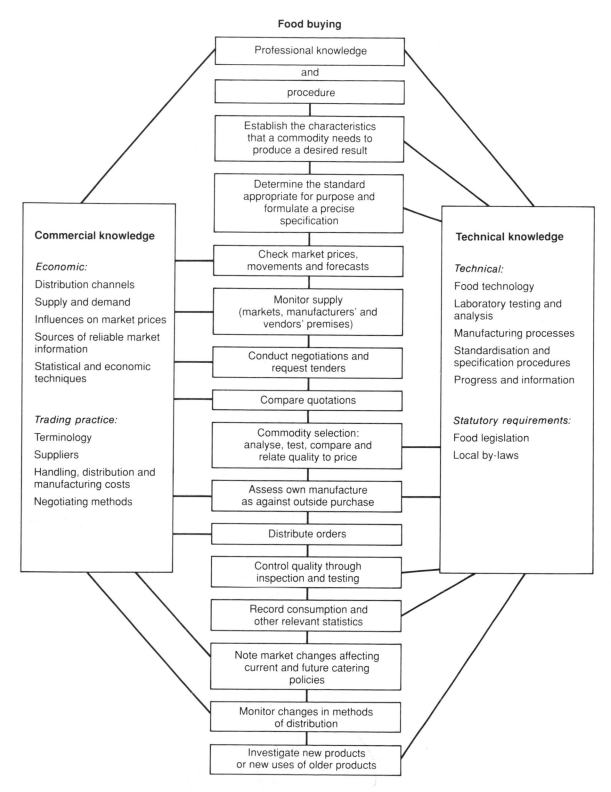

Figure 4.2 *Food buying – professional knowledge and procedure*

and poultry involve a knowledge of meat cuts and joints used in the hotel trade as well as those used in the retail meat trade. The range of fruit and vegetables may include those more exotic than commonly found in the average retail greengrocers' shops. In addition to the perishable items, provisions and grocery items again range wider than the average supermarket.

The purchase decision requires thought, planning and control, supported by knowledge, experience and resources. The decision will be influenced by the type of unit and the location of the establishment. The effective caterer will be conscious of the influence of purchasing activity on the profitability of the operation.

Factors which contribute to poor profitability include:
- bad buying and particularly poor value for money;
- over-purchasing, resulting in stock lying idle and not earning money;
- poor storage, resulting in waste;
- poor quality control, leading to low acceptability and customer dissatisfaction;
- poor portion control (too large, too small or erratic);
- poor preparation, leading to low acceptability and yield;
- bad pricing, resulting in an inadequate gross profit margin and a net loss.

Intelligent buying, by careful specification, not only helps avoid errors in direct buying, but also assists chefs and catering staff in avoiding associated faults. In catering, food wasted represents loss of food at its potential sales price, not cost price. Purchasing, on its own, cannot create profit. The benefit (cost saving) of effective buying only becomes apparent once a sale is made. Even so, it would be foolish to rely on good sales to minimise poor purchasing. Hence, buying procedures must be directed towards total effectiveness.

Information

Clearly, up-to-date information is a major advantage during any purchase negotiations and will enable objective decisions to be made about quotations offered. There are several ways to ensure that purchase decisions are based on up-to-date information.

The supply trade press provide commodity lists and information on current availability, quality and market prices. Trade organisations can be a useful source of information about types and varieties of products available as well as giving advice on the comparative benefits of similar products.

The catering trade press provide up-to-date news, information and market prices, and are particularly valuable for their generally unbiased comment, informative articles and promotional ideas.

The national press provide commodity market news, for example, it gives the price and availability of coffee. A rise in the commodity market price will eventually be passed on to the consumer. Published price indices (changes in commodity prices over a given period) can usefully identify trends and help in arranging early purchases of commodities where price rises might be expected or, conversely, delaying purchases until the prices drop.

Government publications provide essential information on food legislation, surveys and statistics.

Food distribution

It is important for those responsible for food purchase to understand the nature of food supply channels. Some caterers may receive food from all of the supply sources shown in Figure 4.3, but most receive food through at least three.

Whilst caterers may still buy directly from fresh produce markets, they also buy fresh foods from retailers and wholesalers. Convenience food usage has increased the supply to caterers direct from food processing plants (for example, frozen foods), but patterns of supply and purchasing continue to change.

There are two main characteristics to be considered when evaluating supply sources: primary and secondary sources.

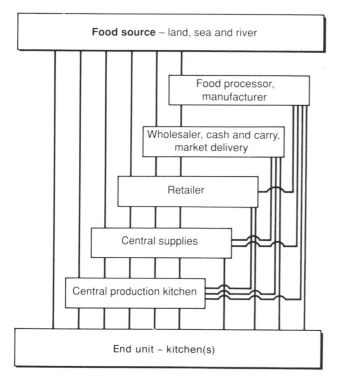

Figure 4.3 *Food supply channels to caterers*

Primary sources include:

- growers – that supply fresh produce with seasonal availability;
- manufacturers – that make products from raw materials;
- processors – that combine fresh and manufactured goods.

Secondary sources include:

- wholesalers – that provide large stocks and delivery, at moderate prices;
- cash-and-carry outlets – that provide easy access and personal selection;
- retailers – that have limited stocks but provide a good service.

The advantage of buying from a primary source is the perceived benefit of quality; the product is fresher, more natural and has no additives. The disadvantage is that availability may be inconsistent, prices may fluctuate and transportation will normally be the responsibility of the purchaser, thus adding to costs.

On the other hand, wholesalers offer a wide range/variety of good and brands and will organise a delivery service to supply requirements in appropriate quantities.

The purchasing decision is based on the identification of operational or company needs and wants, and the expectations of suppliers. By analysing these needs, wants and expectations we can identify the the most suitable supplier.

How do you choose a supplier?

To decide which supplier best meets all the requirements of a caterer, supplier grading is used.

What do you want from a supplier?
Normally the caterer looks for:

- value for money;
- absolute integrity;
- quality and variety of choice;
- timely deliveries;
- accurate information;
- technically-qualified personnel;
- accommodating (large/small) deliveries;
- emergency support;
- efficiency.

What does the supplier want from you?
Normally the supplier will expect:

- technical competence;
- clear, concise instructions;
- authority to buy;
- knowledge of trade procedures/discount systems;
- orders placed on time;
- quick decisions when necessary;
- prompt payment;
- care taken with returnable containers;
- complete integrity.

SUPPLIER GRADING

The choice of suppliers must be determined by their ability to meet the caterer's requirements in three main areas:

- price;
- quality;
- delivery.

Price performance

The cheapest is not always best, on the other hand high price does not always equal high quality. The ideal price performance is a relatively low price for a good-quality product. The rating for price performance may be found by taking the average price charged over a given period for a product of specified quality. A consistently low price (compared to other suppliers) will be given a high rating.

Quality performance

The rating for quality will be based on consistency; the more consistent the supplier the higher the rating.

Delivery performance

This is a measure of the supplier's ability to meet agreed delivery times. Late (or early) delivery may well affect the quality of goods, especially if they are perishable. Inconsistent deliveries will add to pressure of work in a receiving department. Once again consistency of performance is critical, the nearer to delivery date and time the higher the supplier will be rated.

Objective assessment of the supplier's performance in these three areas will determine the supplier grading which will be useful in negotiations and eventual selection of a supplier.

A supplier rated at 6–9–10 (price–quality–delivery) by the buying department would be understood to offer goods at a fairly high price (there are other suppliers who are cheaper), to supply good quality and to have a first-class delivery record. Subjective decisions will have to be made, for example, a comparison of the above supplier with, a 6–10–7 supplier will have to consider whether an increase in consistency of quality warrants the possible disruptions of an erratic or inconvenient delivery time.

For an existing supplier the exercise is a fairly simple one and takes into account purchase history and actual evidence of performance over a given purchase period. The chef and catering staff will be involved in maintaining the records necessary for grading and comparison.

For a new supplier there is often a tendency to be more subjective. However, uncorroborated opinions should, as far as is possible, be avoided in favour of hard facts.

In addition to gathering evidence it is also a good idea to visit prospective suppliers in order to check the details listed above and if possible to meet the management team. This can be a time-consuming exercise, but it is essential for a good business/professional relationship. For the same reason, you should also encourage prospective suppliers to visit your business in order to identify your needs at first hand.

As a result of the supplier-grading exercise you will be able to produce an approved suppliers list which would, quite naturally, require periodic evaluation.

THE COST OF PURCHASING

Whichever supplier is responsible for the provision of raw materials and whatever the method of purchasing used, it is useful to understand how it is possible to negotiate, or influence downwards, the cost of purchases. There is no guarantee that any of these approaches will be successful, it all depends on how the supplier has established the price in the first place and whether or not there is any margin for reduction. There will always be a price below which the supplier will not drop.

The opportunity to negotiate price will, to some extent, be determined by the product in question. If a product is a high-cost item, such as fillet of beef, then the supplier will recognise that the caterer will be price conscious and will probably be prepared to shop around. In these circumstances, the supplier may be prepared to reduce price in order to retain custom.

When dealing with fresh produce the suppliers will want to ensure the product is sold before it begins to deteriorate. There will be a point at which they may be prepared to drop the price in order to ensure a sale. Clearly, in these circumstances, caterers must be certain that they are able to process and sell the product without further loss of quality and careful examination of the goods will be necessary. This is a particularly dangerous area for caterers to get into, many businesses have suffered through the rash purchase of a 'bargain' buy, particularly when large quantities are involved.

When it is not possible to negotiate a lower price the caterer may accept the supplier's prices, but negotiate more favourable credit terms or extended payment schedules, both of which could result in savings for the caterer. Similarly, a discount for bulk purchase or prompt payment may be negotiated. However, discounts are not so common today as they once were. Further savings may be effected by examining stock-holding, order costs and storage costs.

It is essential that stock levels are maintained to prevent running short of items. However, every item of stock on the shelf is money tied up that could be earning interest. It is just as important to make sure that excessive stock is not being held as it is to ensure that stocks are not depleted.

The order cost is defined as that cost incurred every time an order is placed. It is made up of telephone charges, administration of paperwork, wages and salaries of staff involved and so on. It is extremely difficult to establish exactly what these costs are in any operation, but one thing is certain, if fewer orders are placed both time and money are saved.

Storage costs comprise the obvious costs, such as electricity and stock insurance, and hidden costs, such as the potential interest-earning power of money that is tied up in stock and the potential better use that storage space could be put to for revenue-making purposes.

Clearly, order costs and storage costs have opposite effects; as one rises the other decreases. If you try to reduce your order costs by placing fewer orders and, therefore, ordering larger amounts, then your storage costs go up. If you try to reduce your storage costs by holding minimum levels of stock, then you must order more frequently and order costs rise.

Efficient purchasing may be defined as ordering the right amount, at the right time, at the right price.

PRODUCT SPECIFICATIONS

In the United States a specification has been defined as a statement of particulars in specific terms. In the UK's retail trade, the success of companies like Marks & Spencer has been associated with careful specifications for items of clothing, foods and other goods, which accurately meet the demands and pockets of their customers. In catering, similarly keen specifications may be used to achieve costing, pricing and profit targets.

In a catering context a specification provides:
- buying standards for the operation;
- an agreed definition for both the buyer and seller;
- uniformity and consistency in purchasing and receiving.

It is not proposed, in this chapter, to give examples of specifications for each type of food. Each product has different attributes to be considered when purchasing. These will affect what is incorporated into the specification for a particular commodity. Moreover, the specification must accurately reflect the needs of the catering operation in terms of menu style, numbers catered for, storage capacity, control problems, portioning, service style, staff skills and equipment. These factors need to be evaluated relative to the plate or portion cost of what is to be bought.

A specification should, therefore, include detail regarding quality, type, quantity, characteristics, delivery time and frequency. These involve discussing with appropriate staff (i.e. the using and receiving staff) problems linked with checking, storing, issuing, preparing, cooking, portioning, holding and service. In short, key catering staff need to be involved and kept informed to help maintain desired food cost.

Any specification may need to be amended and revised as a commodity becomes scarcer, dearer, cheaper or more abundant. This might prompt the inclusion of further details regarding the country of origin and whether or not the produce is to be chilled or frozen.

Using a specification

A specification's prime purpose is to inform potential suppliers of a caterer's requirements so that they can properly quote prices. Specifications are circulated to possible suppliers to attract competitive market quotations. A buyer seeks the most favourable price, but unit price is never the principal consideration. Certainly, such units as sack, box, punnet and head must be accompanied by weight details.

The true worth of a specification depends on its effectiveness in terms of actual yield and consumer satisfaction. Kitchen tests need to be used to check yield. Consumer satisfaction must be assessed by consistent monitoring.

High-cost items

Buying inevitably tends to concentrate maximum attention on high-cost foods. The cost of low-cost foods should not, however, be overlooked, particularly where these items are consumed in volume. Attention should be given to the total value of any commodity purchased. Although high-cost protein items are often highlighted, low-cost/high-volume commodities, like vegetables and potatoes, with their propensity to waste, should not be ignored.

Specifications must be used consistently to be effective. In small operations, or where market availability reduces volume purchased or wherever factors of this kind make formal specification impracticable, the specification concept can still be used to aid profitable purchasing.

Importantly, those who are responsible within the catering operation itself for checking that the specification has been met, require specification details for their own use. Those within the operation who need this information include the chef (who may well be involved in preparing the specification), the goods receiver and/or storeperson. This is because effective specification buying demands effective specification receiving.

Writing a specification

One problem associated with the writing of purchase specifications is the lack of commonly accepted and understood terms and definitions, although every opportunity should be taken to make use of those that do exists, for example, EEC grading for vegetables and fruit, and systems as used by New Zealand Lamb and the MLC (Meat and Livestock Commission). When writing your own specifications keep the language simple and clear, avoid the use of ambiguous words like 'nice' which are capable of a variety of interpretations, and where necesssary use diagrams and photographs.

Raw material specifications may be influenced by:
- company policy;
- type of production system;
- storage facilities available;
- level of staff expertise;
- menu requirements;
- budgetary and financial considerations;
- service style.

The following may be used as a guideline in drawing up a specification:

- name of product;
- intended use of product;
- specific details – type, grade or brand name, size/weight, edible yield, special notes;
- inspection procedure (intended checks on delivery);
- unit price;
- minimum and maximum order quantity.

Figure 4.4 gives an example of a raw material specification.

Please note that deviation from the standards specified may be taken as breach of contract.

Item	*general description*
Intended use	
Description	*type, brand name, etc.*
Quality	*grade*
Unit size	*pack size, weight, edible yield*
Units per pack	
Unit price	
Min/max order quantity	
Delivery details	
Inspection procedure	
Authorising Officer	Date ....

Figure 4.4 *Raw material specification*

There are some potential problems inherent in the writing of purchase specifications, most of which result from poor preparation and/or planning. Specifications may use a quality standard which is difficult to obtain and, therefore, adds to cost. A geographical specification will involve seasonal fluctuation and, therefore, variations in price. Specific delivery times, if unreasonable, will add to cost and imprecise specifications defeat the whole purpose of the exercise. Over-specifying, including unnecessary detail or impossible demands, can create difficulties for the supplier which may well be passed on as additional cost.

PURCHASING PROCEDURE

Control and documentation of the transaction

When an order is placed it can be done by:

- telephone (usually daily orders of fresh foods);
- in person to a salesperson or representative;
- by post.

Whichever method is used it should always be supported by strict adherence to company policy/procedure. Cash purchases and standing orders should be avoided. Cash purchases are generally a sign of inefficiencies in the system. Standing orders may be seen initially as attractive, as paperwork is reduced and the supplier may even offer a discount, but this is only because the supplier is more likely to benefit from the use of standing orders than the caterer who may well find that the opportunity to buy at a more competitve price has been missed.

Sample procedure

This is outlined in Figure 4.5 (overleaf) and follows the steps below:

- Identify requirements based on menu, dish specification, standardised recipes, raw material specifications, minimum stock and re-order levels.
- Produce a purchase list ensuring that details (raw material specifications) are correct. Identify sources of supply and separate the list as necessary, for example, into dry goods, meat, dairy products.
- Check prices and select a suitable supplier by reference to the supplier rating. In many cases prices may need to be checked by phone in which case, if acceptable, the order may be placed at the same time. Where systems allow, a telephone order may be supported by a faxed copy of the completed order form.
- Complete the order form, usually in triplicate, and dispatch the top copy, by post, to the supplier. One copy will be retained by the purchasing office the other copy should go to the receiving area or stores control clerk.
- Prior to delivery the caterer may receive an advice note. This is likely only in the event of large orders that are placed some time in advance of delivery. The purpose of the advice note is to acknowledge receipt of the order, state when goods will be delivered by the supplier and inform the purchaser of any items which may be unavailable or temporarily out-of-stock.

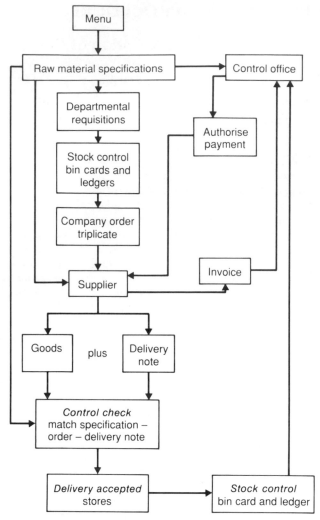

Figure 4.5   *Purchase (control) procedure*

Documentation

This could include any one or more of the following:

- Letter of enquiry (or phone) – a tender or request for information or prices, resulting in an offer by the supplier to sell goods at a specified price.
- Quotation – an offer by the supplier to sell, identifying the price and terms of sale, which may be subject to negotiation. May prove useful in completing the supplier rating.
- Purchase order – an offer to buy or agreement on contract terms, should contain the following details:
  who the order is from (name and address of firm);
  who it is to (supplier name and address);
  the serial number (reference number);
  the date;
  the signature of the person ordering;
  the signature of the person authorising;
  the name, amount and price of each item required;
  the purchase specification (unless previously agreed).

Summary

Whilst the food buyer must remain vigilant, critical and alert, it would be a mistake for any caterer to seek to have anything other than good relations with suppliers. What is of overriding importance is to select dealers of sound reputation from whom one can expect reliable goods and fair service. Skilled meat purveyors and trained grocers have not only the knowledge of their professions, but are as likely to have as high professional standards as conscientious caterers. To seek to develop an atmosphere of mutual confidence and trust with sound merchants does not imply a naive reliance on someone else's judgement, rather it certainly helps in securing a good supplier's expert skill and assistance.

Effective purchasing specifications that match the needs of the menu and are based on knowledge of food grading and standards are vital. Good purchasing records will help to avoid over-buying and will prevent fraud. However, they may be wasted if receiving is entrusted to inexperienced staff. Conscientious weighing, accounting and receipt scrutiny is essential. If such care is not exercised, suppliers and/or delivery personnel may be tempted to under-deliver. Good buying must be supported by good receiving.

In such a diverse industry as catering it is difficult to be prescriptive about the best purchasing system. The optimum system will be the one that best meets the needs of the customer, the caterer and the supplier, resulting in the most efficient method of obtaining clearly specified raw materials at the most economic prices.

In many instances, the basis of the relationship between caterer and supplier will be defined in a written contract. Unit managers and chefs working for large, national companies, will sometimes find that they are bound by contract to a supplier who in some instances charges significantly more than a local supplier. The policy would have been negotiated nationally and the benefits, such as reduced administration and transportation costs, may only be apparent at head office. The role of the unit manager/chef in these circumstances should be to identify the differences and inform head office.

Whether a written contract exists or not, the relationship between caterer and supplier should be one of mutual trust, as noted by J.F. Love in his book (*McDonalds – Behind the Arches*, Bantam Press, 1987) where he refers to the relationship between McDonalds and one of their suppliers:

'Lotman, a major supplier of hamburger, said in response to a comment about his lack of a supply contract "People ask me how I sleep, knowing that I have but one customer and no supply contract. My answer is that a supply contract is only as good as the people who sign it and if those people have honourable intent you don't need a contract. With McDonalds I have never needed a contract!"'

Check list

1. Determine the company policy.
2. Identify levels of authority.
3. Define precise raw material specifications; if possible see and test before purchase.
4. Set maximum, minimum and re-order levels for all stock items.
5. Identify sources of supply and distribution channels.
6. Select suppliers on the basis of supplier grading.
7. Update price lists regularly/frequently and make comparisons between suppliers.
8. Choose a suitable method of purchase and payment.
9. All purchasing must be made through a nominated person, who is known to the supplier, authorised and signed for, before the order is placed.
10. Use a standardised order form.
11. The same person placing orders should not also receive deliveries.
12. Watch market trends and special offers; consult with suppliers.
13. When orders are placed by phone ensure that a written purchase order (confirmation) is completed and processed immediately.
14. Discourage cash purchases; if absolutely necessary then authorise limits.
15. Avoid dependence on standing orders; reassess frequently.

Dairy Produce, Fats and Oils

Dairy produce, fats and oils make a major contribution to the UK national diet. Some products perform a unique function, both in the diet and in cookery processes, and are therefore considered to be indispensable. In the minds of most customers dairy produce infers rich, wholesome ingredients.

Dairy terms have had a history of abuse in relation to enhancing products of lesser quality by applying dairy terms and descriptions to promote these products.

FOOD VALUES

Milk is mainly water (87 per cent), fat (3.9 per cent) and non-fat solids (see Table 5.1), the precise content of which is stipulated by government regulations.

Fat

Milk fat consists of fat globules (suspended as natural emulsion), each protected by a protein membrane. The fat globules are lighter than other milk constituents, hence their tendency to rise to the surface.

Table 5.1 Nutritional chart – dairy produce, fats, oils and eggs

Product	Per 100g				
	Energy (cals)	Protein (g)	Fat (g)	Carbohydrate (g)	Calcium (mg)
Channel Island milk	76	3.6	4.8	4.7	120
Milk, whole	65	3.3	3.8	4.7	120
Long-life UHT	65	3.3	3.8	4.7	120
Milk, semi-skimmed	47	3.4	1.8	4.7	125
Milk, skimmed	33	3.4	0.1	5.0	130
Milk, goats	71	3.3	4.5	4.6	130
Cream, single	212	2.4	21.2	3.2	79
Cream, whipping	332	1.9	35.0	2.5	63
Cream, double	447	1.5	48.2	2.0	50
Butter (salted)	746	0.4	82.0	0.5	15
Yogurt, natural (low fat)	52	5.0	1.0	6.2	180
Yogurt, fruit	95	4.8	1.0	17.9	160
Yogurt, hazelnut	106	5.2	2.6	16.5	180
Cheese, Cheddar	406	26.0	33.5	0.1	800
Cheese, Stilton	462	25.6	40.0	0.1	360
Cheese, cottage (low fat)	96	13.6	4.0	1.4	60
Lard	891	0.1	99.0	0.0	1
Vegetable oil	899	0.1	99.9	0.0	0
Eggs, whole	147	12.3	10.9	0.1	52

Protein

The three principal milk proteins are casein and the whey proteins lactalbumin and lactoglobulin. Together they provide high-quality protein containing all the essential amino acids.

Carbohydrate

Lactose, the milk sugar, is unique to milk. It is readily fermented into lactic acid, by the bacteria naturally present in raw, untreated milk, which causes souring. Pasteurisation and other forms of heat treatment destroy these bacteria and so increase the keeping quality of the milk. Lactose may be deliberately fermented, by the introduction of specific bacteria, during the manufacture of yogurt and soured cream.

Vitamins and minerals

Milk is a good source of vitamins and minerals. Yogurt contains the same nutrients as the milk from which it was produced and so has good food value. It is a particularly good source of protein due to the addition of extra milk solids during manufacture. Yogurt made from skimmed milk lacks the fat soluble vitamins A and D which are naturally present in butterfat, however these are now added to many brands of yogurt so check the label.

Cream is a rich source of energy and vitamins A and D. As the butterfat percentage increases the vitamin and calorfic content increases and the calcium and water content decreases.

Cheese is one of the oldest ways of concentrating and preserving the nutrients of milk. It takes one gallon of milk to make a pound of cheese, which is a concentration of the fat and non-fat solids. Its nutritional content is, therefore, similar to a concentrated form of milk. It contains more protein per ounce than eggs, fish or meat and is a rich source of calcium, vitamin A and riboflavin. The nutritional value of cheese does not alter during cooking.

Butter is a good, natural, source of vitamins A, D and E.

Over recent years there has been a general increase in the demand for fresh dairy produce with reduced fat levels. Healthy eating has generated a demand for skimmed and semi-skimmed milk and low-fat spreads and cheeses.

MILK

The sole sustenance of a young mammal, milk is an almost 'complete' food, containing some of all the nutrients needed to keep the body in good health. Milk contains no additives, the only method of extending its shelf life which is permitted by government regulations is heat treatment.

A. *Veterinary tests* – for disease/illness in the cow:
   1. Mastitis;
   2. Brucellosis.
B. *Control tests*, in the processing laboratory, which may affect payments made to the dairy farmer:
   3. Composition – protein, lactose and butterfat content;
   4. Hygiene – bacterial count of milk samples;
   5. Antibiotics – ensures that milk from cows under treatment is not used.
C. *Dairy/creamery test* for quality:
   6. Extraneous water – based on the difference in freezing point between water and milk (section 36 of the 1984 Food Act makes it an offence to add water to milk);
   7. Butterfat – percentage content;
   8. Non-fat solids – density of the milk (hydrometer reading);
   9. Sediment – filtration;
   10. Hygiene – bacterial activity in the milk (Direct Epifluorescent Filter Technique (DEFT) test – bacteria count).
D. *Designated tests* for heat treatment efficiency:
   11. Phosphatase test – phosphatase (present in milk) inactivated by pasteurisation;
   12. Methylene Blue test – the keeping quality of pasteurised milk;
   13. Colony Count test – bacteria content in UHT milk;
   14. Turbidity test – sterilised milk.

Figure 5.1   *Quality checking system (tests) for milk*

A milk-like fluid is obtainable from nuts, roots and beans. Soya milk, for example, is high in nutritional value and can be used in cooking, but is likely to curdle if used in hot drinks. As it does not taste like dairy milk, being slightly bitter, sugar is sometimes added. It can be acceptable to those with a lactose intolerance.

Source

The main source of milk in the UK is the dairy cow, although milk is obtainable from sheep, goats, camels, buffalo, yaks and even horses. The dairy cow is a herbivorous ruminant which means that it eats grass which it digests through four stomachs.

Quality

Guided by the Milk Marketing Boards and the Dairy Federation the dairy industry has developed stringent testing of both product and production methods (see Figure 5.1 on the previous page). The Ministry of Agriculture, Fisheries and Food (MAFF) carry out regular clinical inspections of dairy herds. All milk-producing herds in the UK are 'attested', that is certified, as being free of tuberculosis and brucellosis.

The quality of milk and milk-based products can be affected by the type/breed of cow, and the type and quality of its feed. However, because of the size of

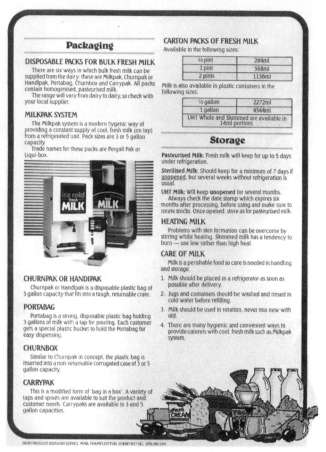

Figure 5.3   *Milk packaging and storage*

modern dairies, the control procedures and the way in which milk is processed, today's milk is of a very uniform standard.

Processing

Various methods of heat treatment are used to improve the keeping quality of milk (see Figure 5.2). Other forms of processing, extending the shelf life, include drying and canning (see Chapter 8 for details).

Function in cookery

Milk is used as a drink, hot or cold, on its own or blended with other ingredients. It is used to enrich soups and sauces and as a basic ingredient for many puddings. The flavour and colour of milk are affected by heat, resulting in caramelisation and the liberation of sulphides.

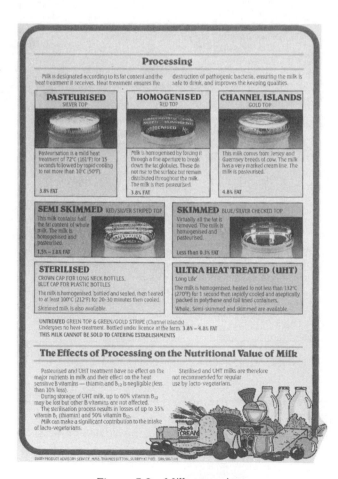

Figure 5.2   *Milk processing*

Purchasing units and specifications

Milk is normally specified by fat content and the type of heat treatment and may be purchased in a wide variety of pack sizes (see Figure 5.3).

Disposable cartons, plastic or waxed card, are preferable to glass bottles, they are lighter and easier to handle, resulting in fewer breakages. There is no additional labour or control, i.e. washing and/or returning.

Storage, hygiene and health

In much the same way as milk was long-regarded as an almost perfect food for human beings, it is also an ideal home for bacteria. Avoid unnecessary exposure to air and sunlight; store under refrigeration, as quickly as possible (see Figure 5.3).

Profitable usage

All too often milk is purchased according to a standard order with no accurate accounting of where, when or why it was used. Major savings can be made by ensuring that milk is only ordered according to specified needs and that once purchased its use is carefully monitored.

Owing to the variety of unit sizes available it is important to adjust all quoted prices to one standard unit in order to make price comparisons, for example, reduce all offers to price per pint regardless of actual unit size.

YOGURT

Yogurt is a soured milk product thought to have originated among the nomadic tribes of Eastern Europe. It was originally a drink made by allowing the natural bacteria in milk to ferment the lactose to lactic acid. Without refrigeration and/or heat treatment to limit the amount of acid production yogurt would become very sour.

Yogurt is now popular world-wide. The UK preference is generally for a semi-solid, mildly acid-flavoured product, although a wide range of textures and flavours are now available. The difference in flavour and texture depends on the type of milk used, the activity of the micro-organisms involved and the control of the conditions of incubation, time and temperature.

Source

Yogurt may be made from the milk of cows, ewes, goats or even buffaloes. Most UK yogurts are made from a skimmed cows milk base to which extra skimmed milk powder is added, improving the consistency of the final product.

Quality

The quality of yogurt is governed by a Manufacturer's Code of Practice for the Composition and Labelling of Yogurt. Control during processing and storage is important. In particular change in temperature can adversely affect quality.

Processing

The basic principle is applied to pasteurised milk which is inoculated with a mixed culture of lacto bacillus bulgaricus and streptococcus thermophilus which ferment the lactose into lactic acid. The yogurt is then allowed to incubate in the carton to give a set-type yogurt or, alternatively, it is allowed to incubate in a large tank where it is continuously stirred to give a stir-type yogurt with a smooth, cream-like consistency. Incubation takes place at 43°C and is continued until the acidity increases to a point (0.8–1.4 per cent lactic acid) where the the product thickens owing to coagulation of the proteins. Bacterial growth is then halted by cooling the yogurt to a temperature of 4.5°C.

Note that unpasteurised live yogurt may be used as a starter culture for the manufacture of home-made yogurt.

All yogurt, unless specified on the label as pasteurised, sterilised or UHT, contains live bacteria which remain dormant when kept at a low temperature. Stored at room temperature or above, the dormant bacteria become active and produce more acid. A high acid content will eventually prevent further bacterial growth, but will have impaired the flavour and caused the yogurt to split.

Function in cookery

Yogurt may be served as a dish in its own right, perhaps accompanied by fruit. It may be used instead of cream, added to soups, casseroles, moussaka, sauces and salad dressings.

Served frozen, yoghurt is a good alternative to ice cream.

Current developments in the yogurt market include:

- yogurt plus fromage frais;
- whipping yogurt and whipped yogurt desserts;
- yogurt with added vitamins;
- yogurt with jelly and/or fruit puree (in separate sachet);
- long-life yogurt;
- yogurt with freshly squeezed orange juice.

Purchasing units and specifications

Yogurt is normally defined by its type (set or stirred), variety (flavour) and fat content (see Figure 5.4).

Purchasing units are generally individual portion tubs, although larger, 450 gm, 2 pt, 4 pt, and 8 pt, catering units are available. Single portion tubs vary in size, usually quoted in grams; check and recalculate costs accordingly.

Natural	– contains no colour, preservative, stabilisers or thickeners.
Natural with ****	– may contain sugar or natural flavourings, fruit, nuts, etc., and may be fortified with vitamins.
Fruit yogurt	– should contain at least 5% of the whole fruit, as pieces or purée. If colours, stabilisers, thickeners or preservatives are used they will be declared on the label.
Live yogurt	– see comments under processing.

Fat content:
Very low fat – contains less than 0.5% fat;
Low fat – contains between 0.5% and 2% (most are 1%) fat;
Otherwise the fat content will be declared on the label.

Figure 5.4   *Yogurt – descriptions (specification) flavours and fat content*

Storage, hygiene and health

As nearly all yogurt sold in this country contains live bacteria it is necessary to refrigerate the product in order to restrict the activity of the starter culture (bacteria). At a temperature of 5°C, yogurt has a shelf life of approximately 14 days. Eventually the yogurt will become separated, showing signs of free whey around its edges and on the surface of the shrunken yogurt.

Fruit yogurts may be contaminated by yeasts resulting in a fermentation of sugars and producing carbon dioxide gas which creates pressure under the cap causing it to expand outwards, similar in effect to a blown can. Any items showing signs of expanded lids should be returned to the distributer.

Yogurt will freeze successfully and keep for up to three months.

Profitable usage

As a relatively inexpensive raw material requiring little or no additional ingredients or labour yogurt can be a very profitable menu item. It may also be used to enhance other, more-expensive dishes, without unduly increasing cost. It is especially useful as an alternative to cream.

If a carton of fresh-set-type yogurt is shaken the curd may break, releasing a small amount of whey. Although this affects appearance it should have no effect on the flavour or nutritional value.

CREAM

Cream may be described as the lighter-weight portion of milk which still contains all the main constituents of milk, but in different proportions. The butterfat content of cream is higher than that of milk, and the water and non-fat solids are lower.

Whereas milk may be considered as a valuable and necessary contribution to the diet, cream is primarily an extravagance eaten for pure pleasure, and used to add richness to dishes. Like whole milk, cream is an emulsion of fat in water. Generally, an increase in the thickness of the cream is associated with an increase in the fat content. However, this is not always true as the viscosity of cream can now be controlled during processing.

Source

In the UK, the primary source of cream is cows milk.

Section 48 of the 1984 Food Act prohibits the use of the word 'cream' to describe cream substitutes.

Quality

The quality of cream is dependent on the quality of the original milk, although many people assume double cream to be better than single the increased butterfat content does not affect the quality as such, but rather determines the use to which the cream is most suited. Colour is sometimes seen as a measure of quality in cream, but again this may be deceptive.

The colour of cream may vary depending on:

- The breed of cow – Channel Island breeds are poor converters of carotene to vitamin A, resulting in milk of a deeper yellow since it contains three times as much carotene as milk from a Friesian cow.
- The type of feed consumed – Milk produced in the UK during the winter may produce paler cream because winter feed is generally a poorer source of carotene than grass.

Processing

As the milk is allowed to stand, its butterfat content, being lighter than the water-soluble content, rises to the surface where traditionally it was skimmed by hand. Modern processing normally involves the use of a centrifuge that can separate and draw off cream at specified butterfat levels.

The Milk and Dairies (Heat Treatment of Cream) Regulations 1983 include statutory specifications for the heat treatment of creams. The method of heat treatment (or lack of it) must be declared on the label. Methods of heat treatment are similar to milk.

Sterilised cream, which is usually tinned, may contain certain additives which must be declared on the label. Homogenisation is used for half cream and single cream, to prevent separation and increase viscosity. Double cream may be slightly homogenised to give it a little extra body, but whipping cream is rarely homogenised as the process reduces the whipping ability of the cream. Homogenisation, in conjunction with controlled cooling, is used to produce the stiff texture for spooning and extra-thick creams.

Aerosol cans are normally a ultra heat treated (UHT) cream with a nitrous oxide propellant which aids the aeration. A 250 g can makes two pints of whipped cream, a volume increase of over 400 per cent. The advantage of the aerosol can is its ease of storage and use together with improved hygiene (no handling of bags and tubes). The problems associated with the product are that as the volume increases so there is a proportional decrease in flavour and body which is easily detected by most consumers. Because of the lack of body the product collapses quite quickly, especially on warm food.

Function in cookery

Cream can add richness and texture and, when whipped, can be used to lighten (aerate) and decorate. The suitability of cream varies with its fat content (see Figure 5.5 overleaf).

Purchasing units and specifications

The Cream Regulations 1970 stipulate that cream must be defined by its butterfat content. The label should bear one of the following descriptions and the actual fat content should comply with the requirement for that description (see Figure 5.6 overleaf).

It may be possible to negotiate with a dairy to supply cream to your own specifications, i.e. a 40 per cent butterfat content, or alternatively to blend your own by combining whipping and double cream; equal quantities of both produces a good result.

Description	Suggested use
Half cream	Ideal in coffee, sauces and soup.
Single cream	Suitable for pouring, puddings, etc.
Soured cream	Incubated with a special, harmless bacteria producing a piquant spoonable cream; ideal in goulash or similar hot dishes or as a base for salad dressings.
Whipping cream	Dessert decoration, cakes and pastries; whipping normally increases volume by 100%.
Spoonable cream	Homogenised to increase viscosity, suitable for fruit desserts or as a 'floater' garnish to soups, etc.
Double cream	Rich pouring cream, ideal for Irish coffee; has an improved finish when whipped but does not produce the same volume as whipping cream.
Double, extra-thick cream	Homogenised for extra viscosity and therefore spoonable, but not suitable for whipping; good with desserts.
Clotted cream	Spread or spooned onto scones and pastries.

Figure 5.5   *Cream – description and usage*

Types of Cream

TYPE OF CREAM	LEGAL MINIMUM FAT %	PROCESSING AND PACKAGING
HALF CREAM	12	Homogenised, and may be pasteurised or ultra heat treated.
CREAM OR SINGLE CREAM	18	Homogenised and pasteurised by heating to at least 72°C (161°F) for not less than 15 seconds then cooled to 4.5°C (40°F). Automatically filled into cartons after processing. Sealed with foil caps. Bulk quantities available according to local suppliers.
SOURED CREAM	18	Pasteurised, homogenised cream is 'soured' by the addition of a 'starter' culture of bacteria to produce piquant acid flavour.
WHIPPING CREAM	35	Rarely homogenised, but pasteurised or ultra heat treated.
DOUBLE CREAM	48	Slightly homogenised, then pasteurised and packaged. This cream is best for piping.
DOUBLE CREAM 'THICK' SPOONABLE CREAM	48 35	Heavily homogenised, then pasteurised and packaged. Usually only available in domestic quantities. This cream will not whip, it is designed to be spooned.
CLOTTED CREAM	55	Heated to 82°C (180°F) and cooled for about 4½ hours. The cream crust is then skimmed off. Usually packed in cartons by hand. Bulk quantities available according to local suppliers.
STERILISED HALF CREAM	12	Homogenised, filled into cans, sealed and heated to 108°C (226°F) for at least 45 minutes or equivalent time/ temperature combination. It is then cooled rapidly.
STERILISED CREAM	23	Processed as above. This cream can be spooned but will not whip.
ULTRA HEAT TREATED CREAM	*12 *18 35	Half, single or whipping cream is homogenised and heated to 140°C (284°F) for at least 2 seconds and cooled immediately. Aseptically packed in polythene and foil lined containers. *Available in jigger packs.
AEROSOL CREAM		UHT cream is filled into aerosol cans under sterile conditions. Nitrous oxide is used as the propellant. This cream starts to collapse soon after applying but can be used on milk shakes, iced coffee etc.

fresh cream

DAIRY PRODUCE ADVISORY SERVICE, MMB, THAMES DITTON, SURREY KT7 0EL DPА/86/145

Figure 5.6   *Types (specification) of cream*

Most creams are available in small tubs, pints, litres or gallons. As with milk and yogurt, translate prices to a standard unit size for comparison.

Storage, hygiene and health

The storage and keeping quality of cream is dependent on the type of cream and the heat treatment it has received.

Pasteurised cream is generally sold in liquid form and should be refrigerated. Under ideal conditions it will keep for approximately ten days, if unopened. Check the date stamps and rotate stock regularly. Frozen pasteurised cream will keep for a year.

Sterilised cream is generally sold in cans and if kept in a cool, dry store should last for up to two years. Once opened the cream should be refrigerated and its keeping qualities will be the same as pasteurised cream.

Ultra heat treated (UHT) cream is most commonly sold in individual packs, cartons or plastic tubs which have been filled under sterile conditions. Unopened UHT cream will keep for between two and four months, depending on the fat content (the greater the fat content the shorter the shelf life). Keep in a cool, dry store and check date stamps and rotate stock regularly.

UHT aerosol cans keep refrigerated for approximately three months.

Freezing cream
Half, single and soured creams do not freeze successfully. Whipping cream is best frozen in small quantities in a partially-whipped state. Double cream will freeze but has a tendency to become buttery if storage exceeds a month.

Caution – frozen cream has a tendency to overwhip.

Cream may be purchased frozen, but check the initial cost and the cost of storage because as an emergency resource frozen cream may not always be cost-effective.

Cream is identified as a major food poisoning risk. Always treat it with care; avoid handling and cross-contamination; ensure equipment is sterile before use. Always keep cream and cream products covered and away from other strong-smelling or high-risk foods.

1. *Fat content*
   An increase in fat content will not increase volume, rather the reverse, but it does produce a better finish for piping. Whipping cream should produce a 100% over-run where double cream will only produce a 50% over-run, although it will whip more quickly. Many caterers use a blend of whipping and double cream, or alternatively, specify a 40% butterfat content.

2. *Availability of free protein*
   The membrane around the fat globules, which acts as a stabiliser, may be affected by homogenisation. Extra-thick double cream will not whip because it has been homogenised to increase viscosity. UHT cream will whip because homogenisation is controlled during processing in order to leave sufficient free protein to stabilise air bubbles.

3. *Temperature for whipping*
   The temperature at which the cream is whipped embraces not only the cream but also that of the room and equipment used. Temperature determines the amount of solid fat. Fat forms clusters more readily at low temperatures; a temperature of less than 8°C is preferable. Although cream with a fat content as little as 30% will whip at a low temperature, it will not hold if the temperature rises.

4. *Viscosity of the cream*
   Solidification of fat globules after heat treatment increases the viscosity. For this reason cream is normally allowed to age in the dairy for 24 hours.

5. *Type of whisk used*
   Thin wire balloon whisks are most effective; the more wire hoops the better as they increase the rate at which air is incorporated into the foam.

6. *Addition of sugar*
   Sugar reduces stiffness and increases whipping time by restricting the denaturisation of the stabilising protein around the air bubbles. Up to 2% is not detrimental to foam formation, but larger amounts reduce the stiffness and stability of the cream. It is preferable to add the sugar when whipping is nearly complete.

7. *Size of fat globules*
   Large fat globules will cluster together more easily and offer more structural support to air bubbles. Channel Island cream will whip more quickly. Homogenisation reduces the size of the fat globules and the formation of clusters of air bubbles is less likely.

Figure 5.7   *Factors affecting the whipping of cream*

Profitable usage

As a high-cost ingredient, cream is often seen as having a significant effect on profitability and yet traditionally it was always hard to control. The use of single portion (UHT) packs has overcome this problem, but with some cost in terms of customer acceptability. Care should be taken with whipping cream as profitability will be affected, not only by the amount served, but also by the type (fat content) of cream and the method of whipping (see Figure 5.7 on the previous page).

CHEESE

Cheese has probably existed since at least 9000 BC when milk yielding animals were first domesticated; the first recorded evidence dates from 4000 BC. The basic principles of cheese manufacture remain almost unchanged, although many of the stages have been successfully mechanised.

Source

Like yogurt and cream, cheese may be produced from the milk of cows, ewes, goats, etc.

Quality

The Cheese Regulations 1970 control the composition, labelling and advertising of cheese. The 'Cheese Quality Mark' can be found on traditional English cheeses which have been checked and passed as selected quality. Stilton has its own certification trade mark, which ensures that it is made only in Leicestershire, Derbyshire and Nottinghamshire.

Most milk used in the manufacture of cheese is pasteurised, thus destroying bacteria. Some people believe that bacteria adds personality to the cheese. Generally, only farmhouse cheeses are made with unpasteurised milk and so long as the process is hygienic there is no problem although cheeses that have only been ripened for a few weeks should be avoided by expectant mothers, the young, the elderly and those in poor health. Unpasteurised cheese can develop a great deal of character, but its quality development is also less controllable. It should, therefore, be purchased with the greatest care.

Buy cheese fresh and not too far in advance; examine and taste the cheeses and, if in doubt, be guided by a good supplier.

Processing

The processing of cheese may be broadly divided into two basic methods; one for hard cheeses and the other for soft cheeses (see Figures 5.8 and 5.9). The enormous range and variety of cheeses result from the degree of pressing and maturing together with the use of added flavours.

Cheddar is normally left to mature for approximately 12 months. Initial grading takes place at six to eight weeks, when the grader is able to tell whether each particular cheese is best sold as a mild Cheddar or left for further maturing and regular monitoring.

A slight change in one or more stages may have a dramatic effect on the final product, providing individual flavours and textures of the regional cheeses.

1. Warm pasteurised milk is soured or ripened by the addition of a starter culture which converts lactose into lactic acid.
2. When the desired level of acidity is reached, the milk is coagulated by the addition of rennet. Rennet causes the protein casein to coagulate, trapping the fat. Vegetable dye, if used, is added at this stage.
3. The coagulated milk is cut, to allow the whey (liquid) to escape from the curds (solid).
4. The curd is scalded by raising the temperature of the vat, which causes the curd (proteins) to shrink and expel more whey.
5. The whey is drained off as the curd settles, shrinks and begins to matt together. The matted curd is then Cheddared, i.e. cut into blocks, stacked and turned frequently until the desired level of acidity is reached. The effect of Cheddaring may be identified when the curd, which is now more compact, may be torn off in strips resembling cooked chicken breast.
6. The curd is then milled to produce shavings of curd which are salted, cooled and filled into moulds. Salt, normally about 2%, helps to preserve the finished cheese and enhances flavour.
7. The curd is pressed to expel further moisture.
8. The immature cheese is placed in the ripening room, in which the temperature and humidity are controlled. During maturation enzymic breakdown of protein and fat is responsible for the change in texture and flavour of the matured cheese.

Figure 5.8   *Manufacturing hard cheese (the Cheddar method)*

There are basically two classifications of soft cheese:
Fresh (unripened) – cottage cheese, cream cheese, quark;
Ripened   – Brie, Lymeswold, Camembert, Feta.

Fresh (cottage) cheese:

1. Skimmed milk is heat treated.
2. Starter culture is added. The cultures are carefully selected as they possess different characteristics, producing desired flavours, aromas and acidity levels.
3. Rennet is added to some cheeses which result in them being both physically and chemically different from cheeses coagulated with acid alone.
4. The characteristic texture is achieved by slowly heating the curd, before washing and draining.
5. Stabiliser or thickener may be added to some cheeses; check the label.
6. A cream dressing is normally added to give a final fat content of 5%. Low-fat cottage cheese has a fat content of about 1.5%.

Ripened (Brie-type) cheese:

1. Milk, which may be pasteurised or not, is slowly heated.
2. Starter and rennet are added and the milk is allowed to coagulate.
3. The curd is gently cut and the whey allowed to drain.
4. The curd is then ladled into a two-piece mould, the top half is removed once drainage has reduced the volume to the level of the lower half.
5. After about two days the remaining section of the mould is removed and the cheese is dry salted.
6. It is then kept in a high-humidity ripening room at a temperature of 15°C and turned daily.
7. For cheese with an edible fleur (white, furry surface), the next process is to spray the cheese with penicillium candidum.
8. After about a week, the cheese begins to develop the characteristic fur-like mould which is initially pure white in colour but tends to darken with age.

Figure 5.9 *Manufacturing soft cheese*

Developments are currently in progress on the so-called 'accelerated ripening process'. Designed to enable the manufacturer to turn over stock more quickly and thus improve cost effectiveness, we have yet to see its effect on the quality of cheeses produced.

Blue cheeses result from the growth of bacteria, sprinkled, sprayed or injected into the curd during processing. Copper rods are not essential to the process, stainless steel rods are now more common. Their purpose is not to transfer the bacteria to the cheese, but rather to ease the passage of the air which encourages bacterial growth.

British soft cheeses are usually marketed in their fresh or unripened state. They are ready for consumption as soon as the manufacturing process is completed and will keep for up to a week if stored in a refrigerator.

Soft cheeses may have a similar appearance, but vary in fat content according to the product from which

The Cheese Regulations 1970 lay down the following standards for the different cheese descriptions:

skimmed-milk soft cheese – less than 2 per cent fat;
low-fat soft cheese   – 2 to 10 per cent fat;
medium-fat soft cheese   – 10 to 20 per cent fat;
full-fat soft cheese   – a minimum of 20 per cent fat;
cream cheese   – 45 per cent fat;
double cream cheese   – 65 per cent fat.

they were initially made, i.e. cream, milk or skimmed milk. Those that are higher in fat content will have a richer, buttery taste.

Ripened cheeses can be further classified as having:

- surface mould, for example, Brie and Camembert;
- surface and internal mould, for example, Blue Lymeswold;
- surface bacteria, for example, Limberger;
- internal bacteria, for example, Cambridge;
- internal bacteria plus preservation in brine, for example, Feta.

In addition to mould, wine, herbs, spices, nuts and smoking are also used to flavour cheeses.

Processed cheese

Processed cheese comes in a wide variety of fat levels, textures, flavours, shapes and sizes. The manufacturing process involves the base cheese, often Emmental but sometimes Cheddar, being ground up, subjected to heat treatment and blended with water and emulsifying salts to produce a cooked, homogeneous, sterile cheese with good keeping qualities.

Processed slices, for burgers and sandwiches, can be expensive and lack the subtlety of fresh cheese, but are more controllable and less wasteful.

Additionally, the caterer may purchase, as a result of customer demand, low-fat hard cheese or vegetarian cheese (produced with a non-animal rennet).

The following terms are used in the manufacture of cheese:

Bleu – external or internal blue mould.
Bloom, flora or fleur – white, furry surface (Brie, etc.).
Brine – salt water bath which encourages the formation of rind and inhibits the growth of mould.
Cheddar – to cut, stack and turn the curd.
Pate molle – smooth paste, soft cheese.
Penicillium roqueforti – blue-vein mould culture.
Penicillium gorganzola – blue-vein mould culture.
Penicillium candidum – white coat.
Rennet – coagulant obtained from calves' stomachs.

Function in cookery

Cheese may be used in soups, soufflés, pastry, sandwiches, salads, pies, flans, pizza, on toast or as a garnish to many dishes. The choice of cheese may be influenced by its country of origin, ripeness, flavour, texture and also its behaviour during cooking (melting/stringiness/fat content). It is valued not only for its flavour but also its ability to bind other ingredients.

Purchasing units and specifications

Cheese is available in a wide variety of shapes, sizes and forms, including the traditional drums and wheels, rectangular blocks, vacuum-packed blocks, wedges of all sizes and single portion units (see Figure 5.10). Each has its merits, advantages and disadvantages. It is difficult to make comparative judgements between them all. However, it is suggested that the influence of modern technology may be used as a rough guide. A truly traditional cheese, bought as a whole wheel, is likely to be of high quality in terms of texture and flavour, but may also be high in price and difficult to control. On the other hand, a modern, vacuum-packed cheese may be relatively less expensive, be far easier to portion and control, but may have little individuality of flavour and texture.

Soft (cottage) cheeses may be purchased in 250 g or 2 kg tubs; continental cheeses come in a variety of shapes and sizes.

Storage, hygiene and health

Cheese is a living food which may deteriorate quickly if not cared for. Storage temperatures can be the cause of some confusion, with the needs of the connoisseur and the hygienist seeming incompatible. Most cheeses benefit from being served and, ideally, stored at room temperature. Current recommendations require that soft cheeses in particular be kept chilled. The problem may be overcome by providing a cabinet in which small amounts of cheese, sufficient for each meal, can be safely brought to the required temperature.

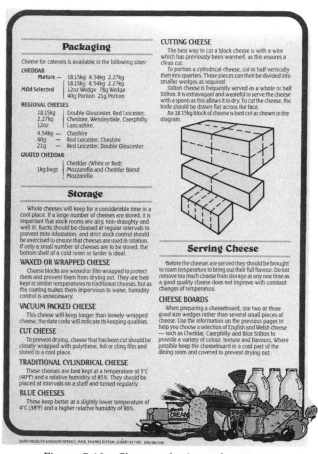

Packaging

Cheese for caterers is available in the following sizes:

CHEDDAR

Mature —	18.15kg	4.54kg	2.27kg
	18.15kg	4.54kg	2.27kg
Mild Selected	12oz Wedge	78g Wedge	
	40g Portion	21g Portion	

REGIONAL CHEESES

18.15kg		Double Gloucester, Red Leicester,
2.27kg		Cheshire, Wensleydale, Caerphilly,
12oz		Lancashire.
4.54kg	—	Cheshire
40g	—	Red Leicester, Cheshire
21g	—	Red Leicester, Double Gloucester

GRATED CHEDDAR

1kg bags	Cheddar (White or Red)
	Mozzarella and Cheddar Blend
	Mozzarella

Storage

Whole cheeses will keep for a considerable time in a cool place. If a large number of cheeses are stored, it is important that stock rooms are airy, non-draughty and well lit. Racks should be cleaned at regular intervals to prevent mite infestation, and strict stock control should be exercised to ensure that cheeses are used in rotation. If only a small number of cheeses are to be stored, the bottom shelf of a cold room or larder is ideal.

WAXED OR WRAPPED CHEESE

Cheese blocks are waxed or film wrapped to protect them and prevent them from drying out. They are best kept at similar temperatures to traditional cheeses, but as the coating makes them impervious to water, humidity control is unnecessary.

VACUUM PACKED CHEESE

This cheese will keep longer than loosely-wrapped cheese, the date code will indicate its keeping qualities.

CUT CHEESE

To prevent drying, cheese that has been cut should be closely wrapped with polythene, foil or cling film and stored in a cool place.

TRADITIONAL CYLINDRICAL CHEESE

These cheeses are best kept at a temperature of 5°C (40°F) and a relative humidity of 85%. They should be placed at intervals on a shelf and turned regularly.

BLUE CHEESES

These keep better at a slightly lower temperature of 4°C (38°F) and a higher relative humidity of 90%.

CUTTING CHEESE

The best way to cut a block cheese is with a wire which has previously been warmed, as this ensures a clean cut.

To portion a cylindrical cheese, cut in half vertically then into quarters. These pieces can then be divided into smaller wedges as required.

Stilton cheese is frequently served as a whole or half Stilton. It is extravagant and wasteful to serve the cheese with a spoon as this allows it to dry. To cut the cheese, the knife should be drawn flat across the face.

An 18.15kg block of cheese is best cut as shown in the diagram.

Serving Cheese

Before the cheeses are served they should be brought to room temperature to bring out their full flavour. Do not remove too much cheese from storage at any one time as a good quality cheese does not improve with constant changes of temperature.

CHEESE BOARDS

When preparing a cheeseboard, use two or three good size wedges rather than several small pieces of cheese. Use the information on the previous pages to help you choose a selection of English and Welsh cheese — such as Cheddar, Caerphilly and Blue Stilton to provide a variety of colour, texture and flavours. Where possible keep the cheeseboard in a cool part of the dining room and covered to prevent drying out.

DAIRY PRODUCE ADVISORY SERVICE, MMB, THAMES DITTON, SURREY KT7 0EL D9A/86/349

Figure 5.10   *Cheese packaging and storage*

Hard cheese has a high acid content and low moisture level making it relatively safe to store. Soft and cream cheeses pose a greater risk and should, therefore, be treated with more caution.

Cheese will freeze but tends to become crumbly once thawed. Grated cheese freezes well and in many respects freezing is a preferable method of storage as refrigeration tends to toughen cheese once it is grated.

Profitable usage

For the customer, the large cheeseboard selection can be a source of great pleasure or great disappointment.

For most caterers it tends to be uncontrollable, a wastage factor in excess of 10 per cent is not unusual.

The cheeseboard can be profitable, but if it is worth doing then it should be done well. Quality rather than quantity is the watchword. Amongst connoisseurs, cheese is treated with great reverence and a restaurant may become known for its cheese in almost the same way that many are noted for the quality of their wine cellar.

Alternative, more cost-effective methods of presentation are a mini-cheeseboard or a cheese menu which allows the customer's selection to be presented without the accompanying debris often associated with large cheeseboards. Cheese portions, by their very nature, are easy to control but may have limited customer acceptance.

BUTTER

Butter is a completely natural food produced from the creamy elements in milk. It takes 12 litres of milk to produce 500 grams of butter.

Source

Although the milk of other animals contains fat, the term butter applies only to fat produced exclusively from cows milk.

Ghee, normally associated with Indian cookery, would traditionally be obtained from buffalo as well as cows milk. It is now widely available in this and other Western countries as a clarified (cows milk) butter.

Quality

Like other dairy products the quality of butter can be influenced by its origin and quality of milk, cattle breed and feed. Colour and flavour, in particular, are influenced by the type of feed.

The quality of butter is determined by government legislation (The Butter Regulations 1966) which specify origin, composition and labelling.

Although not a difference in quality as such, customer preference is influenced by method of manufacture. There are two main forms of butter, sweet cream and lactic, either of which may be salted, slightly-salted or unsalted.

Processing

Churning (revolving, shaking or agitating the container of cream) causes fat globules to cling together and eventually the natural emulsion breaks and the fat (butter) can be separated from the liquid (buttermilk). The only permitted additives are a little salt, which most butter contains unless stated otherwise on the label, and natural colour, which is not often used.

'Sweet cream' butters are traditional to this country and are also produced in Ireland and New Zealand. They are made by simply churning fresh cream. Salt is usually added to enhance flavour and prolong the shelf life.

'Lactic' butters, traditionally imported from the Netherlands and Denmark, are made from cream which has been allowed to ripen a little, giving these butters their distinctive flavour. The natural lactic acid protects against bacteria, allowing the butter to be kept longer.

Function in cookery

Butter is valued for its richness and flavour and is used in a wide variety of cooking methods and dishes.

As a cooking medium it is used for grilling, glazing, shallow frying and sauté-ing. Because the liquid, sediments and salts in butter react differently to the fat when heated, unsalted butters are favoured for cooking and are normally clarified before use.

As an ingredient, butter's unique texture and flavour make it almost essential for many dishes. As a spread, it adds richness and flavour, but also protects the base (bread/biscuit) from any moist filling. In sauces it adds richness, flavour and a smooth gloss; in Hollandaise, Béarnaise, and beurre noisette butter becomes the main ingredient. In baking it enables a fine, even texture and adds flavour. It also has enriching, shortening, creaming, and aerating properties as well as adding moisture and keeping-quality to cakes. As a garnish, flavoured butter complements a number of dishes, particularly grilled meats and fish.

Purchasing units and specifications

Butter may be specified by type (sweet cream or lactic) and salt content, and often the trade name is identified.

As a result of over-production, creating a European butter mountain, a concentrated butter has become available, although its purchase and use may be subject to EEC regulations. Concentrated butter has a 96 per cent fat content; most of the water, non-fat solids and salts have been separated out. Because of its high fat content it has a long storage life of up to six months, or longer if frozen. Although not suitable for spreading, it is excellent for shallow frying and sauté-ing. It is also suitable for use in baking, but recipes should be adjusted, typically to between two-third or three-quarters of the original fat content. A little liquid may need to be added to replace the reduced moisture content of the concentrated butter.

Although butter is available in 20 kg boxes (blocks) it is not generally a sensible or economical form of purchase for most caterers. 500 g packs or even more commonly 250 g packs will be the usual unit of purchase. The 250 g packs may be sold in units of either 40 or 48 packs per case; check the price per case carefully.

For a variety of reasons many caterers will purchase butter for table use in portion-control packs. It is not necessarily more economical, but does have distinct control advantages and is important from a food hygiene aspect.

Storage, hygiene and health

The shelf life of butter is dependent on the type of butter and the type of packaging. Foil packaging (ten to 12 weeks) has a longer shelf life than parchment (six to eight weeks); salted lactic butters keep better than unsalted sweet cream butters.

Although it may be kept in a cool, dark, dry store it is safer to keep butter refrigerated. Butter can absorb flavours so it should be kept away from strong-flavoured foods. Only remove butter from storage in small amounts, if left in the kitchen the rise and fall in temperature can affect the quality. Butter may also be affected by exposure to light, causing it to go rancid which will have a detrimental effect on the vitamin A content.

Butter can be frozen for up to six months if in a foil wrapper and for three months if in parchment. But freezing is unlikely to be cost-effective as any savings made as a result of bulk purchase will be outweighed by the cost of freezer storage.

Profitable usage

Variations in the amount of salt used and the method of processing allow for a much wider variety of textures and flavours in butter than is generally appreciated.

National and regional preferences may be identified. As a result of previous Commonwealth purchasing policies, the British, for instance, became accustomed to saltier butters. The salt was a necessary requirement to preserve the butter on the long journey from New Zealand.

Tastes are now more cosmopolitan and the use of interesting and unusual butters like 'beurre d'Isigny' may add extra value to the meal experience.

Most savings are to be gained by reducing waste. Substituting for cheaper alternatives may not always be cost effective and quality may suffer.

Portion packs can cost up to 50 per cent more, weight for weight, than standard packs. They come in a wide variety of portion sizes and pack designs and, unfortunately, as there is no common standard in terms of portion size, weight may vary from as little as 5 g to as much as 14 g. The weight is not always stated and may or may not include packaging.

It is worth testing a variety of brands and packs in order to discover customer preference, minimum waste level and optimum cost effectiveness.

MARGARINE, FATS AND OILS

Broadly speaking, there is little difference between the basic composition of fats and oils and unless specifically stated the descriptions and comments that follow will apply equally to both.

The single, most obvious difference between fats and oils is that, generally speaking, oils are liquid at room temperature whereas fats are solid. Modern manufacturing/processing techniques have enabled the development of so-called solid oils.

Why do fats differ?
- Source – animal, fish, vegetable.
- Processing – hard, soft, low-fat, plasticised.
- Constituents – fatty acids, saturated, mono-unsaturated, polyunsaturated.

Margarine is essentially a man-made substitute for butter and originally its nutritional content was similar to butter. Modern development, particularly of low fat spreads, means that various so-called margarines may now be quite different in their content (particularly the fat content) and structure, affecting their suitability for certain catering uses. Consequently, careful reading of labels is essential.

Source

Animal fats such as: lard, a refined fat, obtained exclusively from pigs; suet, a natural unrefined fat obtained from the kidney region of most animals, but commonly associated with beef; and dripping, the rendered but unrefined cooking fat of either pork or beef, are all normally identified as butter.

Fish oils are normally obtained from the liver of round fish, particularly cod and halibut. Although fish oils are not usually used as a pure oil in cooking there is a growing body of opinion which suggests that an increase in the consumption of fish oil, or oily fish, could be beneficial to health.

In much the same way that animals and poultry provide high-energy fat for their young, most plants store fat/oil as a high-energy resource for their seeds. It is the seed, therefore, that generally provides the major source of plant/vegetable oil.

Margarine (soft/hard/plasticised) may derive from a combination of animal, plant and fish oils, refined and blended.

Main sources of vegetable oils are:

- corn
- sunflower
- palm
- sesame-seed
- groundnut
- rapeseed
- grapeseed

- coconut
- soya
- cottonseed
- walnut
- safflower
- olive
- poppyseed.

Quality

Judgement of quality, in relation to fats and oils, is normally influenced by intended use, so that the very best frying oil often makes a quite unacceptable salad oil and vice versa. Processing has a major effect on the quality of fats and oils. Olive oil, for example, can vary considerably.

The most important element when considering the quality of fat is identifying the combination of fatty acids that it contains. This is important, not only from the aspect of a healthy diet, but also the effect on the fat during the cooking process. Most fats contain some proportion of all three basic types (saturated, mono-unsaturated, polyunsaturated); the relationship or proportion of each is significant (see Table 5.2).

Table 5.2 Fatty acid levels

	Palmitic (saturated) (%)	Stearic (saturated) (%)	Oleic (mono-unsaturated) (%)	Linoleic (poly-unsaturated) (%)
Beef suet	27.8	26.6	34.3	1.3
Beef tallow	26.9	13.0	42.0	2.0
Groundnut	10.7	2.7	49.0	29.0
Lard	26.8	15.6	40.7	8.7
Corn	14.0	2.3	30.0	50.0
Olive	12.0	2.3	72.0	11.0
Palm	41.5	4.3	43.3	8.4
Rapeseed (high erucic)	3.5	1.0	24.1	15.5
Soyabean	10.0	4.0	25.0	52.0
Sunflowerseed	5.0	6.3	33.0	52.0
Safflower	8.0	2.5	13.0	75.0

All fatty acids consist of a chain of carbon atoms each of which has four bonds (see Figure 5.11): one to link to the carbon atom on the left; one to link to the

right; leaving two free, one or both of which may be linked to hydrogen atoms. Where only one bond is linked to a hydrogen atom the other will join to the adjacent carbon atom to form a double bond. Double bonds are prone to attack by oxygen.

1. Saturated – each carbon atom (C) is linked with two hydrogen atoms (H).

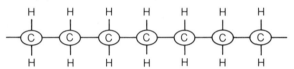

The main characteristics of saturated fatty acids are: they have a relatively high melting point and are therefore generally solid at room temperature; they are comparatively stable and not prone to oxidation (rancidity).

2. Mono-saturated – there is one double bond in the chain.

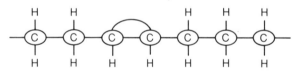

The main characteristics of mono-unsaturated fatty acids are: a lower melting point so they are normally liquid at room temperature; the less-stable double bond makes them susceptible to oxidation. The process of hydrogenation is used to replace the double bond with a hydrogen atom.

3. Polyunsaturated – there is more than one double bond in the chain.

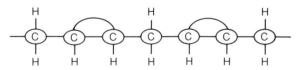

The main characteristics of polyunsaturated fatty acids are: a low melting point; they are susceptible to oxidation in the presence of oxygen.

Figure 5.11   *The fatty acid chain*

In the majority of dietary fats the fatty acids are combined with glycerol to form triglycerides (see Figure 5.12).

The differences between fats are due to the different combinations of fatty acids in the triglyceride. The three fatty acids are seldom the same and the precise melting point of each fat is determined by the proportions of saturated and unsaturated fatty acids.

Processing

Most oils and fats go through a process of cleaning and purifying (as identified in Figure 5.13), so intended use will determine the precise method of processing for each product.

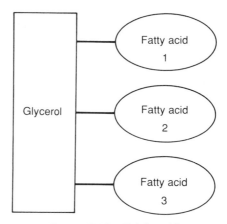

Figure 5.12   *Triglycerides*

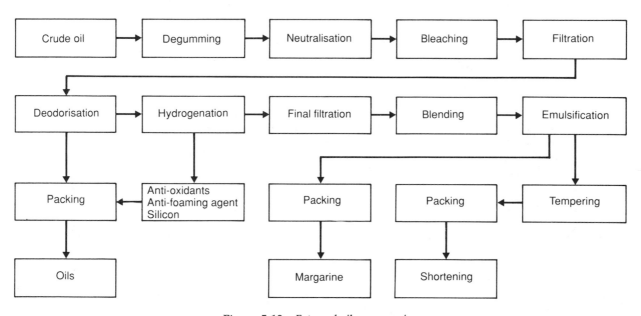

Figure 5.13   *Fats and oils – processing*

Treatment of fats and oils (frying)

Some oils may have anti-oxidants added to prolong shelf life and anti-foaming agents may be added to prolong frying life. Long-life oils are normally semi-solid. The addition of silicon (one or two parts per million) can extend frying life and protect the oil from deterioration. Hydrogenation may also be used to increase hardness and lengthen life by decreasing susceptibility to oxidisation.

Treatment of fats and oils (ingredients)

In addition to refining, fats and oils may have liquids and emulsifiers added to improve their spreadability or reduce their fat content. They may, alternatively, be hydrogenated and/or plasticised to increase firmness.

Treatment of salad oils

Generally, salad oils are left in their natural state, retaining all their natural character and flavour. The only process that may be applied is 'winterising' (subjecting the oil to a very low temperature so that any impurities may be more easily removed).

Function in cookery

Fats are very versatile and serve more culinary purposes than most other nutrients, as a cooking medium, a lubricant for other foods and as an ingredient. Fat is important to the cooking process, providing palatability, flavour and texture. They are used for creaming and shortening in cakes and pastries; protecting and adding moisture during grilling, roasting and shallow frying; and thickening and enriching sauces.

Frying is a very effective method of cookery. As a result of the high temperature involved, heat transfer is fast, imparting qualities of crispness, texture, colour and flavour unobtainable by other methods of cooking.

Oil may be used as an ingredient in marinades, which are used to tenderise and develop flavour in meat, fish and poultry. Fats and oils may also be used as a seal and to protect food during storage.

Purchasing units and specifications

Specifications range from all-animal to all-vegetable products with a wide variety of blends, textures and flavours in between, some of which may contain natural dairy products.

Variety of fats and oils available

- Suet – pastry, steaming, poaching and baking.
- Lard – frying and pastry.
- Dripping – roasting.
- Shortenings – pie crust, flans, biscuits and pastries.
- Plasticised fat – puff pastry and laminated goods.
- Cake margarine – creaming and aerating sponges and puddings.
- Bread fats and emulsions – fermented yeast goods.
- Fat/oil – shallow frying; and deep frying.
- Salad oils – emulsion sauces, mayonnaise, dressings, etc.
- Speciality fats and oils – ice cream, confectionery and toppings.

Margarines designed to replicate butter will contain 16 per cent water. Low-fat spreads contain considerably more water, sometimes to the extent that it becomes the main ingredient (check the label). Purchasing units will be much the same as for butter.

For most fats and oils the choice of pack size will be influenced by operational style/need, number of covers served, cookery function and recipe units. Solid fats may be purchased in boxes of 500 g or 250 g packs; check packs per box and box weight carefully when calculating costs.

Pack size for frying oils will depend on whether the oil is used for topping-up or discarding and replacing. For topping-up small (2 l) containers are preferable, being easier to handle For discarding and replacing the larger (20 l) drums make more sense.

Storage, hygiene and health

Keep fats and oils in a cool, dry store, away from strong light. Once packs are opened, fats and oils become susceptible to oxidisation, resulting from exposure to the air.

Profitable usage

Quality will be a major influence on price and profitability. It is important to define priorities/requirements carefully. It may be necessary to purchase several varieties, to suit differing needs, in order to maintain quality and cost effectiveness. Alternatively, it may be necessary to compromise a little on quality in order to minimise stock-holding. Although a vast range of speciality fats and oils are available, for most caterers it would normally be uneconomic to be too prescriptive. Generally, a selection of mid-range, all-purpose products will be most cost-effective. For example, one product each is sufficient for the following uses: laminated goods (puff paste); creaming and shortening (cakes and pastry); shallow frying; deep frying; and salad oil.

Profitability of fats and oils should be determined by:

- their ability to perform, i.e. to produce volume in cakes, or frying life/unit output;
- customer acceptance – quality.

The most profitable product is the one that best meets both criteria. It will depend on individual judgement, testing and analysis. For frying, the fats/oils absorption rate can be critical, for example, doughnuts are known to have a high absorption rate so it would not, therefore, be wise to use the most expensive cooking oils, but poor flavour should be avoided.

Incorrect use can halve the life of frying oil, in effect doubling the cost (see Table 5.3 and Figures 5.14 and 5.15 overleaf).

Owing to the nature of their composition, some oils and fats tend to be more sensitive to heat and as a result will spoil more rapidly than others. It is, therefore, wise to use fats and oils which have been specifically designed and processed for frying. The most stable oils, for example, groundnut and corn oils, are generally the most expensive. Other oils and blends are more economical, but rather less stable chemically.

Table 5.3 Comparative food-frying temperatures

	°C
Chips (blanche)	166
Chicken	174
Fish	174
Crisps (game chips)	177
Fritters	180
Choux paste	182
Doughnuts	182
Chips (brown)	188

Frying characteristics of fats and oils

	Smoke point (°C)	Flash point (°C)
Solid fats:		
Lard	221	324
Beef dripping	163	302
Palm fat	218	321
All vegetable fat	215	318
Liquid oils:		
Corn	215	224
Cottonseed	238	325
Groundnut	238	325
Rapeseed	218	320
Soyabean	230	320

1. Choose the fat/oil best suited to your operation: some are more suited to day-long cooking, others are better for shorter service periods. Frequent heating and cooling can be just as detrimental as holding at frying temperature for prolonged periods.
2. Filter the oil regularly, preferably after each use.
3. If using long-life oil, top up regularly. Topping up tends to dampen the effect of deterioration in the frying medium. If 20% is added daily the oil is less likely to need changing.
4. Keep equipment clean; do not use iron or copper as both may accelerate deterioration of the oil.
5. Check thermostats regularly, including the over-ride (cut-out) thermometer.
6. Although the thermostat may be set to a maximum temperature of 190 °C, latent heat in the metal of the equipment may continue heating the oil above 190 °C even after the heat source is turned off. Ensure that the maximum attainable temperature does not exceed 205 °C, and if necessary have the thermostat reset.
7. With gas equipment, check that the flame burns evenly to ensure that no hot spots occur.
8. Do not fry food at low temperature. Do not overheat the fat/oil.
9. Ensure correct ratio of food to oil is maintained; one part food to six parts oil is ideal (one part food to eight parts oil if frozen food is being cooked as the temperature of the oil drops more quickly). If a lot of frozen food is to be fried then automatically-controlled, fast-recovery fryers are a worthwhile investment.
10. If only small amounts are cooked, then use a small fryer; it limits both the amount of oil and heat needed, and the more frequent topping up may be better for the oil.
11. Prepare food carefully, especially where moisture is concerned. Dry chips carefully, ensuring frozen chips are free of ice/frost; if a potato whitener is used special care is required – note manufacturers instructions carefully. Handle fragile foods with care; ensure they are effectively coated; if necessary consider double crumbing, but ensure food is free of loose crumb and/or flour. Meat products, sausages, chicken, burgers, etc., should be coated well to prevent the unrefined fat which they contain contaminating the frying medium.
12. Check the absorption rate. Absorption rate for chips is approximately 6% (for every 100lb of chips fried 6lb of fat will be absorbed). For a product like doughnuts it may be as high as 30%. Costing of dishes should allow for absorption of oil.

Figure 5.14 *Cost-effective deep frying*

Stage	Risk	Reaction	Reaction speed
Storage	Exposure to air	Oxidisation	Slow
Standby	Exposure to air Subjected to heat	Oxidisation Polymerisation	Fast Slow
Frying	Exposure to air Subjected to heat Moisture from food	Oxidisation Polymerisation Hydrolysis	Fast Slow Fast

Oxidisation – attacking the molecular chains in the oil at its weakest point(s). Stable oils have fewer weak points. It is possible to use a chemical process, hydrogenation, to reduce the number of points of weakness. The melting point of the oil is also increased, thus hardening the oil. In this way, oils may be changed from liquids to solids – margarine.

Polymerisation – two or more molecules of the same material have joined together, causing the oil to thicken. The resinous substance formed on frying equipment is a result of polymerisation.

Hydrolysis – moisture present in the food, released as steam into the hot fat, breaks down the triglycerides and allows the formation of free fatty acids. The smoke point of an oil or fat is determined by the number of free fatty acids present. They may eventually cause the oil and the cooked food to develop 'off' flavours.

Figure 5.15   *Stages of spoilage (fats and oils)*

Fluid frying media can offer the best of both worlds. Although thick, they are pourable and do not require special melting before heating to frying temperature. They are generally more stable than normal vegetable oil blends.

EGGS

Eggs are one of the most essential and versatile foods used in cookery. They contain all the requirements for life; water, protein, fat, carbohydrate, vitamins, minerals and air.

Eggs are held by some to be the symbol of life and fertility. The giving of Easter eggs, heralding the birth of a new year, pre-dates Christianity.

Food value

There is no difference in nutritional value between free-range and battery eggs, nor between white or brown shells, although free-range eggs are believed to have more flavour. Eggs are easy to digest and relatively inexpensive.

Just as milk sustains the calf, eggs, being the main food source of the developing chick, contain all the required nutritional elements. Unlike milk, which is a single emulsion, the egg contains separate and quite unique parts. Basically, the egg is 12 per cent shell, 58 per cent white and 30 per cent yolk. The white and yolk contain the same elements, but are different

Structure of eggs		
	Yolk (%)	*White (%)*
Water	48.50	87.70
Protein	16.60	10.60
Fat	32.60	0.03
Carbohydrate	10.00	0.90
Minerals	1.10	0.60
Vitamins	A, D, E, K and B group	B group

in their structure, the main difference being the water and fat content. As can be seen, literally all the fat is contained in the yolk in the form of lecithin which has unique emulsifying properties.

Source

Eggs for human consumption are generally obtained from hens, although the eggs of all egg-producing species are edible. The more common varieties are:

- duck;
- partridge;
- guinea fowl;
- pheasant;
- goose;
- quail;
- gull;
- turkey.

Quality

The 1989 salmonella egg scare did highlight a problem with quality testing for eggs in that there is no effective way of determining whether any particular egg is free from harmful bacteria. The quality of eggs is dependent on the conditions affecting production, primarily the health of the hen and the quality of its feed. Tighter controls and inspection procedures have been introduced in the UK, but there is still some concern in regard to imported eggs. Check the label for source/producer.

In all other respects, the quality of eggs is defined by the specific 1973 EEC Regulations. In particular, they identify the following, all of which should appear on the egg packaging label (see Figure 5.16 overleaf):

- grade (A, B or C);
- the number of eggs in the pack;
- the size/weight of the eggs (1–7);
- the registration on the packing station;
- the name and address of the producer;
- the date code, commencing first Sunday of each year as week 1.

Processing

Little processing is required in the case of eggs. The main requirements being inspection, candling, grading, weighing and packaging.

> Candling – the use of a strong light source to see through the egg; observe position and quality of the yolk; the size of the air sack; and check for any impurities.

Further methods of processing are based on extending the storage life of the egg. The oldest method used is to create a non-porous shell by dipping the egg in paraffin wax or oil, or rubbing it with butter. More modern methods involve removing the eggs from their shell and freezing them as a blended liquid, which may be either whole egg, egg yolk or egg white. In some cases a little salt may be added.

> One of the more popular uses for liquid egg is as a quick, simple, and above all, clean method of producing scrambled egg. Whole egg liquid may be purchased in heat-resistant bags which can be immersed in boiling water. After a few minutes cooking the contents of the bag may be emptied into the service dish and lightly broken with a fork, making a quite acceptable product and saving one of the caterer's more difficult cleaning problems, the removal of cooked egg from pans and equipment.

The other principal method of extending the life of the egg is to dehydrate it. Egg powder is available as whole egg, egg yolk, and by far the most popular in catering terms, egg white.

Function in cookery

Eggs are a natural food, which are easy to prepare as a wide range of dishes in their own right. Cooked in a variety of ways they also provide interesting accompaniments to other meat, poultry and fish dishes. However, it is the unique properties of the egg, either whole, yolk or white, that make eggs such an indispensable commodity. No other single product can provide for so many functions in the kitchen. It is questionable whether the wealth of dishes that we are used to would be possible if the egg did not exist.

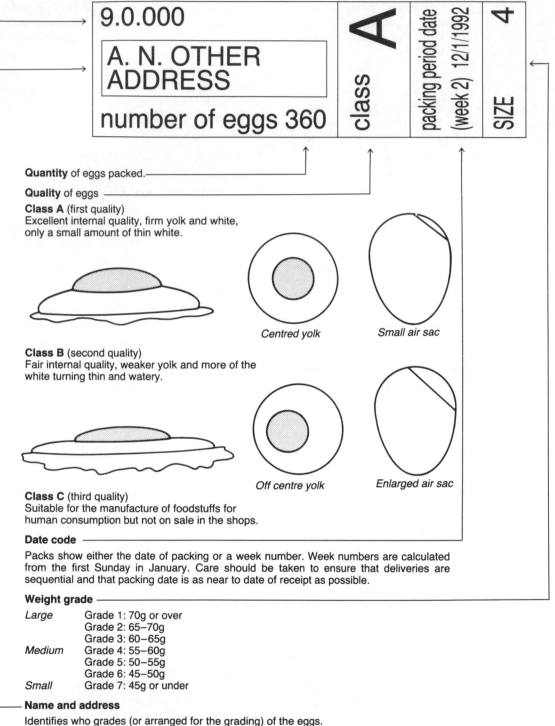

Quantity of eggs packed.

Quality of eggs

Class A (first quality)
Excellent internal quality, firm yolk and white,
only a small amount of thin white.

Centred yolk   *Small air sac*

Class B (second quality)
Fair internal quality, weaker yolk and more of the
white turning thin and watery.

Off centre yolk   *Enlarged air sac*

Class C (third quality)
Suitable for the manufacture of foodstuffs for
human consumption but not on sale in the shops.

Date code

Packs show either the date of packing or a week number. Week numbers are calculated
from the first Sunday in January. Care should be taken to ensure that deliveries are
sequential and that packing date is as near to date of receipt as possible.

Weight grade

Large	Grade 1: 70g or over
	Grade 2: 65–70g
	Grade 3: 60–65g
Medium	Grade 4: 55–60g
	Grade 5: 50–55g
	Grade 6: 45–50g
Small	Grade 7: 45g or under

Name and address

Identifies who grades (or arranged for the grading) of the eggs.

Registered number

Identifies the packing station. All UK packing stations being with 9 followed by a regional
number and finally the individual packing station identification number.

Figure 5.16   *Egg package labelling (detail and quality information)*

> The function of eggs are to:
> - flavour
> - coat
> - emulsify
> - stabilise
> - shape
> - bind
> - foam
> - liaise
> - colour
> - glaze
> - thicken
> - clarify
> - add texture
> - aerate
> - set/coagulate
> - smooth/enrich.

The proteins in egg white break and expand when whipped, forming elastic-walled cells that trap air which expands when heated. The protein eventually sets, retaining shape and form. The resulting foam is used to lighten and aerate.

The protein in the yolk is used to bind, thicken and liaise. The yolk is less stable than the white and when exposed to excessive heat the proteins shrink and harden, and the fat and water molecules separate, resulting in curdling.

Purchasing units and specifications

The wholesale price for eggs may be quoted as 'per long hundred' (10 dozen), per 180 (15 dozen) or by the case. The catering case contains three long hundreds (360) packed in 12 trays of 30. Half cases (180) can be purchased or, alternatively, eggs may be purchased by the dozen.

Specifications will be based on the pack labelling standards as discussed above (see the section on Quality). Note particularly the date coding.

Liquid egg (whole/yolk/white) may be purchased in tubs or bags ranging from ½ kg up to 25 kg. 2 kg of liquid whole egg is approximately equivalent to 40 standard eggs.

Liquid egg may also be blended with milk, whey, oil and or sugar to caterers' specifications. These may be sold as custard mix, omelette mix or scrambled egg mix.

Storage, hygiene and health

Eggs will keep refrigerated for up to four weeks, alternatively they may be kept in a cool, dry store. Because the shell is porous, eggs are subject to attack by bacteria and they will deteriorate over time. They should be kept away from strong-smelling foods. Egg liquid will freeze and may keep frozen for up to nine months.

Most bulk liquids are sold as pasteurised and have a life of up to four days. Pasteurisation does not kill all bacteria. Like many products there is a high risk of deterioration once the product is on the caterer's premises. The strictest rules of hygiene should always be observed when handling eggs and egg products.

Profitable usage

The price of eggs will be determined primarily by their size. As price may differ by as much as 20 per cent between largest and smallest, it is important to be specific about size requirements. If, as is often the case, the eggs main function is as part of a full English breakfast then perhaps a small egg is sufficient. However, caterers tend to buy medium-size (size 4 or 5) standard eggs, often on the basis that recipes call for standard eggs. Depending on the size and style of operation it may be possible to specify two egg standards, i.e. small for cooking (fried, boiled, etc.) and medium for recipes. Alternatively, caterers may choose to specify small eggs and adjust recipes so that egg is measured by liquid volume; a pint of egg contains approximately 10 standard or 12 small eggs.

> Measuring egg by liquid volume has the added advantage of increased accuracy which can have a significant effect on quality of the end product. Choux paste, for example, can be adversely affected by a small inconsistency in the amount of egg used.

Buying direct from the packer can effect considerable savings, although it may be necessary to take larger, less-frequent deliveries. Some saving may be made through the purchase of grade B eggs, but as reduced quality may be easily identified by the customer, this is not to be recommended.

LEGISLATION

The following is a list of the relevant acts and regulations:

The Food Safety Act 1990;

The Milk and Milk Products (Protection and Designations) Regulations 1990;

The Food Act 1984 (a consolidation of the Food and Drugs Act 1955);

The Milk (Special Designation) Regulations 1988;

The Milk (Semi Skimmed and Skimmed Milk) (Heat Treatment and Labelling) Regulations 1988;

The Weights and Measures Act 1985;

The Food and Environmental Protection Act 1985;

The Eggs (Marketing Standards) Regulations 1985;

The Food Labelling Regulations 1984;

The Milk Based Drinks (Hygiene and Heat Treatment) Regulations 1983;

The Milk and Dairies (Heat Treatment of Cream) Regulations 1983;

The Importation of Milk Act 1983;

The Condensed Milk and Dried Milk Regulations 1977;

The Drinking Milk Regulations 1976;

The Milk and Dairies (Milk Bottle Caps) (Colour) Regulations 1976;

The Trade Descriptions Act 1968 and 1972;

The Cream Regulations 1970;

The Cheese Regulations 1970;

The Margarine Regulations 1967;

The Ice Cream Regulations 1967;

The Butter Regulations 1966;

The Liquid Egg (Pasteurisation) Regulations 1963;

The Skimmed Milk with Non-Milk Fat Regulations 1960;

The Milk and Dairies (General) Regulations 1959;

The Milk and Dairies (Channel Islands & South Devon Milk) Regulations 1956.

Summary

The purchasing and use of dairy produce, fats and oils may be a totally convenience, totally fresh or a mixed activity. Product preference, purchasing methods and profitability will ultimately be influenced by policy as defined in earlier chapters. The wise caterer will observe customer preference and be influenced by trends such as healthy eating.

In most cases, it will be desirable to provide fresh, quality foods. Fresh farmhouse produce can be used to merchandise dishes and enhance the menu, particularly where there are local specialities.

Precise product specifications are essential, but they will be unique to the needs of each and every individual establishment. The examples provided are descriptive rather than prescriptive. Effective cost comparison can only be made if all quotations are based on a standard unit size, regardless of the actual unit or packs delivered. Consider carefully unit size, delivery and storage requirements.

Fish, Meat, Poultry and Game

Buying inevitably tends to concentrate maximum attention on high-cost items. Although specifications apply to a wide range of catering commodities, they are particularly needed for fish, meat and poultry.

At one time, hotels and large restaurants prepared and portioned much of their own fish, meat and poultry. Today, these important foods are increasingly purchased in cut form as steaks, fish fillets and ready-trussed poultry. Nevertheless, it remains important not only for the food buyer to have a knowledge of the structure of the animals from which meat cuts are taken, but also that chefs should

appreciate the nature of fish, meat and poultry so that they are better able to ensure that raw materials properly meet specifications. Moreover, a knowledge of commodities remains highly important in understanding cooking treatment.

The flesh of fish and meat differs in two ways (see Figure 6.1). First, the fish muscle consists of short fibres separated by large sheets of very thin connective tissue (flakes). There is little connective tissue in fish (3 per cent of its weight) compared to meat (15 per cent). Secondly, the colour of the flesh, which is influenced by the presence of myoglobin (colour

Meat: bundles of long fibre surrounded by connective tissue. Young flesh = fine fibres; old flesh = coarse fibres. Tough meat has more flavour.

Muscle: signals from the nervous system shorten and relax the fibres, generating movement in the limbs of the living animal.

Connective tissue: collagen (white) dissolves during cooking adding moisture and flavour; elastin (yellow) does not dissolve and has to be removed, sliced, diced or minced to make it digestible.

Fish: short fibres between layers of connective tissue.

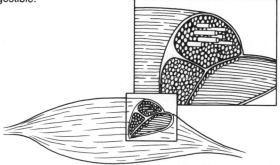

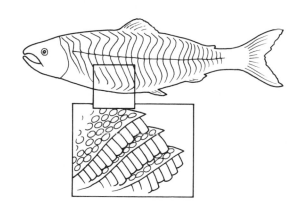

Figure 6.1   *Composition of meat and fish (muscle fibre)*

pigment) used to store oxygen needed for muscle activity, is different. Because it weighs less in water and hence there is less need for muscle activity, fish has little myoglobin. The effect is also noticeable in the difference between leg and breast meat in chicken, for much the same reason.

The muscle tissue of meat is made up of long thin fibres, bound by thin sheets of connective tissue. The individual fibres can be as long as the whole muscle and some may exceed 30cm in length. The bundles of fibres are organised into groups to form an individual muscle which is anchored to bone by other connective tissues. The longitudinal structure of the muscle fibres account for what is called the grain of the meat, normally running parallel to the bone. Shortening the

grain by cutting, slicing, dicing or mincing the meat helps to improve the eating quality/texture.

FOOD VALUES

Fish and meat, in their various forms, are generally accepted as sources of high, biological value protein. The type and proportion of amino acids are particularly suitable for growth and repair in the human body.

In addition to protein, (see Table 6.1), the main nutrients supplied are B group vitamins, thiamin, riboflavin and nicotinic acid (niacin) and minerals (iron and zinc). Vitamins B1 and B2 provide vitality,

Table 6.1   Nutritional chart – fish, meat and poultry

| Product | Per 100g | | | |
	Energy (cals)	Protein (g)	Fat (g)	Calcium (mg)
Fish, white (cod fillet)	76	17.4	0.7	16
Fish, oily (herring)	234	16.8	18.5	33
Oysters	51	10.8	0.9	190
Bacon (dressed carcass)	352	13.0	33.3	7
Bacon (back rasher)	428	14.2	41.2	7
Beef (dressed carcass)	282	15.8	24.3	7
Beef (sirloin)	272	16.6	22.8	9
Lamb (dressed carcass)	333	14.6	30.5	7
Lamb (loin)	377	14.6	35.4	7
Pork (dressed carcass)	228	13.6	31.5	8
Pork (loin)	329	15.9	29.5	8
Chicken (meat and skin)	230	17.9	17.7	10
Chicken (meat only)	121	20.5	4.3	10

releasing the energy value from food. Vitamin B12, which is not found in plant foods, is required for the formation of red blood cells and the normal function of the nervous system.

Pork, lamb, poultry and especially fish all contain

less saturated fat than beef and consequently appear softer at room temperature (see Table 6.2). Fat, especially the marbling in beef, helps to tenderise meat, as well as adding moisture and flavour.

FISH

There are up to 100 varieties of edible fish. Traditional British conservatism is dying and a greater variety of seafood, including squid, shark and swordfish, is now common in shops and on the caterer's menu.

Table 6.2   Typical composition of fish and meat

	Water (%)	Protein (%)	Fat (%)
Fish	70	20	10
Beef	60	18	22
Veal	58	32	10
Lamb	56	16	28
Pork	42	13	45
Bacon	69	24	7
Turkey	58	22	20
Venison	59	35	6

Recent years have not only seen changes in taste but also in price and availability. Farmed salmon is now as cheap as cod. Developments in fish farming techniques mean that other types, such as trout, mussels and oysters, are plentiful. Efforts are being made to farm turbot, sole, halibut and carp, but it is likely to be some time before we see any effect on the market.

Source

There is more than one way of classifying fish. Nutritionists, for example, are concerned with the difference between white and oily fish; the fishing industry differentiates between surface (pelagic) and bottom (demersal) swimmers. In buying, perhaps, it may be convenient to consider three main classes, round fish, flat fish and freshwater fish, as shown in Figure 6.2.

As a result of world-wide availability, processing at sea and developments in fish farming techniques, seasonal availability (see Table 6.3 overleaf) is now less significant than it once was.

Round fish	
White	
Bass	Ling
Cod	Monkfish
Coley	Pollock
Haddock	Whiting
Hake	
Oily	
Anchovy	Salmon
Gurnard	Salmon trout
Herring	Sardine
Mackerel	Sprat
Mullet (red)	Tuna
Mullet (grey)	Whitebait
Pilchard	

Flat fish	
Brill	Megrim
Dab	Plaice
Flounder	Skate
Halibut	Sole
John Dory	Turbot

Freshwater fish	
Bream	Salmon
Carp	Salmon trout
Eel	Sturgeon
Perch	Tench
Pike	Trout

Note: Salmon, sturgeon and salmon trout are available in fresh water during the spawning season.

Figure 6.2   *Classification of fish*

Quality

Owing to the many varieties of fish it is desirable to summarise the general points indicative of freshness and quality that should be looked for when buying.

There are two main sources of spoilage in fish, enzymes and bacteria, both of which can be inhibited by a reduction in temperature. At a temperature of 0°C, bacterial activity is considerably reduced and fish may remain good for up to six days (one to two days for herring). Crushed ice has the benefit of being relatively cheap and easy to produce and retains ideal temperature and moisture levels. Ice is used on most trawlers to maintain quality. Modern freezer trawlers are able to gut, fillet, skin and freeze their catch within five hours. Most species freeze well with little deterioration to quality.

With the exception of herring, all sea fish are gutted before sale and this may be done at sea or at the docks prior to marketing.

Quality control checking, packing, storage and icing procedures should be built in to the specifications, especially when dealing with inland wholesalers where delays could occur. Speed of delivery, from port to table, is important.

The Sea Fish Authority helps to maintain quality through its Advisory Inspection Service and Quality Assurance Section. It also provides advice on specification and fish quality monitoring (see Figures 6.3 and 6.4 and page 91).

The Sea Fish Inspected Processor Award covers:
- reception and storage;
- design of premises;
- hygiene and cleaning;
- machinery and equipment;
- product handling;
- packaging and dispatch.

Table 6.3   Fish and shellfish seasons

Commodity	Season	When best
Anchovy	All year	
Bass	September–May	
Bream, sea	June–February	Autumn
Bream, river	July–March	Autumn
Brill	June–February	
Carp	July–March	
Catfish	All year (spawns late autumn/early winter)	February–July
Cockles	All year	
Cod	All year (especially October to February)	December
Coley	See Saithe	
Conger eel	All year	October–January
Crab	April–December	Summer
Crawfish	April–September	June, July
Crayfish	All year	Spring
Dabs	August–December	
Dace	December–June	
Eel, fresh water	All year	September–November
Flounder	All year	August–November
Gurnet (Gurnard)	July–April	October
Haddock	All year (especially May to February)	November–February
Hake	June–March	June, July
Halibut	All year	July–April
Herring	All year (according to area)	May–February
Huss (Dogfish)	All year	
John Dory	All year	Winter
Ling	August–March	
Lobster	All year	Summer
Mackerel	August–April	Winter
Megrim	August–March	Autumn and Winter
Monkfish	All year	
Mullet, grey	September–February	
Mullet, red	All year (especially September to February)	
Mussels	September–March	Winter
Oysters	September–April	Winter
Perch	July–March	July–January
Pike	July–March	October–February
Pilchard	November–February/April	
Plaice	All year	May–November
Pollock	All year	Late Summer, Autumn
Prawns	February–October	
Queens scallops	All year	
Saithe	All year	September–February
Salmon, English	February–October*	
Salmon, Imported	All year (chilled or frozen)	
Salmon, Scotch	February–August*	July–August
Salmon trout	March 2–August 31	May
Scallops	All year	
Scampi	All year	April–November
Shrimps	All year (especially February to November)	March–October
Skate	All year (especially May to February)	September–February
Sole, Dover	All year (especially May to March)	September–February
Sole, lemon	All year (especially May to March)	December–March
Sprats	September–March	November, December
Squid	May–October	
Sturgeon	August–March	

Table 6.3   *(cont.)*

Commodity	Season	When best
Tench	July–March	Autumn
Trout	March–September (all year from hatcheries)	April–July
Tunnyfish	June–December	Autumn, Winter
Turbot	All year (especially April to February)	May–July
Whelks	February–August	
Whitebait	February–September	February–July
Whiting	All year (especially June to February)	December–February

Note: * Opening and closing dates may vary for different rivers.

Sea Fish Industry Authority sample specifications include:

■ Scope of specification, e.g. species – cod, haddock, etc.

■ Definition of product, e.g. fillet.

■ Specification of product – detailed description (requirement) of the following:
  ● colour;
  ● appearance (bones, skin, belly lining/flap);
  ● worms and parasites (tolerance levels);
  ● size;
  ● eating quality;
  ● packaging;
  ● temperature at delivery.

Figure 6.3   *Fish specification*

The following points are an indication of good quality.

For whole wet fish check the following:

● Bright, clear eyes, no discolouration, slime or cloudiness.

● No abrasions on the skin.

● The gills, if present, should be bright red with no discoloured slime or objectionable smell.

● The flesh should not retain the indentation when pressed with a finger.

● The skin should not be gritty, scales should not be easily removed. It should have a good, not dull, sheen. No discoloured slime.

For fillets of wet fish (which may have been previously frozen):

● The flesh should be translucent; firm and not ragged or gaping; and should not retain an indentation when pressed with a finger.

● There should be no smell of ammonia or sour odours.

Freezer burn

This may be identified as a change in the texture of any flesh which has been exposed to freezing conditions, especially direct contact with freezing equipment.

Belly lining

Burst bellies

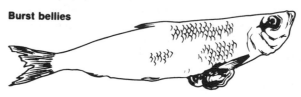

Example of excess belly flab

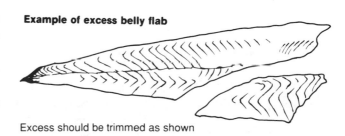

Excess should be trimmed as shown

Figure 6.4   *Examples of defective products*

Parasitic worms (cod)

These are normally identified by inspection (by the processor) but can be found, in the occasional fillet, by the caterer. Although they are unsightly, there is no evidence to suggest that their presence in fish, once cooked, could be harmful.

- There should be no bruising or blood clots.
- There should be no areas of discolouration.
- The maximum tolerance for cod worms is three per 3.2kg (7lb).

For frozen fish check the following:
- If packaged, the packaging should be undamaged.
- There should be no evidence of freezer burn.

- There should be no evidence of partial thaw and refreeze.
- Thawed fish should be firm and not ragged or gaping.

Processing

Fish farming has had a significant influence on the availability and quality of produce suitable for the menu.

Salmon: farmed versus wild

Wild salmon start life in rivers before migrating to the sea. They return after several years to spawn. This lifestyle causes seasonal fluctuations in price and availability, but also in quality. The development of the salmon farming industry has progressed to a point that quality may now rival that of the wild variety. In particular, purchasers can be sure of consistent, pre-determined quality; in addition to year-round supplies at a consistent price.

Freezing

Fresh fish can be prepared, packed and frozen so quickly that there is almost no loss of quality during the process. Although fish is less susceptible to rupture of cell structure spoilage can occur at or just below 0°C and large ice particles may form if the process is too slow.

Glazing

This is the method whereby products are dipped in (or sprayed with) water prior to freezing. This causes a lining, or skin, of ice to form around the fish which protects it during storage in the freezer. This ice should normally be in addition to pack weight. Look for net weight products. Water emanating from frozen products during defrost results from either glaze or drip which should not exceed 5 per cent of total weight. Excessive drip may result from poor storage.

Freezer burn

This is the dehydration (drying out) of flesh resulting from either direct contact with freezer components or unprotected fish losing moisture through condensation, resulting in frost in the freezer. Freezer burn may be identified as white, cotton-wool-like patches.

Other methods of processing include drying, salting, canning (oily fish), irradiation (shellfish) and smoking.

In addition to its preservative function the smoking process provides for interesting developments in flavour. However, good quality smoked fish should not be over-salty or unpleasantly smoky. Its appearance should be free of smuts and dirt. Although the dyes used by some processors are not harmful they can result in uneven drying such that flavour and keeping quality are adversely affected.

Good quality smoked fish will be firm, fairly rigid and springy to the touch. White fish (cod and haddock) should be fairly dry. Oily fish (for example, kippers) should appear slightly oily.

Uniformity of colour and texture throughout a batch of fish is generally a good indication of good processing and hence keeping quality.

Purchasing units and specifications

Fresh fish is associated with quality but it can be difficult to handle. Frozen fish, purchased according to appropriate specifications, provides an acceptable alternative which is clean and simple to handle. In either case, the caterer must decide on the unit of purchase – whole, fillets or portions. The choice will be influenced by staff availability and skills, size and design of preparation area and storage capacity.

Fresh fish should, ideally, be delivered daily, if possible direct from the market. Look for clean new boxes or request non-returnable containers that are more hygienic and will not require washing, storage or a deposit. Look for specialist vehicles, especially insulated vehicles for frozen products.

Storage, hygiene and health

Fish requires careful handling and storage or it will spoil rapidly. Prepare and cook fish as soon after delivery as possible. If it is not used at once, refrigerate at about 0°C, cover with crushed ice where possible, making sure that it is kept away from other foods (using a separate refrigerator where possible). The method of storage should allow for the free drainage of liquids such that the fish does not lie in water as the ice melts. Separate the different species as much as possible. White fish keeps better than oily fish.

Frozen fish

Even at a temperature of −30°C fish will eventually deteriorate. Therefore, keep stocks to the minimum and turn stock over frequently, at least every three weeks.

Frozen fish is best defrosted in a refrigerator, rather than at room temperature, allowing approximately 24 hours per kilo.

Profitable usage

Filleting and skinning in-house can be wasteful unless staff are competent and the customer recognises the added value and is prepared to pay for the benefit.

When purchasing whole fish for in-house preparation waste should be accounted for in costings. As a general rule, allow for 60 per cent on round fish and 50 per cent for flat. Exceptions are salmon (as little as 35 per cent) and monkfish (as much as 75 per cent).

Price for fresh fish will be subject to availability and caterers are thus faced with the choice of firm or fluctuating price. A fixed price, short-term contract, with tight specifications to ensure that quality does not drop, if/when price increases, is desirable. Market pricing is possible where menus change daily. For set menus, frozen product prices are likely to be more stable.

SHELLFISH

Some types of shellfish may cause trouble to diners who have allergies. Shellfish also tend to be prone to infection in the case, for example, of contamination by typhoid germs as a result of sewage discharging near oyster beds. Particular vigilance is required, therefore, in selecting shellfish.

Mussel farming
Under the right conditions, farmed mussels yield better meat at a faster production rate than in the wild. Various methods are used depending on the geography of the coast:

- raft (floating culture) in Spain;
- bottom culture in the Netherlands;
- pole (bouchot) culture in France.

Both raft and bottom culture have been successfully developed in the UK. Seeds are transplanted to protected beds, suspended on ropes or in net tubes in deep sheltered water with a rich supply of plankton. The growing period lasts 20–24 months.

Source

Shellfish may be classified as, crustacea, molluscs or cephalopods (see Figure 6.5).

Many species of shellfish are now farmed successfully.

Quality

Between prawns and shrimps there is some confusion as to size, but shrimps are generally accepted as being the smaller, browner species. Prawns may range in size from 400 per kg up to 800 per kg and may be identified as warm water, cold water or fresh water.

Crustacea	
Shrimp	Crawfish
Crayfish	Dublin Bay prawn (scampi)
Crab	Lobster
Prawn	

Molluscs	
Univalve – one shell	
Winkle	Whelk
Bivalve – two shell	
Cockle	Mussel
Queen	Scallop
Clam	Oyster

Cephalopods (internal shell)		
Octopus	Squid	Cuttlefish

Figure 6.5   *Classification of shellfish*

- Warm water prawns account for 80 per cent of the market and are cheaper. Some brands may require additional cooking.
- Cold water prawns are normally sold fully-cooked and peeled. Their flavour and texture are considered best for prawn cocktail.

Prawn farming is on the increase and now accounts for 16 per cent of the market. Hand-peeled prawns are more expensive, but machine peeling can damage the prawns.

Lobsters are obtainable all the year round, but are most abundant and best in the summer. They must be alive when purchased, to test their freshness pull back the tail which should close smartly.

Crabs are similarly obtained all year, but are most abundant in the spring and early summer when they are at their best. Unlike lobsters they should be killed before boiling otherwise they tend to cast their claws. Avoid crabs that are discoloured and are of a faded appearance. Stickiness of the claws at the joints is also a danger sign.

Mussels, though in season from July to April, are at their best from August to November. They are generally considered more prone to infection than oysters, but can be cleansed from contamination by being placed in clean water for a period of not less than four days.

A mussel bed is an enormous biological filter. A mussel pumps large quantities of sea water through its system (45–70 litres in a 24-hour period) in order to feed on minute planktonic organisms, including bacteria, viruses and/or toxic chemicals. Consequently, the mussel has been seen as a health risk. Most producers now use a purification system to cleanse the product.

Pasteurised, rope culture mussels with smooth, clean shells are now available frozen and vacuum packed.

Though foreign oysters may be obtainable all the year round, there is a close season for native varieties and they are only eaten when there is an 'R' in the month. During the rest of the year spawning takes place and the oysters are indigestible and of poor taste and body. Natives such as Whitstables are considered to be in prime condition between four and five years old, though foreign oysters, such as Portuguese ones, when relaid in UK coastal waters come to maturity earlier. The smallest natives should not be less than 6.35 cm (2.5 in.) and primes should be between 7.5 –11.5 cm (3–4.5 in.) in diameter.

Processing

In addition to forms of processing already identified for fish, it is common to purchase shellfish as a ready-cooked product.

Cooked shellfish

Where the product has not been dressed or peeled:

- the shell should be intact with no cracks;
- shells should not leak excessive amounts of liquid;
- there should be no signs of discolouration;
- there should be no unpleasant aroma (ammonia).

Frozen cooked shellfish, once thawed, should not be refrozen.

Purchasing units and specifications

Shellfish may be purchased in the following units:

- individual – lobsters and crab;
- dozens – oysters;
- kilos or pounds – crayfish, scampi, mussels and prawns;
- litres or pints – prawns, shrimps, cockles and whelks.

Specify all shellfish by size or weight range.

Judge crustacea by weight rather than size. They should be heavy for their size with no excess water and the shell should be intact, not cracked or holed.

With all molluscs, look for tightly closed shells or, in the case of any slightly open, immediate closure on handling. Open shelled fish should otherwise be rejected as dead. When opening, the shell of a fresh oyster should close noticeably upon the knife and the stronger this closing the better chances of having a sound oyster.

All shellfish should be bought live or frozen. Shellfish should be in a cool, moist condition and reasonably lively. Dead or dying shellfish should never be used.

If buying locally, check where and how your supplier receives deliveries, as poor handling and transportation can affect the quality of shellfish. The mortality rate of shellfish is often due to poor handling, causing them stress.

Storage, hygiene and health

Ideally, shellfish should be used on the day of purchase. Where storage is considered necessary then keep fresh shellfish alive, cool and moist (by covering with seaweed). Do not attempt to keep oysters or lobsters in water unless it is oxygenated. Oysters may keep out of water for up to seven days.

Once cooked, all shellfish will keep well under normal refrigerated conditions. Apart from the known risk of eating molluscs from sewage-contaminated waters, properly-cooked seafood is generally safe. Any problems which do arise with crab meat, prawns or molluscs can usually be linked to poor storage, preparation, handling and/or cooking.

Profitable usage

Glazing, a skin of ice, is essential to protect the quality of frozen shellfish. However, it can range from anywhere between 10 per cent and 40 per cent of the packed product. Most experts consider that between 12 per cent and 15 per cent is perfectly adequate to maintain quality. Look for net weight packs, which may appear more expensive but will give an accurate measure of consumable product and will be more controllable and cost effective.

MEAT

Meat is still one of the most expensive items on the budget and therefore a great deal of care and thought should be put into choosing it wisely. Butchers' meats are largely a product of selective breeding and feeding techniques producing well-fleshed yet compact animals.

Consumer requirements, affected by social and economic trends, the animal's anatomy and to some extent religious custom, affect the way the butcher prepares and cuts the carcass. Butchery techniques vary considerably, not only between countries, but even within cities and towns. Continental or seam butchery (cutting between the muscles where it is easier to remove fat and gristle) has become more popular in this country. The resulting joints ensure more even texture on cooking and improved carving. The butcher still has to make some return on carcass fat, gristle and bone so that these joints are likely to be more expensive, but equally they should be more cost-effective.

Plate waste is significantly reduced when using boned and trimmed meats, compare two 170 g (6 oz) traditional pork chops, resulting in approximately 30 per cent plate waste, with one 225 g (8 oz) lean trimmed (boned) chop, where there is no potential waste. Each portion would probably cost the same to purchase and would sell, on the menu, at a similar price.

Butchers do not always appreciate the idiosyncracies of the caterer, so it is wise to deal with a supplier that specialises in catering cuts, including traditional 'French' cuts.

Meat is a natural not uniform product, varying in quality from carcass to carcass. While flavour, texture and appearance of the meat are largely determined by the type of animal they can also be influenced by muscle activity, age, type of feed and fat distribution, as well as by method of slaughter. It has long been recognised that a stressed animal, and the subsequent change in body chemistry, can affect the quality of butchered meat.

The most useful guide to tenderness, flavour and quality is a knowledge of the cuts of meat and their location on the carcass. In principle, the leanest and tenderest cuts come from the back (loin) and rear (rump) of the animal. Coarser cuts are found on the shoulders/neck, legs and tail, i.e. those parts of the animal that have plenty of muscular exercise, where fibres have become hardened and there is a greater proportion of connective tissue, especially elastin.

Processing

The slaughter process should include the following hygiene and inspection rules:

- The animals are all inspected before slaughter for signs of disease/distress.

- Stunning – large animals are dispatched by captive bolt and pithing (a long, thin rod inserted into the brain to prevent reflex activity); smaller animals by electrical stun which passes a current through the brain making the animal unconscious for up to 1.5 minutes; pigs are treated with carbon dioxide (gas and air) which renders the animal unconscious and results in more efficient bleeding.

- Bleeding – the animal is hung by its hind legs and the main artery in the neck is severed causing the removal of blood/oxygen from the heart and brain, resulting in death.

- Skinning and dressing (the removal of gut and organs (offal)) – to reduce the risk from BSE (commonly known as Mad Cow Disease) the brain and spinal cord are removed and disposed of.

- Inspection of the carcass and particularly the offal for signs of disease; this may involve cutting into the lymph nodes and liver.

- Storage – both carcass and offal are tagged (to match one another) before being transferred to store.

During slaughter animals are drained of about half their blood (blood being prime material for bacterial growth); removing the blood decreases the spoilage. Halal and Kosher methods are designed to remove the maximum amount of blood. Bacterial growth may be further deterred by curing, smoking, drying and/or cooking.

Blood and life

Kosher butchery originates from the edict 'though shall not eat flesh with its life'; life was taken to mean blood. The method used is to sever the trachea, oesophagus, jugular vein and carotid arteries, resulting in the fullest outpouring of blood. Any blood that might remain is removed by the cook, through soaking and/or salting.

Tannahill R., *Food in History*, Penguin, 1988

Most animal protein benefits from some delay between slaughter and cooking. The process of hanging meat allows for the dissipation of rigormortis and the onset of enzymatic action resulting in the breakdown of muscle tissue which contributes to the tenderness of the meat. Hanging has little effect on tough connective tissue; consequently shin and similar cuts do not benefit greatly.

Electrical stimulation of the carcass may be used to reduce hanging time, and allow for more rapid chilling.

Beef carcasses may be injected with papain (from pawpaw fruit) prior to slaughter, the enzyme helps to break down the protein producing more tender meat. The process of injection is likely to become illegal by 1992, although it may still be possible to introduce tenderisers (pawpaw, figs or pineapple) into the animals' feed.

Vacuum packing extends the shelf life of better cuts and joints, although the maturation process will still continue.

Traditional seasons for meat are shown in Table 6.4.

BEEF

Domesticated cattle have developed over thousands of years, although recent times have seen more selective breeding in order to produce leaner, more tender cuts.

Source

- Bull – entire male (for breeding) but admired by some as good, lean eating meat.
- Bullock/steer – castrated male, generally accepted as the best producer of meat for the table.
- Heifer – female that has not produced young; provides acceptable meat.
- Cow – female that has produced young; may produce acceptable meat when young but can be anything up to five years old in which case the meat is poor.
- Veal – calves under 12 months (milk-fed).
- Bobby calf – under 12 weeks, normally used for manufacture.
- Barley beef – reared on cereal to promote growth, providing expensive but sought-after meat.

Traditional steer beef is fed grass through the summer and silage in the winter (silage produces a heavier carcass than hay). The animal is slaughtered at 20–24 months.

Table 6.4 Traditional seasons for meat

Meat	Traditional season
Beef	All year
Lamb	April–July
Mutton	November–December
Pork	September–April
Rabbit	All year (farmed)
Veal	All year
Venison	All year (farmed)*

Note: Now that fresh meat is imported from the EC and other European countries, and frozen and chilled meat from Australia, New Zealand and other parts of the world, the question of season no longer really arises. Moreover, in the United Kingdom, production methods have eliminated the season for pork, which is available and eaten throughout the year. On the other hand, there is so little demand for mutton that it is almost unobtainable on a regular basis. Nevertheless, the seasons which used to apply still have some relevance in indicating when naturally-reared, home-produced stock is at its best, and are thus included.

* Farmed venison are defined as animals grasssed in fenced enclosures; they will also have been tagged and tested for disease.

Intensive production

Cattle are housed throughout, fed on an all-concentrate diet and slaughtered at ten to 12 months old.

Quality

The chef has traditionally looked for marbling in beef, that is to say, the appearance of particles of fat in the lean section of the meat which indicates a well-fed animal. This fat gives, in effect, internal basting during cooking which no external basting alone can do. Good quality beef should have bright, firm and fine-grained lean meat and its fat should be creamy white rather than yellow, although this latter factor is affected by the breed and is certainly not an inflexible rule. Light-coloured meat with the appearance of oozing is indicative of toughness.

Scotch breeds of beef, such as Aberdeen-Angus and Beef Shorthorn, are specially reared for the table and are highly esteemed. Home-killed Scotch beef is, therefore, a menu item which should be exploited to the maximum. However, imported breeds raised from similar strains can give excellent results. Signs of quality are similar whatever the origin.

The following are commonly used quality terms:

- Prime – meat from young heifers or steers; compact muscle, firm, smooth red meat; white, brittle fat; bones soft and porous with some evidence of blood.
- Choice – heifers or steers; slightly darker flesh; firm white fat.

The Meat and Livestock Commission (MLC) has produced a system of carcass classification based on fat distribution and muscle confirmation (see Figure 6.6). For example, a U3 carcass has quite good confirmation and is fairly lean, whereas a R4L classification is an average carcass.

There are two standards for fat specifications:

- the visible fat content over the surface of meat;
- a chemical test for the fat content in minced meat.

Conformation Class		Fat class — Increasing fatness →							
		1	2	3	4L	4H	5L	5H	
Improving conformation ↑	E								
	U+			U3					
	−U								
	R				R4L				
	O+								
	−O								
	P+								
	−P								

Figure 6.6   *MLC beef classification (grading of carcass).*
Note: The most common type of clean beef carcase is R4L. A U+3 carcass is quite good conformation as well as being fairly lean.

Beef products, for example, minced beef and hamburgers, may vary considerably in quality. It is wise to draw very detailed specifications, particularly in relation to source/joint and fat content, and acceptable additives.

Processing

Dissection of meat varies in Britain according to the custom of the retail meat trade in a given area. Where the bone remains, joints are generally easy to recognise; once boned, recognition becomes more difficult. Larger operations may purchase beef by the side or quarters. This enables these operations to use traditional French cuts or to exploit the side or quarter more economically than when it has been dissected for the retailer's profit. It is not practical to give all the variations of cut possible, but Figures 6.7 and 6.8 shows the principal cuts together with an indication of their approximate weights (see Tables 6.5 and 6.6 and page 100).

Table 6.5 Carcass weights and uses for beef

	Uses	*Average weight from a side of beef approx. 113.5 kg (250 lb)*	
Beef cuts (English and French)		kg	lb
1 Shin (Jambe)	Gravy, stock, stewing	6.35–6.80	14–15
2 Topside (Tranche Tendre)	Roast, braising, carbonade, paupiette	8.60–9.10	19–20
3 Silverside (Gite à la Noix)	Salting, boiling	9.10–10.4	20–23
4 Thick flank (Tranche Grasse)	General purpose, braising, stewing, pies	9.10–10.00	20–22
5 Rump (Culotte), including head fillet	Grill, roast, braising	9.10–11.35	20–25
6 Sirloin (Aloyau)	Roast, grill, including fillet (filet) and contrefilet	7.25–8.15	16–18
7 Thin flank (Bavette d'Aloyau)	Stewing, pie	5.45–7.25	12–16
8 Wing ribs (Côte d'Aloyau)	Roast, braising	4.55–5.45	10–12
9 Fore ribs (Côte Première)	Roast	8.15–9.10	18–20
10 Middle ribs (Côte Decouverte)	Roast, pot roast	8.15–9.10	18–20
11 Brisket (Poitrine)	Stewing, salting, mince (sausage meat)	9.10–11.35	20–25
12 Flat ribs (Plat Decotes Decouverte)	Boiling, mince, sausage	6.80–8.15	15–18
13 Chuck ribs (Côte de Collier)	Pot roast. stew, pie	8.15–9.10	18–20
14 Neck (Collier)	Stew, mince	7.25–8.15	16–18
15 Shank (Jarret de Devant)	Gravy, stock, stewing	4.55–5.45	10–12
Beef offal (which, except for kidney, are not included when buying a side or quarter)		kg	lb
Heart (Cœur)	Stuffing, braising, bake	2.50	5½
Tail (Queue)	Soups, stewing, braising	0.90–1.35	2–3
Kidney (Rognon)	Soups, sauté, pie, pudding	0.70	1½
Brain (Cervelle)	Boiling, fried, hors d'œuvres		
Tongue (Langue)	Boiling, braising, pickling	2.75	6
Tripe (Tripes)	Boiling, stewing, sauté		
Liver (Foie)	Frying, sauté, stewing, braising, terrine, pâté	2.25–3.20	5–7
Sweetbread (Ris)	Frying, stewing, sauté		

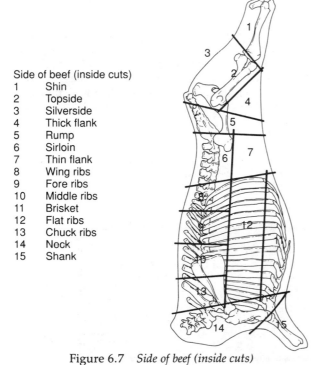

Side of beef (inside cuts)
1   Shin
2   Topside
3   Silverside
4   Thick flank
5   Rump
6   Sirloin
7   Thin flank
8   Wing ribs
9   Fore ribs
10 Middle ribs
11 Brisket
12 Flat ribs
13 Chuck ribs
14 Neck
15 Shank

Figure 6.7 *Side of beef (inside cuts)*

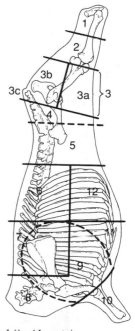

1   Shank
2   Knuckle
3   Leg
3a   Thick flank
3b   Cushion
3c   Under cushion
4   Rump
5   Loin
6   Best end
7   Low cutlets
8   Neck
9   Shoulder
10   Knuckle
11   Breast
12   Tendons

Figure 6.8 *Side of veal (inside cuts)*

Table 6.6 Carcass weights and uses for veal

	Uses	Average weight from a side of veal approx. 77 kg (170 lb)	
Veal cuts		kg	lb
1 Shank (Crosse)	Stock and jelly	} 1.80–2.70	4–6
2 Knuckle (Jarret Derrière)	Osso Bucco, sauté		
3 Leg (Cuisse)	Roast, braise, escalopes, sauté	13.60–15.90	30–35
3a Thick flank (Noix Patissière)	Roast, escalopes	} Parts of leg	
3b Cushion (Noix de Veau)	Roast, escalopes, fricandeau		
3c Under cushion (Sous Noix)	Roast, escalopes		
4 Rump (Cul de veau)	Escalopes, roast		
5 Loin (Longe) (two comprising a saddle)	Roast, grilling (chops, noisettes)	7.25–8.15	16–18
6 Best end (Carré)	Roast, grilling (cutlets)	5.45–6.35	12–14
7 Low cutlets (Côtelettes Decouvertes)	Stewing	} 5.45	12
8 Neck (Collet)	Stewing		
9 Shoulder (Epaule)	Roast, stuffed, braised, stew	6.80 each	15 each
10 Knuckle (Jarret)	Osso Bucco, sauté	1.35–1.80	3–4 each
11 Breast (Poitrine)	Stewing, bone and stuff, galantine	3.65–4.55	8–10 each
12 Tendons (Tendrons)	Blanquettes, goulash	Part of breast	
Veal offal		kg	lb
Head (Tête de veau)	Boiling, frying, hors d'œuvres	4.55	10
Tongue (Langue)	Boiled, stewed, cold, salad	0.70–0.90	1½–2
Liver (Foie)	Sauté, grilled, brochette, terrine	1.35–1.80	3–4
Brain (Cervelle)	Boiled, sauté, ravigote	0.35–0.45	¾–1
Kidney (Rognon)	Grilled, fried, sauté	0.20–0.30	8oz–10oz each
Heart (Cœur)	Braising, stuffing	0.35	¾
Feet (Pieds)	Boiling	2.70	6 (a set)
Sweetbreads (Ris de Veau)	Braising, frying	0.70	1½

Purchasing units and specifications

Much meat is now purchased ready dissected into joints for roasting, braising and boiling or in small cuts for grilling and frying. The Meat and Livestock Commission (MLC) has prepared sample material for specifications and at least one large meat purveyor has similarly produced an illustrated set of sample specifications; such material can be consulted for further guidance. The specification details that this material incorporates helps caterers and suppliers to have a stable relationship and allows caterers to assess more fairly the merits, cost and value of meats. Closer identification of cost aids predetermination of profit. An example of a sample specification (for entrecôte steak) is given in Figure 6.9 with a diagrammatic specification shown in Figure 6.10, but details can, and should, be varied to meet the needs of a particular operation.

In summarising several specifications for one supplier a form may be arranged to suit the operation (see Figure 6.11).

> The MLC have developed a coding system for meat cuts, providing a clear standard for a wide variety of joints and trims. The MLC coding is based on a three-figure number; the first number denotes the animal, the second two identify the joint, for example, 200 = lamb carcass, 300 = pork carcass, 400 = veal carcass and 500 = offal. A fourth number may be added to denote a special trim, for example, 100 = beef, 112 = beef sirloin (on bone) and 1125 = beef sirloin, boned and rolled.

Entrecôte steak

Origin: From a striploin.
Backstrip gristle: Leave intact.
Side chain: Leave intact.
Length of 'tops': Not to exceed 25 mm (1 in.).
Cutting: Across/against the grain of the 'eye' muscle so that both cut surfaces will be reasonably parallel to ensure consistent thickness of each portion.
Thickness: Dependent upon the steak size specified.
Surface fat: Not to exceed a thickness of 133 mm (½ in.).
Recommended weights 115 g (4 oz), 140 g (5 oz), 170 g (6 oz), 200 g (7 oz).

Note: A photograph or clear drawing of the cut specified is a useful accompaniment to the specification.

Tolerances
For a consistent and viable degree of accuracy for both purchaser and portioners, weight tolerances may be applied as follows:

Weight specified	*Tolerance*
Under 170 g (6 oz)	± 7 g (¼ oz)
170 g (6 oz) but less than 340 g (12 oz)	± 14 g (½ oz)
340 g (12 oz) but less than 450 g (18 oz)	± 20 g (¾ oz)
565 g (20 oz) plus	± 28 g (1 oz)

Example
If 225 g (8 oz) portions are specified, then individual portions weighing between 215 g–240 g (7½ oz–8½ oz) are acceptable.

Source: Sample specification as originally produced by Harrison and King of Kettering, Northants.

Figure 6.9   *Specification (description) for sirloin steak*

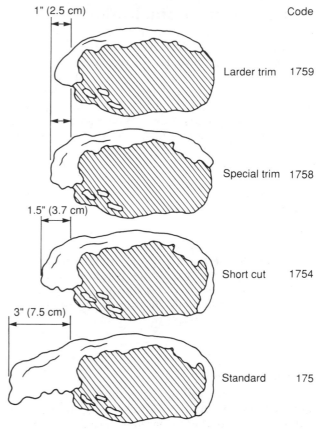

In addition to diagrams, MLC sample specifications also include full descriptions of source joint, depth of external fat and method of cutting.

Source: The Meat Buyers' Guide for Caterers. Moore, Stone and Tattersal, International Thompson Publishing Ltd.

Figure 6.10   *Specification (diagram) for sirloin steak (MLC)*

Item ref.	Item	Grade	Country of origin	How purchased	Weight or count	Tolerance	Delivery requirements
1	Steak: preportioned fillet	Home-killed, first-quality, prime ox	UK/EC	From fillets trimmed of fat silver tissue chain and tail	20 steaks @ 200 g (7 oz) each	± 15 g (½ oz) per steak	Weekly (Friday am)
2	Striploin: boneless	First-quality, prime ox	UK/EC	25.41 cm (10 in.) flank trim	5.45–8.15 kg (12–16 lb)	N/A	
3							

Figure 6.11   *Itemising specifications (summary sheet)*

Storage, hygiene and health

Every time that meat is cut a loss of weight occurs, the larger the cut surface the greater the loss from both drip and evaporation. Even under optimum refrigeration, losses can be considerable. As an example, a rump matured for 14 days can lose 4–5 per cent of its initial weight. Losses will be greater under poor storage conditions. There is much debate among chefs as to the relative advantages of hanging meat as opposed to laying it flat, on clean trays. The generally accepted view is that hanging is preferable for carcasses and larger joints, particularly while still on the bone. Storing on trays is better for small, trimmed/boned joints.

Ideal temperature for fresh meat storage is 2°C at a relative humidity of around 90 per cent; chilled meat should be stored at −2°C. Safe storage times under hygienic conditions at these temperatures will be up to three weeks for beef and one to two weeks for veal. Frozen meat should be stored at a temperature of −18°C.

Profitable usage

Cost effectiveness will be determined by the quality and skill of purchasing. Whole loins, bought for grilling as sirloin steaks, may have excessive flap/fat/gristle, or may be cut high into the rump or wing rib, making it difficult to get good steaks at either end.

Value for money from beef will be dependent on the skills used in cutting and preparation before cooking, traditionally those of the larder chef or hotel butcher, so remember to cost for labour. Preparing steaks in-house from loins bought on the bone may add as much as 150 per cent on to the original cost of the meat.

VEAL

Veal is the meat from young dairy calves slaughtered between 12 and 20 weeks.

Source

Historically, most veal comes from the continent, particularly Holland. In Britain, the emphasis has been on raising beef cattle, though there are signs of greater concentration on veal production. Native veal is available all the year round, although it is considered to be at its best in summer.

Quality

The lean part of veal should be a clear, pale pink with the fat firm and pinky-white. Milk-fed calves produce the palest flesh. Colour develops as the animal ages and is particularly associated with a change in feed. Any evidence of softness or moistness in the fat means staleness and is to be avoided. Further positive signs of quality are:

- the kidney (well covered with fat);
- bright blue veins in the shoulder;
- it should be possible to separate the muscles (cushions) on the hind leg without the aid of a knife.

Processing and purchasing specifications

The joints of veal and their approximate weights and uses are identified in Figure 6.8 and Table 6.6 on pages 99 and 100.

Storage, hygiene and health

This is the same as for beef above.

Profitable usage

Traditionally, there has always been a greater demand in catering for cushions, the muscles on the hind leg, from which escalopes are produced. Carcass veal is considerably cheaper but the caterer must be confident that the whole carcass can be used in menu items that sell.

LAMB AND MUTTON

Seasonal variations in lamb and mutton buying are less important than formerly because of chilling, cold storage and the availability of imported carcasses. Home-killed lamb is at its best in spring (April and May). Mutton makes good eating all the year round, but as it is decreasingly reared for the table it may be difficult to obtain.

Home-killed lamb
Mountain breeds produce late-maturing carcasses, available through autumn. Lowland and downland breeds provide the early spring lamb.

Source

- Lamb – either sex under 12 months old (normally four to six months);
- Hogget – maiden ewes or wethers up to two years (or 26kg);
- Mutton – adult sheep (not hogget or ram).

Lamb is normally sent for slaughter when it reaches half of its anticipated mature weight, for example, about 36 kg (80 lb), resulting in a 18 kg (40 lb) dressed-weight carcass.

Quality

Lamb is one of the most natural meats available, being raised on natural grass feed with no hormone or other such treatment. Native lamb and mutton, particularly Southdown, is highly esteemed, but imported meat, especially from New Zealand, reaches high standards. The reputation of New Zealand Lamb for consistent quality is based on strict controls. There are clear grading standards (see Figure 6.12) and because the product is frozen there is less seasonal variation in prices.

Local British lamb, being fresh and seasonal, should be used to enhance the menu. There are also many varieties of British lamb. Hill sheep work hard to put on weight and are generally slaughtered late; they have a firmer, darker flesh. Other varieties include those that graze on salt flats and are prized for their distinctive flavour (in France they are termed 'pre sale' on menus). Milk-fed and spring lamb may look similar but are, in fact, quite different. Milk-fed lamb grows quickly producing soft pale flesh similar to veal, but at a high cost. The Meat and Livestock Commission (MLC) have their own grading system for British carcasses (see Figure 6.13 overleaf).

The appearance of good lamb is pink rather than red with fine graining in the lean meat. The fat should not only be creamy-coloured but have a clear, crisp appearance. Pulled apart, knuckle joints of lamb shoulders and legs have a bluish tinge when the animal is young. Bones should be pink; the breast bone pliable. Mutton will have, by virtue of its coming from an older animal, darker red meat with white and waxier fat, and white and brittle bones.

	Fat content						
Weight	A almost devoid	Y light	P medium	T heavy	F excess	C mixed	M mixed
Less than 9.0 kg	A						
9.0–12.5kg		YL	PL	TL	Used		
13.0–16.0 kg		YM	PM	TM	for		
16.5–20.0 kg		YX	PX	TH	manufacture		
20.5 kg and over		YX	PH	TH			
Mutton	MM	MX	ML	MH	MF		

Notes: The PX grade is normally recommended for caterers, but response to customer demand may determine YX or YM in the future.

New Zealand lamb is graded and marked accordingly with a 'NZ Lamb' stamp on each of the main carcass joints, legs, loins, best-ends and shoulders (eight stamps in all). Mutton is marked in only six places.

Figure 6.12   *Classification (grading) of New Zealand lamb*

Conformation Class		Fat class	Increasing fatness					
		1	2	3L	3H	4L	4H	5
E								
U								
R				R3L				
O								
P								

Figure 6.13 *Classification (grading) of British lamb (MLC)*
Note: Conformation class is described first followed by the fat class, eg R3L.

Processing

Lamb is slaughtered, dressed and sold fresh, chilled or frozen. If frozen it will keep for up to 12 months with no deterioration in quality. Freezing may also be associated with band-saw cutting which has the advantage of being a cheap and efficient method of breaking up the carcass. However, this method cuts through (rather than between) bones, resulting in portions containing oddments and splinters of bone, and so it may be considered by some caterers to be unacceptable.

Fresh carcasses may be sold whole or jointed. There are differences in cutting technique: square cut across the muscle; and round (French) cuts, between muscle seams and through natural muscle joints. Some joints (legs, saddle and loins) may be obtained as short or long cuts. A new development is for larger-boned joints, often including two or more traditional joints, for example, leg plus loin, loin plus best end; these may be ideal for the carvery trade.

The cuts of lamb and mutton with their approximate weights and uses are identified in Figure 6.14.

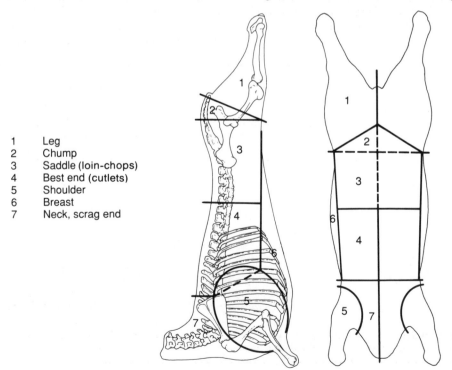

1   Leg
2   Chump
3   Saddle (loin-chops)
4   Best end (cutlets)
5   Shoulder
6   Breast
7   Neck, scrag end

Figure 6.14 *Lamb or mutton cuts*

Table 6.7 Carcass weights and uses for lamb or mutton

	Uses	Lamb: approx. 17.24 kg (38 lb)		Mutton: approx. 22.70 kg (50 lb)	
Lamb and mutton cuts		kg	lb	kg	lb
Leg (Gigot)	Roast, boiling (mutton)	1.80–2.25	4–5 each	3.20–3.60	7–8 each
Chump*	(Chops) grilling, roast	0.70–0.90	1½–2	1.60–2.00	3½–4½
Saddle (Selle)†	Roast, grill (in chops) noisettes	2.25–2.70	5–6	3.20–3.60	7–8
Best end (Carré)	Roast grilling	1.80–2.25	4–5	2.95–3.40	6½–7½
Shoulder (Epaule)	Roast, stuffed, braised, poêlé	1.35–1.80 each	3–4 each	2.00–2.50 each	4½–5½ each
Breast (Poitrine)	Stew, epigrammes, bone, stuff	1.80–2.25	4–5	2.95–3.40	6½–7½
Neck, scrag end (Cou, collier)	Stewing, navarin	1.35–1.80	3–4	2.00–2.50	4½–5½
Lamb offal (which, kidneys excepted, are not included when buying a carcass)		kg	lb	kg	lb
Liver (Foie)	Fried, sauté, stewed, braised, terrine, pâté	0.35–0.45	¾–1	0.90–1.35	2–3
Kidney (Rognon)	Sauté, stewed, grilled	0.15–0.20	6 oz–8 oz	0.20–0.30	8 oz–10 oz
Head (Tête)	Boiled	1.35	3	1.80–2.25	4–5

Notes:
* Unless required for chops, the chump is either left on the leg to give a long leg for roasting or left on the saddle (especially when the latter is to be carved in the restaurant).
† Split down the middle the saddle makes two loins.

Purchasing units and specifications

Lamb and mutton may be purchased by the carcass or as whole joints, prepared joints, cutlets and chops. New Zealand lamb may be purchased in boxed cuts, where it is weight-graded as (L)ight, (M)edium or (H)eavy.

Storage, hygiene and health

As for beef and veal (up to two weeks).

Profitable usage

Profitable usage will depend on efficient and effective purchasing of the correct cuts. In-house preparation may be used to advantage, but will have a cost which must be identified. Portion control, particularly of carved joints, will be significant and a skilled craftsperson will considerably affect the profitability of any carving operation. Carving skills must be supported by the purchase of properly-prepared joints.

PORK AND BACON

Use of pigs as a source of meat is thought to have originated in China, where there is no word, other than the Chinese for pork, to describe meat. Most domestic breeds of pig are descended from Asian stock.

At one time, pork was a highly seasonal animal and was rigorously excluded from restaurant menus when there was an R in the month. The importation of pork from other countries and the use of freezing and refrigerated storage, together with developments in breeding and rearing of pigs, has eliminated the seasonal aspect. The UK is one of the most efficient producers of pig meat in the world. The predominant production method is indoor rearing on a concentrated diet. As with the battery farming of hens, there has been some criticism of this method of production. The development of free-range techniques will be influenced primarily by the consumer who may be driven by social values as much as by price and quality of meat.

Pork and bacon production has now developed to such a degree that pigs are bred and reared to specification. Larger organisations, like Marks & Spencer, Sainsbury's and some of the larger catering operations, can specify precisely weight, size, shape and fat distribution of the animal/carcass (as well as production technique) and farmers are able to meet those requirements precisely.

Source

Pigs, having only one stomach, are efficient converters of feed to body weight; six pounds of feed producing about one pound of flesh. They may be slaughtered at between 16 and 30 weeks; lighter for pork, heavier for bacon. Because most of the animal is used, it provides a comparatively high dressing-out weight of about 80 per cent.

Quality

A pork pig, as distinct from a bacon pig, should, though young and well-fed, be small rather than excessively fat. The lean meat should be a pale rather than bright pink, of firm and fine-grained texture, making it feel resilient to the touch. The skin should be thin and the underlying fat white, firm and fine-grained.

Whilst a cut surface should appear slightly moist any excessive weeping or moisture is an unfavourable sign. In older animals, the flesh is coarser, darker and of a drier appearance.

The grading of pork is based on the use of an introscope which is a probe to measure the depth of fat at specified points on the carcass. The amounts are added together and expressed (in mm) as a total which is stamped on the carcass (see Figure 6.15).

Less than 28 mm	= Q
29 – 34 mm	= A
35 – 40 mm	= B
More than 40 mm	= C

Figure 6.15   *Pork grading*

The presence of trichina, a parasitic worm, led to the tradition of always cooking pork 'well done', often drying out the meat in the process. The eradication of trichina, together with improved cooking techniques and particularly the use of probes to measure internal temperatures (an excess of 76°C is sufficient for pork) should now make it unnecessary to overcook pork.

Bacon

Bacon is prepared from pigs older and better-developed than those used for pork. They are usually specifically bred for the purpose. The type of cure affects purchasing considerations and green (unsmoked) bacon differs obviously from smoked. General signs of quality are a smooth, thin, flexible rind, a good pink colour of the lean meat with firm, clean-looking fat, tinged with pink from the brining process but not showing signs of any yellow marks. Bone taint may be encountered in bacon and should be sought by inserting a skewer deeply into the flesh adjoining the bones.

The Quality Assurance Scheme for Charter Quality Bacon may provide the basis for determining source and quality of bacon and bacon products. The scheme is monitored by MLC inspectors who assess bacon production plants for temperature control, hygiene and housekeeping, process control, equipment and structure/finish of the building/premises.

Processing

Bacon is normally cured in a brine tank and dry curing is less common, being more difficult to control. In addition to salt, brine would normally contain a proportion of salt petre and it is this which gives bacon its pink colour. The drying method may take up to six weeks with a further two weeks to mature. The brine method may be completed in about five days with a further seven days to mature.

Traditional methods are time-consuming and large stocks of meat in process is not an efficient use of financial resources. There has been some development of rapid curing techniques in order to turn stock over more quickly. These techniques include injecting brine, curing slices and tumbling (joints) in a drum, such that the brine is 'massaged' into the flesh.

Table 6.8 Carcass weights and uses for pork

	Uses	Approx. average from side of pork weighing approx. 27.25 kg (60 lb) headless	
		kg	lb
Pork cuts (English and French)			
1 Leg (Cuissot)	Roast, boiling (pickled)	6.80–7.25	15–16
2 Hand and spring or shoulder (Epaule)	Boiling, roast (excluding knuckle)	3.20–4.10	7–9
3 Belly (Poitrine)	Pickling, boiling grillette	4.10–4.55	9–10
4 Spare rib (Basse-Côte)	Roast, braising, pickling	4.10–4.55	9–10
5 Loin (Longe)	Roast, chops (grill and fry)	6.80–7.25	15–16
Pork offal			
6 Trotters (Pieds de porc)	Boil, grill (after boiling)	0.70–0.90	1½–2
Liver (Foie)	Terrine, pâté	0.90–1.35	2–3
7 Head (Tête)	Brawn	2.25–2.70	5–6

During smoking, surface drying helps to preserve the meat by further inhibiting bacterial growth and reduces the tendency toward rancidity in the fat. It also develops colour and flavour.

Purchasing units and specifications

Pork may be bought as a whole or half carcass, by the joint or in small cuts. Specifications should detail acceptable amount of fat and bone, normally as a proportion of the eye muscle (see Figure 6.16 for joints, and Table 6.8 for weights and common uses).

Bacon may be purchased as a side, jointed or sliced and vacuum packed (see Figure 6.17 overleaf for joints and Table 6.9 overleaf for weights and common uses).

Ham is the hind leg of a pork pig cured and smoked separately, as for bacon. For many varieties of ham the curing process will be prolonged to improve flavour.

Gammon is the hind leg of a bacon pig, removed after the side has been cured and smoked. The hind leg may be cut straight (as gammon normally is from a side of bacon), (sections 7 and 8 on Figure 6.17), but some hams (for example, York hams) are removed with a rounder cut which takes in additional meat from the rump end.

Storage, hygiene and health

This is generally the same as for other meats, although extra care is often applied to pork. Pork is best used soon after purchase; it does not improve with keeping.

Bacon sides and joints (legs and shoulders) are best

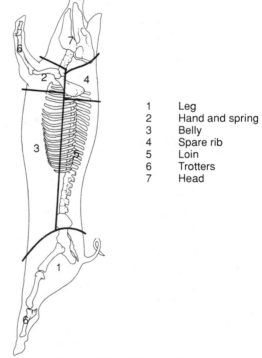

1	Leg
2	Hand and spring
3	Belly
4	Spare rib
5	Loin
6	Trotters
7	Head

Figure 6.16 *Side of pork*

kept hanging. Middles, once boned, should be stored on flat trays.

Vacuum-packed bacon rashers will store successfully in the freezer.

Profitable usage

The most expensive pig carcasses come in the 36–45 kg (80–100 lb) range, heavier pigs are referred to as cutters due to the fact that they are often cut up in the abattoir prior to distribution.

Table 6.9   Carcass weights and uses for bacon

Bacon cuts	Uses	Weight kg	lb	*Approx. number of averge size rashers: from average side total weight = 25 kg (55 lb)*	
1 Fore hock	Boil, grill	4.10	9	} 64 × 2 oz rashers	0.55 lb
2 Collar	Boil, grill	3.60	8		
3 Thick streaky	Grill, griddle, fry		9½	155 × 1 oz rashers	0.28 lb
4 Thin streaky	Grill, griddle, fry				
5 Back and ribs	Grill, griddle, fry		15	160 ×1½ oz rashers	0.42 lb
6 Long loin	Grill, griddle, fry				
7 Gammon	Boiling and grilling		13½		
8 Corner gammon	Boiling and grilling				

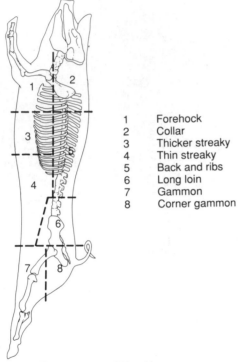

1	Forehock
2	Collar
3	Thicker streaky
4	Thin streaky
5	Back and ribs
6	Long loin
7	Gammon
8	Corner gammon

Figure 6.17   *Side of bacon*

As with other meats, profitability is influenced by quality and selection of cuts, allied to skilled cookery and portioning by the caterer.

POULTRY

The broiler industry and the prevalence of chilled and frozen poultry, bred to standard size, has obviated at some levels of catering the need for traditional types of judgement in selecting birds. The trend towards standard products is likely to continue, yet there will be occasions when even the most modest type of catering operation will need to know something of the points of quality in poultry selection. Under the designation of poultry are, of course, included all domestic birds specifically reared for eating or for their eggs, for example, chickens, ducks, geese, turkey, pigeons and guinea fowl.

Traditional seasons for poultry are shown in Table 6.10.

Source of chicken

Several types of bird are used in catering, dish suitability being determined primarily by age (size):

- Poussin – spring chicken; one per portion, may be grilled or roasted.
- Poulet – young chicken, may be sauted or roasted.
- Poularde – fattened, young but larger bird up to about 2.75 kg (6 lb) in weight.
- Poule – a hen of indeterminate age, usually used for boiling.

Capon (a castrated cock bird) is no longer available, the process now being illegal. The term 'capon-style' may still be used to describe large-breasted birds.

Source of turkey

There are several species, the most common of which is the Broad Breasted White. Turkey is now eaten all year round and breeding and processing has been developed with this in view. The better, full-grown birds weigh 3.6 – 5.5 kg (8–12 lb) and hens are generally regarded as being more delicate in flavour than cocks, though some chefs consider the cock bird to be superior as far as tenderness goes. Larger birds, i.e. those over 6.4 kg (14 lb), are usually selected for catering for reasons of economy.

Table 6.10 Traditional seasons for poultry

Poultry	Traditional seasons	When best
Chicken	April–June	Spring
Chick (poussin)	January–May	
Duck	All year	September, October
Duckling	March–September	May, June
Goose	September–February	November, December
Gosling	May–August	May, June
Guinea fowl	All year	Summer
Pigeon	All year	
Turkey	August–March	November–January

General note: poultry of all types and sizes are available all year. Seasons above thus refer to old-style rearing.

Source of duck and duckling

These weigh between 1.5–3 kg (3–7 lb). Duckling are usually killed at seven weeks, just before the second feather stage (which differentiates between duckling and duck).

Source of goose

Although available throughout the year, geese are still considered to be seasonal (September–December). By December a mature goose weighs about 8 kg (18 lb) and because of its large rib cage it provides less meat than chicken or turkey, so allow about 1lb per person when ordering oven-ready birds.

Source of guinea fowl

This bird weighs 1–2 kg (2–4 lb) and tastes like a cross between chicken and pheasant. They are considered to be in season from early spring to early summer, although they may begin to appear on menus as early as February.

Source of quail

As a wild bird, quail is a protected species, but they are now farmed in the UK and elsewhere. A Japanese species is now bred specifically for the table. Allow one 140 g (5 oz) bird per portion.

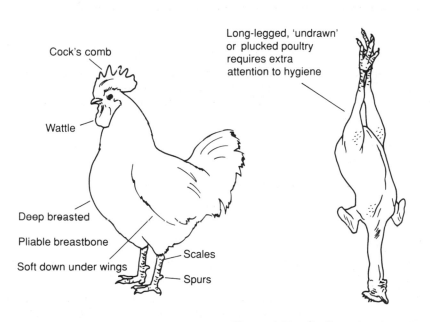
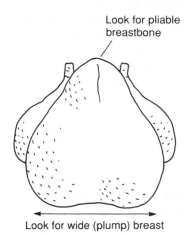

Figure 6.18 *Quality points in poultry*

Quality

Generally speaking, the skin of chicken should be smooth and supple, its breastbone should be pliable. Plump-breasted, unblemished, creamy-white flesh with a pinkish tinge and with a deeper pink to the legs is desirable. The colour of fowl is not necessarily a mark of quality, it may be influenced by the type/breed or by feed. Indeed, yellow, corn-fed chicken is prized for its flavour. Other signs of youth, and hence tenderness, are small spurs, combs and wattle (see Figure 6.18 on previous page) with abundant small, shiny scales over legs which should be flexible and smooth in appearance.

Signs of age are general coarseness of appearance, particularly coarse scales on the feet, rough skin and long hairs. A hard, unyielding breast bone is a certain indication of an old and tough bird. There are times when an old fowl will be required for the stockpot and similar purposes, but whatever the age of the bird it should be fresh, clean and in good condition.

Similar quality points may be identified in other poultry although skin tone, in particular, will vary.

> General points to look for, irrespective of age or species, are good appearance of the eyes (particularly avoid those with sunken eyes) and unblemished skin of a regular colour (avoid birds of patchy or discoloured appearance).

Finally, sense of smell must be relied on for indication of freshness. Poultry should smell wholesome and clean.

Although birds should be hung for a day at least, they should not be allowed to develop a noticeable gamey smell.

> Frozen poultry is generally of a good, uniform standard; there will be some weight loss during defrosting.

Processing

Poultry are hung on shackles on an overhead conveyor, then stunned and killed, and plucked and eviscerated by machine. The edible offal and neck are packed, and inedible produce is removed. If a bird is to be frozen it is first immersed in a water chiller to bring the temperature down to 4.4°C as rapidly as possible. It is then placed on a drip line to allow excess moisture to drain away, before it is blast frozen. The dressed weight includes giblets, if sold with the bird.

Purchasing units and specifications

Most poultry can be purchased either whole, jointed (legs and breast) or boned as brown and/or white meat and supremes. Check size (portions) are as follows:

- 100–150 g (4–6 oz) boneless raw meat per portion;
- 340 g (12 oz) oven-ready weight per portion.

Duck and goose, because of their lower meat to bone ratio, require 450–560 g (16–20 oz) oven-ready weight. Water birds generally have a larger carcass and more fat.

Storage, hygiene and health

Freezer storage times are:

- chicken and turkey – 6 to 9 months;
- duck and goose – 4 to 6 months.

Rancidity develops in the natural fat of water birds even at sub-zero temperatures.

Always ensure that frozen poultry is thoroughly defrosted, check that the legs are flexible and free of ice crystals (see Table 6.11).

Table 6.11 Defrosting times for poultry

Weight kg	(lb)	Room temperature	Refrigerator
1.0	(2¼)	8 hours	20 hours
1.4	(3¼)	10	24
1.8	(4¼)	12	28
3.2	(7¼)	18	30
5.4	(12¼)	30	48
7.2	(16¼)	36	60

Poultry is a high-risk rood so good hygiene should be maintained at all times. Avoid cross-contamination by using separate, colour-coded equipment, and thoroughly wash hands and work surfaces.

Profitable usage

Poultry remains a popular and relatively inexpensive menu item. Combining good portions, efficiently prepared and cooked, and served with interesting sauces and garnishes, which sell at a premium price, is likely to have the most profitable effect.

GAME

Game is not confined to birds but embraces all flesh brought to the table as a result of hunting or sport (usually within a specified season determined by the creatures' breeding cycles) as distinct from domestic rearing or herding. Some species, like wood pigeon, that are shot all year round are, according to some, not true game, but they are generally treated as such for culinary purposes.

Feathered game

There are a large number of game birds and only those that are commonly brought to table will be dealt with here. However, some general considerations have wide application in selecting game birds. As birds are often sold unplucked, it is harder to estimate their age and condition than poultry. Points of quality and youth to be looked for are easy breaking or penetration of the beak with a finger, smoothness and suppleness of legs and toes, ease of removal of spurs and shortness of wing quill feathers. Hens are considered to be juicier than cock birds, whilst the latter are more flavoursome.

Source of pheasant

Pheasant are easy to rear and consequently relatively cheap. The hen, like many species, is smaller and less-colourful than the cock bird which weighs 1.2–1.6 kg (2.5–3.5 lb), sufficient for two to four portions. They are at their best through November and December.

Source of partridge

Of the two types of partridge, the grey variety is regarded as a bird to be eaten young, when the feet should be of a good yellow colour and the whole appearance of the flesh smooth, soft, plump and white below the breast feathers. Red-legged partridge are eaten when more mature and signs of age are not, therefore, so important. Order one bird per portion.

Source of grouse

There are several species of grouse, the red or Scottish grouse being the smallest. Its unique flavour results from the heather on which it feeds. Birds shot in their first season are best; older birds may be tough and dry. Though grouse may be hung to gamey flavour, it is generally considered best eaten when freshly shot rather than high. Order one bird 450 g (16 oz) per portion.

Source of wild duck

Wild duck (mallard) and teal and widgeon have less fat and darker meat than domestic duck.

Source of snipe and woodcock

It is customary to roast these birds undrawn with their long necks twisted back so that the long beak may be pushed through the legs and body to truss the bird.

Furred game

Wild rabbit, as opposed to the domesticated variety, generally betrays itself by having a herby flavour according to the pasture on which it has fed. The flesh is pale and the fat should be clean and white. At about 1.5–2 kg (3–4 lb) in weight it may feed two to four depending on the cutting/cooking method and garnish. It has only about 4 per cent fat.

Hare is identified as being larger than rabbit with large (longer) hind legs and ears. One-third of its weight will be lost in dressing; a 3–3.5 kg (6–7 lb) hare will feed four. Hares are brought to the table towards the end of summer up to early spring. They are best young, under two years old, and long claws are a sign of age. Hare flesh is darker and drier than rabbit.

Venison may be wild or domesticated. Four types of deer are available in Britain: Roe, Fallow, Red and Sika (from game parks). Season depends on the breed, sex and origin (part of the country). Deer meat of one form or another is available most of the year.

Venison meat, though dark in colour, should be of clean appearance and accompanying fat should be abundant, bright and clear. It is generally accepted that older animals provide fuller-flavoured meat which should, of course, be well-hung. Venison provides a very fine-textured flesh of dense, dark red meat with little surface or marbled fat. Developments in deer farming and more adventurous eating habits are likely to result in the availability of younger animals and milder, less full-flavoured meat.

Quality

Other than seasonality (see Table 6.12) the most important factor when buying game is to know its age since this will have the greatest effect on texture and quality of the meat.

Table 6.12   Seasons for game

Game	Seasons	When best
Duck, wild	1st September–31st January	November, December
Grouse	12th August–15th December	September
Hare	1st August–28th February	October
Partridge	1st September–1st February	October, November
Pheasant	1st October–1st February	
Quail	All year	September, October
Rabbit, wild	1st September–30th April	
Snipe	12th August–30th June	October, November
Teal	1st September–31st June	November, December
Venison	May	
buck	August	
doe	March, April	
hind	Winter	
Widgeon	1st September–31st January	October, November
Woodcock	1st October–31st January	October, November

Generally with feathered game, look for clean, soft-textured feet with rounded spurs. A soft, pliable breastbone and a soft beak are also good signs. Look also for 'downy' feathers on the breast and under the wings.

For hare and rabbit, soft-textured ears which can be easily torn and a lower jaw which cracks easily when pressed between the fingers are good signs.

Processing

Hanging of game, in a cool, dry, airy place, is accepted as being a significant contributor to eventual quality of the cooked meat. Tastes vary as to the necessary length of time that is required, the following are offered as guidelines:

- grouse – 3 to 4 days;
- pheasant – 6 to 14 days;
- partridge – 7 to 8 days;
- wood pigeon – 2 to 3 days;
- snipe/woodcock – 7 to 10 days;
- hare/rabbit – 2 to 3 days;
- venison – 3 weeks.

As a result of their diet and general lifestyle, game have certain enzymes in their tissue (more abundant than in poultry) which break down or metabolise meat proteins. These enzymes, which become active about 24 hours after the animal has been killed, soften the meat, making it gelatinous and palatable, and giving it that 'gamey' flavour.

While the enzymes are at work the carcass hosts anaerobes (micro-organisms which help to break down the protein). Provided that there are no dangerous staphylococci present the bacteria that affect game meat are harmless.

Purchasing units and specifications

Purchase pheasant by the brace (cock and hen). The hen is considered to be the more tender of the two.

Fresh game is traditionally bought on sight or trust from a local supplier; weight and quality may vary, but terms and definitions will be understood by both parties.

There has been some growth in the dressed game market with a variety of standardised, portioned and trimmed cuts available through wholesalers.

Feathered game may be purchased unplucked, rough-plucked (feathers removed from body with head, wings, legs and gut left intact), or dressed ready for cooking.

Venison may be purchased by the forequarter, hind-quarter (haunch) or jointed (for example, saddle, loin or leg). Hare may be purchased whole and unskinned, skinned and paunched (eviscerated), or jointed.

Storage, hygiene and health

Fresh game should be cleaned and prepared quickly and efficiently. Feathers and or skins should be disposed of as they may contain parasites. Hands and work surfaces should be thoroughly cleansed, and avoid cross-contamination.

If game has been shot, it should be examined carefully for lead shot which may cause problems for the consumer.

Increasing concern with health and hygiene results in less game being hung, dressed and portioned on the caterer's premises. Prepared, oven-ready birds and portioned meats have become the rule rather than the exception.

Venison, hare and rabbit all freeze well.

Profitable usage

Game is generally considered a high-value, speciality item and although it can be more expensive than poultry to purchase it can be equally profitable. Customer acceptance is important and products must be of good and consistent quality. Random purchases are unlikely to be productive, particularly if they are over the back door.

Caterers are also cautioned with regard to their legal liability if game happens to have been poached.

OFFAL AND MEAT BY-PRODUCTS

The offal of meat, those items of the animal that are separated from the carcass, such as vital organs, is similar to carcass meat in that the older the animal the tougher, yet more flavoursome, the meat (muscle). So that whereas lamb kidney and liver may be shallow fried or grilled, the kidney and liver of ox will need to be braised.

The pig, by tradition, provides the greatest variety of offal products (see Figure 6.19 overleaf), including cheek and trotters. The same items from other animals would be unacceptable as a menu item though at one time (and perhaps still in some areas) ox cheek and cow heel are consumed.

Offal should not be stored for longer than seven days. Good quality offal, bought in small quantities and used while fresh, can result in interesting and highly-profitable dishes.

Processing (meat by-products)

Although the meat from the cheek of a beef carcass would not appear as a menu item, butchery techniques, prompted by the high price of meat, have developed to such a degree that this meat will not be wasted. Mechanically Recovered Meat (MRM) is a process whereby every last ounce of flesh is stripped from the bones of the animal. Although such meat may not be sold directly, it is widely-used in the preparation of sausages, continental sausages, pâtés and other cooked-meat products.

Purchasing units

Generally speaking, offal and meat by-products are purchased by the kilo/pound. However, some items (cheeks, trotters, tail and heart) may be purchased by number.

Profitable usage

Compared with carcass meats, most offal items are relatively inexpensive. As a cheap item offal and meat by-products do not usually enhance the menu or aid profitability. However, sold at a good price, as a

	Beef	Veal	Lamb	Pork	Game	Poultry
Brain*		✓		Brawn		
Cheeks				✓		
Tongue	✓	✓	✓	Brawn		
Sweetbreads		✓	✓			
Heart	✓	✓	✓	✓		
Liver	✓	✓	✓	✓	Pâté	✓
Kidney	✓	✓	✓	✓		
Tripe (stomach)	✓		✓			
Intestines				Sausage skins		
Tail	✓					
Feet		Calves' foot jelly		Trotters		

Note: * Prior to BSE: restrictions are now being imposed.

Figure 6.19 *Uses for offal*

novelty or speciality item or from the point of view of food value (for example, iron in liver), using imaginative recipes and presentation, the caterer may be able to take full advantage of these generally low-cost items.

LEGISLATION

The following is a list of the relevant acts and regulations:

The Food Safety Act 1990;
The Food and Environmental Protection Act 1985;
The Food Labelling Regulations 1984;
The Food Act 1984;
Public Health (Shellfish) Act 1934;
Meat Products and Spreadable Fish Products Regulations 1984;
The Meat (Treatment) Regulations 1964;
The Poultry Meat (Water Content) Regulations 1984;
The Poultry and Meat (Hygiene) Regulations.

Summary

Despite changing attitudes to the national diet, fish, meat and poultry remain the most popular source of protein and the most common main-meal item. Fish and animal protein foods are frequently the price determinants on the menu.

Carcass knowledge, variety, cuts and uses of fish and meat are an essential prerequisite to the efficient preparation of specifications which in turn will have a significant influence on profitability. Use of the various advisory authorities in providing guidance is to be recommended.

Protein foods are, initially at least, high-risk foods. All fish, meat, poultry and game, whether fresh, chilled or frozen, should be refrigerated immediately upon delivery. Storage methods should avoid the risk of cross-contamination between raw and cooked foods.

Vegetables and Fruits

Plants are the ultimate source of life, for they form the base of the food chain. The animals that provide our meat require plant life, grass, cereals and/or other vegetation for nourishment.

Fresh vegetables, herbs, potatoes and fruits are dynamic, living organisms that require constant observation and attention during purchasing and storage. Essential in purchasing, quality control and profitable usage of fresh produce is an appreciation of the inherent perishability of the products. Subject to temperature and moisture control, enzymic reaction will continue, even after harvesting, resulting in changes to appearance, texture, flavour and nutritional content.

> It is now common practice to extend the shelf life of a variety of fresh produce by controlling storage temperature, humidity and atmosphere (using inert gases, carbon dioxide and nitrogen).

Almost all fruits and vegetables are at their best and most nutritious when they are ripe. Thus availability and quality are influenced by season and local weather conditions.

The sophistication of transportation and storage methods, and world-wide availability of fresh produce have, to some extent, reduced the emphasis on seasons, seasonal availability and fluctuation in price. This has not, however, made the caterer's job any easier. Now the caterer must be concerned with a far greater variety of fresh produce, quality control and storage techniques. The caterer will not only need to be aware of each product's characteristics, but also be able to predict and respond to changes in price and availability.

It may often be desirable to compare the cost of fresh produce with convenience alternatives. The caterer's purchasing knowledge should include an understanding of percentage loss in trimming and yield per unit or per kilo (per pound).

In the purchase of all commodities it is important to become familiar with the customary units of weight or measurement at which items can most favourably be bought. In the case of potatoes, vegetables and fruit confusion may arise between the use of metric (kilograms) and imperial (pounds) measures to describe the weight of a sack. Further confusion may arise from such terms as 'head' of celery or 'bunch' of parsley. Whatever systems are used the purchaser should ensure that interpretation is consistent and aids accurate calculation of precise cost. Agree with each supplier the precise definition by weight of box, chip, punnet, bag, crate, tray and sack, and write it into the specification.

Fresh produce is normally specified by item, grade, size (per unit, count per outer/number per box, portion yield) and usage; inspection on delivery is essential. Contracts for fresh produce should always include words to the effect 'grade specified should be the condition upon delivery'.

Reliable greengrocers, who value their connection with the chef or caterer, will not stoop to petty deceptions, but there obviously remains great advantage in personal selection of those fresh commodities which quickly go out of condition and which may be offered in indeterminate units of measurement.

Despite general benefits there are, of course, some drawbacks in buying at market. Personal purchasing particularly consumes time which might be used for other purposes. There is also the possibility of having to make bulk purchases which may be larger than that normally required. Sometimes, also, minor price advantages are lost in the added cost of transportation and handling charges. It is the type and style of the establishment, the amount of business done and the best use of staff time which must be considered when determining fresh produce purchasing policy.

FOOD VALUES

The nutritional value of vegetables depends on the particular type/species but generally speaking vegetables are a good source of vitamins, particularly C, B, A and E, minerals (copper, iron and calcium), dietary fibre and, in some cases, protein. The nature, structure, texture and nutritional content of each type of vegetable is influenced by its function as part of the plant.

> Vegetables begin to lose vitamins as soon as they are harvested. On average there is a 50 per cent loss of vitamin C over a seven-day period. This may be as high as 85 per cent in the case of spinach or as low as 20 per cent in the case of sprouts.

- Roots absorb and conduct moisture and store food supplies (starch). Consequently, they are a good source of carbohydrate, vitamins and minerals.
- Tubers main function is to produce the shoots (young stems); they contain high proportions of starch.
- Bulbs are actually the leaf base; their role is to store water and starch.
- Stems conduct water and nutrients and support the leaves.
- Leaves produce food (sugar) through the process of photosynthesis. They have a maximum surface area with very little storage tissue. Green leaves are associated with mineral content, vitamin C and carotene. The vitamin C content is highest in the darker outer leaves and comparatively low in the heart. Therefore, care is required when trimming.
- Flowers are the reproductive organ of the plant.
- Fruits carry the seed for the next generation.
- Pulses are important, particularly to vegetarians, as they are a prime source of vegetable protein which when combined with cereal results in a first-class substitute for meat. Some, like soya, may contain fat/oil.
- Fungi may be edible or poisonous. They feed off living, dead or decaying oranic matter, and contain no fat or carbohydrate. They are a good source of vegetable protein, B vitamins and minerals.
- Herbs have, historically, been associated with medicinal as well as culinary value. With the exception of parsley, which contains vitamin C, most herbs have little nutritional value but they are considered important in the diet as they aid the digestive process. Their scent, flavour and colour can promote the appetite and flow of gastric juices.
- Marine plants are highly nutritious, they contain vitamin C, E and B group, and are particularly rich in minerals, calcium, iodine and iron, with good proportions of magnesium, potassium, sodium, copper and zinc. Seaweed also provides a high-quality protein.

Fruits are noted for their vitamin content. However, it may not be generally known that the juice of an orange contains only 25 per cent of the vitamin C of the whole orange as most vitamin C is concentrated in the zest and pith. Weight for weight, blackcurrants are the best source of vitamin C. Dried fruits contain no vitamin C.

Most fruits are a valuable source of cellulose (fibre).

> Sage is considered to aid the digestion of fat – hence sage and onion stuffing with pork.

POTATOES

Potatoes are a type of vegetable, a tuber, which may be described as the swollen part of an underground stem. Tubers differ from root vegetables in that they are the source of the new shoot and a store for the food which aids its growth. This tuber is most popular with consumers and because of its regular and relatively high consumption rate, is significant nutritionally. Caterers must regard potatoes as important, both as a source of consumer satisfaction and profit. They are often seen as a filler or 'bulk' item that contributes to profitability. However, careless purchasing, storage and use can result in the loss of their profit potential.

Food value

The nutritional value of a potato (see Table 7.1) will depend on its age, the length of storage and method/quality of the peeling process, as many nutrients are contained in, and just below, the skin. It is now more acceptable, particularly with the small, new varieties, to cook and serve potatoes in their skins.

Potatoes contain a complex form of starch (carbohydrate) which is slow to digest, they are therefore more satisfying over a longer period than other vegetables. Because of the amount consumed, potatoes, especially the new varieties, are an important source of vitamin C. However, vitamin C levels fall gradually during storage.

Source

Originally from the Americas, potatoes are now grown all over the world. Capable of surviving in a variety of climates they prefer cool to cold conditions. Most potatoes used in this country are home-produced, with some imported varieties appearing as early, new potatoes.

Table 7.1   Nutritional content of potatoes

Water	78.8%
Starch	15.6%
Protein	2.1%
Fibre	1.7%
Sugar	1.3%
Thiamin	–
Riboflavin	–
Niacin	–
Iron	–
Calcium	–

Harvesting of the first new (home-grown) potatoes begins in May and continues through June. Second earlies are lifted in July and August. Harvesting of the main crop normally begins in September and these potatoes are usually sold direct. The bulk of the main crop is lifted in October, possibly November, and these potatoes normally go into store for sale through the winter.

An autumn new potato has now been developed; specialised growing techniques are necessary to enable this unseasonal harvest.

Quality

In addition to sponsoring research into production and marketing the Potato Marketing Board (PMB) ensures that potato planting in this country is sufficient to meet expected demand. The Board also sets and enforces quality standards for British potatoes. Registered growers sell through licensed wholesale merchants. Strict penalties are incurred if quality standards are not maintained.

New potatoes		Main crop	
Early	*Second early*	*Waxy*	*Floury*
Maris Bard	Estima	Maris Piper	Pentland Squire
Pentland Javelin	Wilja	Pentland Dell	Pentland Crown
Ulster Sceptre	Marfona	Cara	Pentland Hawk
Arran Comet	Jersey Royal	Desiree	King Edward
Alcmaria	Penta	Romano	
Home Guard			
Epicure			

There are many other varieties, both home-grown and imported. One of the less-common varieties is Pink Fir Apple which has an unusual elongated shape. It is a firm, waxy potato that has a particularly good flavour.

Figure 7.1   *Sample varieties (classification) of UK potatoes*

Quality considerations are primarily influenced by season (early or main crop) and variety (waxy or floury).

Potatoes must be named by variety (see Figure 7.1 on previous page), either at point of sale or marked on the sack (Food Labelling Regulations 1983).

Variety is important because it is a significant influ-ence on the quality of the cooked product, in that certain varieties are favoured for chips and others for mash or jacket potatoes. The reason for the difference between waxy and floury varieties is not known, although the floury varieties do contain more starch. Waxy potatoes may be identified by their smooth, creamy-yellow flesh. Floury potatoes have a whiter, starchy appearance.

In a solution of 11 parts water to one part salt, waxy potatoes will float whereas floury potatoes will sink.

The characteristics of main crop potatoes may be influenced by soil and growing conditions to such an extent that the same variety grown in a different part of the country may produce differing attributes.

With early/new potatoes they should feel damp and their skins should be removed easily by rubbing. As new potatoes lose their flavour quickly, they should be purchased in no more than two days supply at a time.

With Ware standard (main crop) potatoes they should be tight-skinned, not dry or wrinkled. The skin will not rub off mature potatoes. Greening of the skin or flesh results from exposure to light, forming toxins under the skin. Potatoes should be free from scab, disease, rot, misshapes, growth cracks, machine damage, pest damage, frost damage, greening and hollow heart. The Potato Marketing Board determine minimum and maximum sizes; normally no larger than 80 mm and no smaller than 40 mm. Tolerances may be modified by the Board in exceptional circumstances.

Potatoes that are smaller are termed 'mids' and extra-large potatoes are referred to as 'bakers'.

Checking quality
Take a random sample. Empty the contents of the whole bag and examine the potatoes for size, disease and/or damage, check the amount of earth and stone. Refuse delivery if the sample exceeds 5 per cent unacceptable potatoes.

Seek advice from the wholesaler with regard to availability, best varieties and quality. If in doubt, ask the Potato Marketing Board.

Processing

Traditionally, potatoes would have been stored in clamps or earthed-up mounds, either in the field or in barns or sheds. Today storage is highly-specialised, designed to maintain the potatoes in peak condition by controlling the temperature and humidity.

Prior to storage, surplus soil is removed and potatoes may be treated with chemical fungicides and sprout-suppressants. Additional processing, prior to sale, may involve washing and drying the potatoes or, as a further convenience, they may be peeled and vacuum packed.

Function in cookery

Owing to the numerous ways in which they can be cooked and served potatoes perform an important function on the menu. They complement and contrast with fish, meat and poultry, and absorb sauces and juices. They may be used in recipes to bind or top other ingredients. Although they are often seen as merely providing bulk, they can be used to provide a variety of light and interesting dishes.

Purchasing units and specifications

Potatoes are often purchased in very large quantities because of the nature of the supply channel. However, the benefits of bulk purchase must be measured against any drop in quality resulting from prolonged storage. The problems of handling and storage of large quantities of potatoes should not be ignored.

Stock turnover should be at least once a week, although this will depend on size and frequency of deliveries which may be influenced by discount pricing.

Although a standard product will be required, specifications (see Figure 7.2) should be renewed regularly

---

A CONTRACT made on the .... day of .... 19 .... between .... (hereinafter called the Supplier) on the one part and .... (hereinafter called the Buyer) on the other part, whereby it is agreed that the Supplier shall sell and the Buyer shall purchase potatoes as contracted hereunder on the following conditions –

1. *Period*

The Contract shall be for a period of .... commencing on ....

Should either party wish to terminate this Contract within the agreed period, they shall give notice in writing to the other party at least 30 days before the proposed date of termination.

2. *Grading*

All potatoes delivered shall be 'dressed' to the standard (for ware or new potatoes as the case may be) laid down by the Potato Marketing Board and currently in force at the date of delivery.

3. *Quantity, Description and Delivery*

The Supplier shall deliver each week and the Buyer shall receive potatoes to the quantity and description as given in the following schedule during the currency of this Contract –

Quantity	Variety or Type of Potato	Delivery Address

All potatoes shall be delivered free of charge to the address or addresses shown in the above schedule and delivery shall be given at the Supplier's risk.

Each delivery shall be accompanied by a Delivery Note which shall show the weight of the quantity delivered, the price per hundredweight and, if the containers are chargeable, the number of such containers.

4. *Price*

The price to be paid by the Buyer to the Supplier for all potatoes delivered under this Contract shall be in accordance with the following schedule –

Variety or Type of Potato	Period	Prices per Hundred Weight

or

the wholesale price for the variety (or type of potato) of good quality ruling at the date of delivery at .... Market (or town) as shown in the Potato Marketing Board's Daily Price Schedule

or

the wholesale price for the variety (or type of potato) of good quality ruling at the date of delivery at .... Market (or town) as shown in the Commodity Price List in .... (nominate a trade journal, e.g. *Fruit and Vegetable Trades Journal*, etc.).

All prices quoted shall be subject to ..... per cent discount if payment is made to the Supplier within 30 days of receipt of the invoice by the Buyer.

5. *Containers*

Potatoes shall be delivered in dry, clean and sound hessian or paper sacks which have not previously been used for fertilizers or other chemicals. Other types of containers may be used only with the Buyers' prior approval.

All sacks or containers, other than those specified, shall be deemed to be non-returnable unless specifically shown on the Delivery Note.

Type of Container	Charge to be paid by Buyer if not returned within 30 days of delivery

6. *Rejection*

The Buyer shall have the right to reject on delivery, without any liability, any potatoes which do not conform to the conditions of this Contract.

7. *Arbitration*

Any dispute arising out of, or in connexion with, this Contract shall be referred for arbitration to two independent persons, one appointed by the Buyer and the other appointed by the Supplier. In case the arbitrators so appointed are unable to agree, an umpire shall be appointed by them before they hear the dispute. This clause shall be deemed to be a submission to arbitration under the provisions of the Arbitration Act, 1950, or any statutory modification thereof or (where both parties carry on business in Scotland) under the law of Scotland.

Signed ....
stamp

Witnessed ....

Source: Potato Marketing Board

Figure 7.2 *Potato specification (sample contract)*

through the year, particularly when varieties are specified by name as each will vary in quality and performance through the year. It is important to identify their intended use to suppliers, in which case they will be able to provide the variety most suited to that particular purpose, at any point in the season.

Storage, hygiene and health

Despite their seemingly hardy appearance, potatoes damage easily so they should be handled with care.

Keep them away from light to prevent greening. Store in a cool, dark, dry area with good ventilation. Warmth and humidity promote sprouting. Dirt and damp spread disease and mould.

Most kitchens require a ready supply of peeled potatoes. The fact that potatoes discolour quickly (enzymic browning) once peeled may cause an additional storage problem for some caterers. Large areas of sink space or the provision of mobile (heavy-duty plastic) tanks is often required.

Enzymic browning is a reaction between tyrosine in the potato and oxygen in the air. Methods of prevention include the following:

- exclude the air (vacuum packing);
- sodium sulphite solution (potato 'whitener' (powder)) – use whiteners carefully, as directed by the manufacturer, taking particular care with soaking times and rinsing and draining procedures;
- blanche in water, steam or oil – once blanched the potatoes should be covered and chilled;
- cover with water – ensure that the water is changed frequently. Never mix freshly-peeled potatoes with older stock.

Profitable usage

Potatoes are a classic example of how caterers are often confused by the value (price) of the product as compared to the cost of consumption. It is easy to see the difference in price between 170 g (6 oz) of steak and 170 g (6 oz) of potato. However, it is the figures on the balance sheet that are really important. Purely due to the volume consumed, potatoes will rank as one of the most important individual items of expenditure.

A 10 per cent saving on potatoes alone will make a significant difference to the profitability of many operations. A saving in this area is often relatively easy to achieve by improved training of staff, greater supervision, and better servicing and maintenance of equipment. It does require greater vigilance and attention to detail.

Some caterers will take the view that whilst the fresh product is more desirable the convenience alternatives are easier to control.

OTHER VEGETABLES AND HERBS

Today's caterer is faced with a wide range of veg-etables and herbs to choose from. World-wide availability has not only increased the choice of vegetables, but also extended the variety within each group. For example, there are at least six onion types in common use and a dozen or more lettuce to choose from.

Each variety will offer different characteristics of colour, texture, shape, size and flavour, all of which could influence the quality and appearance of a dish. Different varieties with special characteristics will also demand a premium price. Selection of vegetables can be the most complex aspect of the caterer's purchasing activity. Being relatively cheap, the influence of vegetable purchasing on profitability is often overlooked.

The volume of vegetables used by most caterers and the possibility/probability of high levels of waste should be the cause of greater consideration and concern.

Some caterers, particularly those with static menus, will be influenced by year-round availability in order to achieve consistent product quality, rather than picking speciality produce which may only have a short season.

Sales of organic produce have increased by over four times and although this is mainly as a result of

Choosing between varieties

If prawn cocktail and salad are on the menu, it may be sufficient to order lettuce at the best price and use this for both the cocktail and the salad. However, when we consider the difference in texture between some varieties of lettuce we can see that using a variety that will hold its shape, together with the weight of the prawns and sauce, can be more cost-effective. A lettuce which wilts and sinks will cause either the staff to add more lettuce/prawns/sauce or the product to appear less than generous to the customer.

The same lettuce that is so cost effective in the prawn cocktail may be rather bland and unappealing in a salad. Choosing a different variety with more colour and/or flavour will help to increase sales of a profitable menu item. Similar arguments may be developed for each type of vegetable so that menu usage must be a major influence on final specification.

domestic purchases the underlying trend will undoubtedly be reflected in the catering industry. Although organic produce will increase the cost of purchase, such produce will add value to the menu and may be actively promoted at a premium price. The availability of consistent and reliable supplies is likely to be the only factor inhibiting its wider use by caterers.

Source

Vegetables may be defined as a plant or part of a plant. They are commonly divided into categories based on the particular part of the plant used in cooking (see Figure 7.3). The following lists vegetable categories and gives common examples of each:

- Roots – carrot, parsnip, beetroot, turnip, swede, radish;
- Shoots – alfalfa, bean sprouts;
- Tubers – potato, Jerusalem artichoke;
- Bulbs – onion, shallot, leek, garlic;
- Stems – asparagus, celery, chicory (Belgian endive);
- Leaves – cabbage, lettuce, spinach, sprouts, curly endive;
- Flowers – cauliflower, broccoli, globe artichoke;
- Fruits (edible flesh surrounding seed) – tomato, avocado;
- Gourds – marrow, cucumber, courgette;
- Pulses (legumes/seeds) – peas, beans and lentils, which are often purchased in dried form;
- Cereals – sweetcorn, rice;

- Fungi – mushroom, flap mushroom (cepe), morel (morelle), cantharellus mushroom (chanterelle), truffle;
- Herbs – grasses, stems, flowers and leaves;
- Marine – seaweed, kelp, laver (bread), agar-agar.

Availability will be influenced by season (see Table 7.2 overleaf). Almost all varieties in common use are grown in this country. There is an increasing availability and use of imported tropical species. A number of sub-tropical/Mediterranean varieties are produced in this country under hot-house conditions.

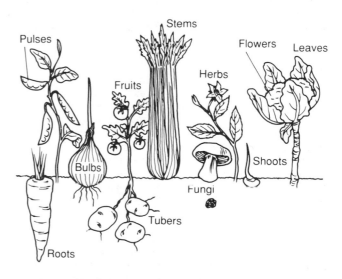

Figure 7.3 *Categories (classification) of vegetables*

Table 7.2 Vegetable seasons

Vegetables and salads	Season	When best/notes
Artichokes, globe	July to October	August
Artichokes, Jerusalem	November to June	December
Asparagus	May to June	May
Asparagus, forced	December to April	
Aubergines	All year	September, October
Beans, broad	July, August	August
Beans, French	July to October	August
Beans, runner	July, August, September	August, September
Beetroot	All year	Autumn
Broccoli	October to April	November to February
Brussels sprouts	October to March	October to December
Cabbage	All year	Spring and Summer
Cabbage, spring	March, April, May, June	
Cabbage, red	September to January	November, December
Capsicums	May to August	
Carrots	All year	April to June
Carrots, new	April, May, June	
Cauliflower	March to November	July
Celeriac	October to March	
Celery	August to March	December
Chervil	December to May	
Chicory	October to March	
Chives	June	
Corn, green	October, November, December	
Corn, Indian	August, September, October, November	
Courgettes	May to August	
Cucumber	All year (especially February to November)	June to August
Cress, mustard and	All year	
Cress, water	All year	February
Endive	November to March	November (from Italy)
Fennel	April to July	
Flageolet	July	
Greens, spring	February, March, April	
Horse-radish	October to June	Winter
Leeks	All year	Late summer
Lettuce	All year	Home grown in summer. Dutch and other imported in winter
Marrow, vegetable	July to October	September
Mushrooms, field	July to September	
Onions	All year	Summer and Autumn
Onions, Spanish	January to April	
Onions, spring	All year (imported)	April to June
Parsnips	October to May	Winter
Peas, garden	Late April to September	July and August
Potatoes	All year	Autumn
Potatoes, new	May to August	June, July
Potatoes, new (imported)	December to July	From Channel Isles, Mediterranean, etc.
Pumpkin	September, October	October
Radishes	March to November	
Salsify	December to April	
Savoys	November to March	December, January
Scotch kale	March, April	
Sea kale	January to June	February and March
Shallots	November to January	
Sorrel	April to September	

Table 7.2 (*cont.*)

Vegetables and salads	Season	When best/notes
Spinach	All year	
Swedes	All year	
Tomatoes	April to September	Summer
Tomatoes, imported	October to May	Southern Europe, Canaries, etc.
Truffles	Autumn and winter	November to December
Turnips	All year	Summer
Turnips, new	May to June	
Turnip, tops	January to February	

Tomatoes – fruit or vegetable?
Confusion arises between botanical definition and catering use. One definition has had the benefit of a United States Supreme Court ruling which upheld a 10 per cent import duty imposed, by customs officials, for the import of vegetables. There was no duty applicable to fruit at that time. The decision was based on the grounds of accepted common usage. Tomatoes were served with meat and not eaten as a dessert. They were, therefore, defined as a vegetable in this case.

A few caterers will have the opportunity to utilise their own gardens to produce fresh vegetables. However, it is likely that they would have to make use of in-house conveniencing processes (blanching and freezing) to gain full advantage of a well-stocked garden.

Quality

Good quality vegetables are generally clean, compact and crisp with a bright colour, no bruising or damage and no signs of blight or disease. Disease and bruising are quickly passed on when vegetables are packed tightly together.

The flavour and texture of most vegetables starts to deteriorate from the moment that they are picked. The cells go on using nutrients even though the plant has now been cut off from its source of food and water.

Peas lose up to 40 per cent of their sugar in six hours at room temperature. Asparagus and broccoli go on using sugar and as a result produce tough, woody, fibres with increasing maturity.

The texture of vegetables is dependent on the structure of the cell walls and the amount of water present. As the vegetable ages it dries out, water loss results in the destruction of cell walls, there is a reduction in pressure and the vegetable wilts and becomes limp. This is normally most noticeable in the leaf varieties, but even carrots will show a tendency to bend rather than snap if they are less than fresh. As a result of aging, enzymic reaction destroys vitamin C and off flavours and discolouration will develop.

Smell is often a good indication of quality. Try removing and smelling the stalk from a tomato. Little or no smell suggests little or no flavour, good 'bright' smell indicates good flavour.

EEC gradings are often used to identify quality, although not all produce is graded and not all classes (grades) operate at all times. Some produce will have such wide tolerances that the grading system appears to be of little help to the uninitiated. It is generally best to agree definitions with suppliers before placing any orders.

> **EEC gradings**
> Extra   = top class, specially selected.
> Grade I   = good quality, shape, size, appearance.
> Grade II = reasonable, slight deviation from Grade I, some blemishes and/
>   or misshapes.
> Grade III = poor but marketable, only used if supplies are short.

The description of what is meant by 'Grade I – good quality' obviously varies for each different vegetable. Generally, the definition relates to shape, size, conformity, colour, texture and absence of blemishes. As a simple guide, good-quality vegetables should appear ready to eat.

Some more general points which the purchaser/receiver should observe are:

- absence of yellow and/or discolouring leaves;
- reject withered commodities;
- clean produce, free of excessive soil;
- sound, ripe produce, not over-ripe or soft;
- fresh smell.

Organic produce may be subject to far greater risk of attack by pests. Even where insecticides are used the perennial greenfly may still cause problems in such produce as lettuce. This may, indeed, be beyond the control of the supplier, yet it would be wise for an alternative variety to be specified in the contract should the usual variety succumb to infestation.

Processing

Fresh vegetables are not generally subjected to any processing in the sense of manufacture. Processing primarily involves harvesting, cleaning, trimming, grading and packing. However, a variety of techniques are now applied in an attempt to retain quality and nutritional value.

Temperature is an important factor in quality control. Harvesting of most produce takes place when the weather is fine and consequently the produce will be relatively warm. Vacuum cooling is used to reduce field temperature and this is normally followed by controlled atmosphere storage.

Irradiation is now accepted in many EEC countries. It extends the shelf life of highly-perishable raw materials. Strawberries may keep 'fresh' for weeks, once irradiated. The produce must, however, be in perfect condition in the first place. If the process is to be used, it should be applied immediately the produce is harvested before there is any deterioration.

Function in cookery

The traditional role of the vegetable is to complement and contrast with main, protein items. Developments in healthy eating have given a new life to beans and lentils (pulses). They and many other varieties of vegetable are now presented as a dish in their own right as soups, hors d'oeuvres and main courses. Additionally, vegetables (bulbs, stems and roots in particular) provide the essential foundation and flavouring in stocks, sauces, stews and braises. They may also act as a dish ingredient or garnish.

Vegetables provide balance in the form of colour, flavour, texture and/or nutritional content to the meal.

> Mushrooms may be obtained in four main categories:
> - button – small, white, firm and tightly closed;
> - closed cup – slightly more mature, larger, more flavour;
> - open cup – further growth, gills exposed, full flavour;
> - large flat – fully matured, darkened gills completely exposed, rich, full flavour;

Purchasing units and specifications

Purchasing units vary widely (see Table 7.3). Specifications are often based on EEC gradings, see **Quality** above.

Ideally, specification should result in the purchase of vegetables which are ready to eat, with the minimum of trim. Generally, vegetables should be clean, fresh, crisp and compact with good 'bright' colour. Root vegetables should be free from soil.

Vegetable containers should be clean and dry with no visible signs of damage, mould or infestation. Where vegetables are delivered in sacks or nets, a sample should be closely examined. Open the sack and spread the contents, it may be necessary to cut into some vegetables in order to reveal defects.

Table 7.3 Purchasing units/weights of vegetables

Item	Pack type	UK (lb)	Imports (kg)
Artichokes	Count		
Asparagus	Bundle	1/2	5/6/10
Aubergines	Count		5/6
Avocados	Count		4
Beans, French	Chip	5	3
	Box	10/20	5/6
Beetroot	Bag	28	10
Brocolli	Box	10/15	3/5/7
Brussels sprouts	Net	10/20	5/10
Cabbage	Net	26/30	13/25
Capsicum	Count	11	5/10
Carrots	Bag/net	28	10
Cauliflower	Count		
Celery	Count		6/10
Chicory	Count		3/5/10
Courgettes	Box	10/12	3/5
Cucumber	Count		5
Curly endive	Count		15
Fennel	Count		5
Leeks	Crate	10	1/5/10
Lettuce	Count		
Marrow	Count		
Mushrooms	Chip	2/3/4	1/4
Onions	Bag/net	25	20/25
Parsnips	Bag	28	10/12
Peas	Bag/box	20/30	3/5/6
Potatoes	Bag/sack		5/10/20/25/50
Spinach	Crate	10	4/5/10
Swede	Bag	28	
Sweetcorn	Count		7/20
Tomatoes	Chip/box	12	5/6/7
Turnips	Bag	28	

Note: Weights vary according to country of origin.
Source: *The Fresh Produce Desk Book*, Lynda Seaton (Ed.), Lockwood Press (1991).

Storage, hygiene and health

There are two primary causes of food spoilage (a change in taste, texture and/or safety) of vegetables and fruits:

- infection by microbes – mould rather than bacteria;
- action by the plant's own enzymes.

Mould spores are present in the air. Their growth on food only occurs when/where large numbers are present. This may be where there is already some evidence of mould or where the plant has been damaged, bruised or cut, exposing the nutrients in the food to the spores in the air. Handle fresh vegetables with care, to avoid damage or bruising. Dispose of any damaged or mouldy produce.

As living organisms vegetables need to 'breathe'. Lack of oxygen causes cell damage. Do not use sealed polythene bags to store vegetables.

Ripening is the beginning of inevitable decay. Spoilage may, to some extent, be slowed by refrigeration (except for some tropical plants and fruits, such as avocado and banana). Humidity level is important; high humidity will prevent wilting.

Generally, vegetables require cool dry storage, on racks, to allow for the circulation of air. Most vegetables, particularly the harder types, will keep for several days, but may lose appearance, flavour and nutritional value. Keep mushrooms for a maximum of three days and preferably obtain a fresh daily delivery. Store fresh herbs on damp kitchen paper in an open polythene bag.

Clean storage areas, fridges and racks regularly/frequently to avoid the risk of transferring mould spores.

Domestic fridges contain a covered box (salad crisper) to maintain humidity. The same effect may be achieved in caterer's large, walk-in fridges by covering such items as boxes of lettuce with dampened greaseproof paper.

Profitable usage

Vegetables generally add value to other menu items. They may also be sold as extras. In both cases they are likely to generate a high margin of profit (difference between purchase and selling price). It is, therefore, advisable to consider finest quality produce; savings on poorer quality will be more than lost in trimmings and time wasted, not to mention customer dissatisfaction and loss of sales.

For caterers in some sectors of the industry, the time spent in choosing unusual vegetables, and developing and promoting interesting and imaginative dishes and accompaniments will be an important influence on profitability.

FRUITS

Fruit may be described as the edible flesh surrounding the seed or seeds of a plant. In much the same way as some fruits are commonly accepted as vegetables so to there are examples of vegetables which are generally used as fruits, for example, rhubarb.

Nuts are the seeds of certain trees. Some are surrounded by flesh, but in most cases this is not used as a food. Nuts are usually dried and processed, in which case they may be treated as a convenience product.

Source

Fruits are obtained from all over the world. Some species are synonymous with the tropics; some like apples and berries are associated with more temperate climates. Some fruits are identified with particular countries or regions, for example:

- oranges – Spain/Seville;
- kiwi fruit – New Zealand;
- lychees – China.

Fruits are commonly identified by type:

- soft – melon, date, fig;
- hard – apple, pear;
- stone – plum, peach, cherry, mango, apricot, nectarine;
- citrus – orange, lemon, lime, grapefruit, mandarine;
- berry – strawberry, raspberry, gooseberry, blackcurrant, grape;
- vegetable – rhubarb;
- tropical – banana, pineapple, kiwi.

As with vegetables, the availability of fruits will be influenced by season (see Table 7.4). Although developments in harvesting, processing, storage and transportation techniques have resulted in year-round availability of most items, price and quality will vary considerably.

Table 7.4 Fruit seasons

Fruit and nuts	Season	When best
Almonds, green	May–July	
Apples	All year	October, November
Apricots	June–September	August
Bananas	All year	
Blackberries	July–September	August
Cherries	June–August	July
Chestnuts	November–January	December
Cobnuts	August–September	
Coconuts	All year	
Cranberries	November–January	December
Currants	June–September	August
Damsons	September–October	October
Figs (fresh)	July–September	August
Filberts	August–September	
Gooseberries	June–August	August
Grapes	All year	
Grapefruit	All year	
Greengages	August–September	August
Hazelnuts	August–September	
Kumquat	November–June	
Lemons	All year	
Loganberries	July–August	
Lychees	June–August	
Mandarins	November–June	
Melons	All year	June–October
Nectarines	May–October	October
Oranges	All year	
Oranges, Seville	February–March	
Passion-fruit	July–August	
Paw paw	All year	May–August
Peaches	April–October	June–September
Pears	September–March	October, Novevmber
Pineapples	All year	August
Plums	July–October	September
Pomegranate	August–January	
Pumpkins	September–November	October
Quinces	September–October	October
Rambutan	May–August	
Raspberries	June–September	July
Rhubarb	March–July	April
Strawberries	June–September	July
Tangerines	November–February	
Ugli fruit	December–May	
Walnuts	September–February	

Avocados will not ripen if left on the tree, they will only ripen once picked.

Quality

Good fruit will be bright, shiney and tight-skinned. It should be heavy for its size. Fruit showing any evidence of bruising, mould growth, skin split or insect depredation should be rejected.

As fruit ripens, pectic enzymes soften the cell walls, a process very noticeable in pears which are, therefore, usually picked prematurely. Ripening usually results in a change of skin colour, texture of flesh, an increase in sugar and a decrease in acid and starch levels. Melons, pineapples and citrus fruits contain little starch and therefore do not sweeten after picking or during storage. Most fruits, one exception being pears, are best if ripened on the tree. Peaches, if picked early and stored, become woolly and fibrous.

Fruit continues to ripen after it has been picked. Generally speaking, fruits do not improve with keeping. Soft fruits deteriorate quickly.

Processing

The harvesting and storage processes that were discussed for vegetables may also be applied to fruits.

There is a practice of picking some fruits (including tomatoes) while they are still green and hard (making transportation easier) and then gassing them with ethylene to promote the ripening process. The precise reason for fruit ripening in the presence of ethylene is not known. The process does result in evenly-ripened produce at a reasonable price, but at some cost with regard to flavour. Such 'unripened' fruit is often bland as compared to properly-matured, more pungent, fresh local produce.

Skins of citrus fruits are often treated with fungicide to extend the shelf life. If the rind (zest) is to be used then the fruit should be thoroughly cleaned.

Function in cookery

In addition to being a dessert course in their own right, fruits serve a useful purpose throughout the menu. They have obvious applications in sweet dishes, adding bulk, sweetness, flavour and texture to dishes such as pies, flans, tarts, pancakes, bavarois and ices, where they may be used individually or in combination with other fruits. In savoury and main course items it is generally the natural acidity of fruit which gives purpose to its use. Lemon juice may be used as a marinade prior to cooking, or during cooking as in a blanc. The acidity of a cooking apple helps to counteract the fattiness of pork and thus aids

digestion. A fruit such as pineapple which has both a sharp acid taste whilst at the same time being sweet is suited to gammon, helping to both soften the saltiness of the meat and speed the breakdown of proteins.

Purchasing units and specifications

As with vegetables, there are an assortment of unit measurements for the purchase of fruit (see Table 7.5). The EEC grading system also applies to fruits. Size requirements may feature more prominently in the purchase of some fruits which may be sold by number per case or in range bands of 5 mm (see Table 7.6).

Buy fruit regularly in usable quantities. There is an arguement for buying under-ripe fruit and allowing it to ripen to perfection on the premises. The rule should be 'buy today what you expect to use today and make sure you sell it today'. In which case produce must be in peak (perfect) condition on delivery.

Soft fruits deteriorate quickly. When purchasing berries check the base of the carton to see if it is stained in which case the bottom layer of fruit is likely to be over-ripe and/or damaged or squashed. Like vegetables, some fruits should be examined more closely by peeling or cutting into the flesh.

Storage, hygiene and health

Like vegetables, good storage of fruit requires an understanding of infection by microbes and action by the fruit's own enzymes. The saying 'one rotten apple in the barrel' should not go unheeded. Cool, dry, well-ventilated storage is required. Fruit, like vegetables, requires oxygen, so sealing fruit in polythene bags may result in cell damage and brown spot.

Hard and citrus fruits, if individually-wrapped or separated by liners, may be left in their boxes. Unblemished hard and citrus fruits may keep for up to two weeks if stored in the refrigerator. The skin of citrus fruits may toughen and wrinkle and essential oils may be lost from the zest.

Stone fruits should be delivered and stored in trays.

Berries should be bought for immediate consumption, in which case there is no need to remove them from their punnets. Berries have a natural protective layer 'bloom' so do not wash them until ready to use.

Soft fruits are susceptible to dampness and mould, and deteriorate quickly.

Table 7.5 Purchasing units/weights of fruit

Item	Pack type	UK (lb)	Imports (kg)
Apples	Box	30/40	8/12/18/20
Apricots	Tray		4/5
Bananas	Coffin	28/33/40	
Blackberries	Punnet	14 × 8oz	
Cherries	Chip	6/12	5/6
Currants	Punnet	14 × 8oz	12 × 200g/8 × 500g
Gooseberries	Chip	10/12	8 × 500g/4/5
Grapes			5/7/10
Grapefruit	Count/box		15
Kiwi fruits	Count/tray		3.6
Lemons	Count/box		5/10/15
Limes	Count		3/4
Mangos	Count		4/5
Melons	Count/box		5/10
Nectarines	Count/tray		4/5
Oranges	Box		15/18/20
Peaches	Count/tray		4/5/10
Pears	Box/tray	20/30	12/15/18
Pineapples	Count/box		10/16/20
Plums	Chip/tray	12	5/6/10
Raspberries	Punnet	12 × 4oz	8 × 200g/12 × 250g
		18 × 4oz	
Strawberries	Punnet	14 × 8oz	8 × 200g/12 × 250g/10 × 500g
	Chip	8 × 1lb	2/3

Note: Weights vary according to country of origin.
Source: The Fresh Produce Desk Book, Lynda Seaton (Ed.), Lockwood Press (1991).

Table 7.6 Apple sizes

Bramley (mm)	Dessert (mm)
70–80 (approx 6 per kilo)	55–60
80–90	60–65 (approx 10 per kilo)
90–100	65–70
	70–75
	75–80

Profitable usage

There is little to be gained by the purchase of sub-standard fruits. In most instances, fruit requires little preparation but can be sold at a premium price, if it is in perfect condition and well-presented. The trend for healthy eating places a greater demand on the caterer to provide good, fresh fruit.

SEASONALITY

The seasonal lists (see Tables 7.2 and 7.4) should be read against a background of continuing and rapid change. New sources of supply can quickly change the seasonality of a food. Developments of pre-prepared convenience foods also diminish the caterer's concern with seasons. Garden peas have a season, but frozen and canned varieties are always available. On the other hand, catering organisations which undertake their own cook-freeze or conveniencing production have their buying interest in the seasons reawakened.

Just as food processing, which brings year-long availability, changes attitudes, so transportation affects season. Cheaper more efficient means of food transport have brought caterers in the Western world greater opportunity to use imported food in new or extended seasons.

Many vegetables are nowadays available from various countries all year round. These include beetroot, celery, cabbage, carrots, cauliflower and many more. The English season for celery, for example, is extended by imports from Spain and even California, but good catering will still take advantage of the home season for best price and flavour value.

Other economic developments can also extend our seasons. For example, Israel has increased its produc-

Sources	January	February	March	April	May	June	July	August	September	October	November	December
UK	*(in store)* ────────────────────────────────►							▓	▓	▓	──────────►	
France	▓	▓	▓					▓	▓	▓		▓
Canada	▓	▓	▓								▓	▓
Denmark	▓	▓	▓									
Israel										▓	▓	
New Zealand					▓	▓	▓	▓				

Notes:
1. Other sources include Germany, Bulgaria, Hungary, Italy, South Africa and USA.
2. Seasons, particularly for home grown produce, may be extended by cold storage so that UK apples would be available through to June.

Figure 7.4   *Yearly availability of apples*

tion of citrus fruits, avocados and cantaloup melons which gives these fresh commodities a longer season in the UK. The Americas, Cyprus, Italy and the West Indies also supply citrus and other fruits to give varying seasons.

Home crops of dessert fruits have variable harvests so that the demand for apples and pears are met by imports from Europe and the New World (see Figure 7.4). Green and yellow honeydew melons are largely imported from Spain, but these are augmented by Ogens from Israel, Cantaloups from Holland and Charentaise from France.

The speed of change makes it difficult to provide permanent guidance about season; what is valid one year may not endure. Import licences and political factors may alter supply sources and hence season. Previously, change fostered by political, economic and technological factors was less emphatic. Seasonality, even in one country, was tempered by geography. Even in a small country like the UK there will be a difference in season between Scotland and Cornwall. Quality may also be influenced by geography, weather and soil conditions, such that certain districts become identified with particular crops which may in turn have their own season, for example, the orchards of Kent and the potato fields of the Channel Islands.

Nevertheless, the caterer should seek to exploit seasons, both to satisfy the consumer and for reasons of economy. Price is normally at its most favourable in full season and certainly trimming and waste is less than when using foods which are approaching their season's end.

LEGISLATION

The following is a list of the relevant acts and regulations:

The Horticultural Produce Act 1986;
The Food Labelling Regulations 1984;
The Agriculture and Horticulture Act 1964.

Summary

If the maximum benefit is to be obtained from good-quality fresh produce, caterers need to become acquainted with the various varieties and strains of produce and their appropriate uses. In addition to the normal fruits and vegetables, caterers will be encouraged by the wide variety of exotic and unusual produce now available to enliven the menu. Rare vegetables, fruits, herbs and flowers, such as borage, rose petal and nasturtium, will add value to simple meats. There is a greater demand from customers for organic produce, salads and crisp, young vegetables.

A caterer must acquire the knowledge to recognise and identify all these. In smaller towns, it may be necessary to deal through one supplier who can be kept up to the mark and, indeed, brought under instruction with regard to the rarer products. To extend their knowledge, chefs and caterers should not hesitate to make use of gardening or horticultural manuals and even guides produced with the domestic cook or market gardener in mind.

Much is to be gained by regular visits to the market to examine and purchase usable quantities of any produce which is in peak condition, in which case fruit and vegetable specifications may appear superfluous.

Where substantial quantities of fruits and vegetables are regularly purchased consideration may be given to placing contracts under specification. This is especially applicable to potatoes which, as a staple dietary element, have a predictable use in most forms of catering. The Potato Marketing Board (PMB) can provide a specimen contract. Other boards and associations may also be approached with regard to similar advice for their produce. Buyers will appreciate that marketing boards are also concerned with the interests of the producers.

The National Federation of Fruit and Potato Trades also produce a handbook (for which a charge is made). This lists UK distributors, importers and growers, and also provides the addresses, trading hours and function, of wholesale fruit markets in major towns.

Bearing in mind seasonal availability, the caterer will draw specifications for potatoes, vegetables and fruits based on the demands of the menu. Good purchasing policy will be supported by careful examination and storage of produce once delivered.

Convenience and Grocery Foods

Almost all grocery items involve some level of convenience, processing or manufacture. Even items not normally associated with convenience, flour for instance, may involve a high degree of processing. For most products, the processing involves the use of one or more methods to inhibit or delay the onset of food spoilage. Some processing may involve the use of additives.

Current issues relate to the supposed abuse of food by food technologists and whether additives, in particular, are necessary, natural or unnatural, healthy or harmful. It is possible to argue that many additives are better for us than the natural ingredients which they replace. This may indeed be true if you are inclined to the belief that refined sugar, for instance, is bad for you. Despite what many people believe, the adulteration of food is not a modern disease. The Romans were known to add potash to wine and bakers from early times 'improved' their bread by adding chalk and bonemeal. Almost since man learned to cook, herbs and spices have been used to preserve and enhance dishes and recipes. Some more modern additives, for example, emulsions and preservatives, may be considered to be essential to the quality of the product. Others, such as colours and flavours, may be less essential.

Additives

Additives are used to prevent food spoilage, assist processing and preparation, enhance flavour, texture and appearance, and improve or maintain nutritional value. They include the following:

- preservatives
- antioxidants
- flavour enhancers
- artificial sweeteners
- stabilisers
- emulsions
- thickeners
- colourings.

Whilst most caterers accept that there are benefits to be derived from the use of additives some doubt does exist, amongst chefs and gourmets alike, about the over-use of colourings and flavour enhancers in particular. When using additives, as well as when purchasing foods where they may have already been used, refer to the requirements placed on food manufacturers.

For example, additives should be:

- safe;
- effective (in their intended use);
- used in only the minimum quantities necessary;
- of nutritional value, wherever possible;
- must not be used to mislead the consumer.

Ultimately, the consumer will determine the acceptability of additives in dishes. At some levels, convenience products which, for some, have strayed far from their fresh counterpart may indeed be the accepted norm. Tomato soup (powdered or tinned) is highly popular, yet may owe much of its colour, flavour and consistency to additives rather than the real thing. In other areas, consumers may be highly receptive to additive-free products. As with many other aspects of catering, the wise caterer may seek to educate, but will do this tacitly.

Where the caterers seek to purchase ingredients, grocery and convenience items, they have the support of a wealth of information, not only on the product label (ingredients and E numbers), but also in the various publications produced by government bodies and other interested parties.

Today we have a greater knowledge of the effect of various additives and the public is protected by a range of food manufacturing, hygiene and labelling legislation.

CONVENIENCE FOODS

Convenience foods may be defined as those foods which have been carried to an advanced stage by the manufacturer and which may be used as a labour-saving alternative to less highly-processed products. The caterer using such products to any extent must look to some staff rationalisation or labour reduction to justify the higher cost. Buying must take into account the advantage of eliminating preparatory processes in, for example, the larder and vegetable preparation areas. The buyer should study the relationship of 'convenience' foods to the food–service operation as the method of prefabrication or pre-preparation may determine portion size and service style.

Basically, most convenience or ready-to-use food products constitute what the chef would prepare in his or her own kitchen. Because foods are processed at some previous time and in a distant locality, preservation is often required. This usually involves freezing, dehydration or canning.

Preservation

This involves the control of moulds, yeast and/or bacteria by the control of temperature and/or the removal of moisture and/or oxygen.

Moulds are simple plant life which require warmth, oxygen and moisture for growth. They are killed by heat and sunlight. They can grow where there is too little moisture for yeast or bacteria. They are most commonly found on jams, pickles, bread and fruit. Although they are not harmful, they are undesirable.

Yeasts are single-cell plants or organisms, larger than bacteria, which grow on food containing moisture and sugar. Fruit juices often ferment as a result of yeasts being present. They do not cause transferable food poisoning, but can cause stomach upset and are therefore undesirable.

Bacteria are minute organisms which require food, warmth, oxygen and moisture to grow. They may be easily transferred from one food to another. Bacteria spoil food and leave harmful waste deposits – toxins (poisons) – in the food. Bacteria can be destroyed by heat (cooking), but some of the spores (toxins) that they leave behind are resistant to heat.

Methods of processing/preservation include:
- cleaning
- drying
- chilling
- salting
- canning
- sous-vide
- cutting
- bottling
- freezing
- smoking
- irradiation
- vacuum packing.

Today, most of the main groups of foods are available in ready-to-use form with the following being the most-widely handled:

- prepared or partly-prepared foods –
  raw, pre-peeled potatoes and vegetables;
  pre-portioned meat and fish.

- dehydrated and accelerated, freeze-dried foods –
  stocks and sauces;
  soups and soup bases;
  eggs (whole, yolk or white);
  fish, meat and meat products;
  vegetables and potatoes;
  fruits;
  pre-mixes for bakery and confectionery goods;
  instant tea, coffee, milk and chocolate;
  condiments, herbs and spices.

- cured (salted) and/or smoked foods –
  fish, meat, bacon and poultry;
  cheese;
  nuts.

- bottled foods –
  pickled vegetables, eggs and fish;
  potted fish and meats;
  whole, halved and sliced fruits;
  preserves, jams, marmalades and curds;
  condiments, vinegars, oils and sauces.

- canned (tinned) foods –
  condensed and evaporated milk;
  soups and concentrated soups;
  fish (oily varieties in oil, brine or sauce);
  meat and meat products (meat pies/puddings, mince, pie filling);

  poultry and poultry products;
  vegetables;
  sweet puddings and fruit pie fillings;
  whole, halved, sliced, diced or pulp fruits (solid pack, in syrup, in water or in fruit juice).

- chilled and frozen foods (raw, cooked, portioned or bulk packed) –
  fish and fish products;
  meat and meat products;
  poultry and game;
  vegetables, potatoes and potato products;
  fruits and fruit products;
  puddings, pastries and gateaux;
  bread and yeast products;
  dairy products;
  ices and ice cream.

Cleaning, which involves trimming and cutting of produce, is a level of convenience associated with the sale of fresh produce and is an additional service offered by fishmongers, butchers and greengrocers. Similarly, the chilling and/or vacuum packing of such produce may be a normal part of the service offered.

Salting – the process of filling wooden barrels with layers of fish, meat or vegetables, between layers of salt – is one of the oldest methods of food preservation. Today, however, its use as the single method of preservation has almost disappeared. Salt, particularly in the form of a solution (brine), is still widely-used in combination with other forms of processing. Salting, or curing, is most commonly associated with the smoking process.

Osmosis (the drawing of water from one body to another)

Any liquid with a high salt, acid, sugar or alcohol content will have the effect of drying out any bacteria present, thereby restricting food spoilage.

Smoking, another of the early methods of food preservation, is currently experiencing a revival in popularity. In addition to bacon and fish, a wide variety of produce is now smoked, not so much as a means of preservation but more to enhance colour and flavour.

Foods may be hot- or cold-smoked and some foods are more suited to one method than the other. Hot-smoking cooks the food, resulting in a dryer texture and slightly longer shelf life.

Note that some foods may be painted or sprayed with colour and/or flavouring to enhance the product without the effort or expense of the traditional process, but this does not achieve the same, satisfactory flavour.

Drying varies in process from traditional sun drying, often associated with fruits, to more technological methods like tunnel drying, spray and roller drying of liquids, and accelerated freeze drying (AFD).

Tunnel drying
Particularly associated with small, even-sized items like peas or diced carrot. The food is placed on a moving bed which vibrates as it passes through a heated tunnel, resulting in rapid and even dehydration.

Puff drying
Small items of food, such as diced carrot, are pressurised. The sudden release of pressure, combined with heat, results in dehydration. Products treated in this way rehydrate (absorb water) very quickly. A similar process is used for breakfast cereals, for example, puffed wheat.

Roller drying
Associated with liquids and slurries (milk, soups, potato) which are poured over a heated drum. As the drum revolves, the water content evaporates and the resulting dried solids are scraped off.

Spray drying
Liquids are sprayed through a fine nozzle at the top of a heated chamber. As the droplets fall, water evaporates and the dehydrated solids fall to the floor. The process has the advantage of a less-cooked flavour and so is particularly good for milk.

Accelerated freeze drying (AFD)
This involves the process of sublimation, taking a product from its frozen state to a dehydrated state without it passing through the liquid phase. AFD is used to produce dried food which, once reconstituted, is generally accepted as being closest to its original form (flavour). The process is most frequently associated with coffee granules. AFD products normally rehydrate quickly and effectively.

Application of the drying process to milk

Various forms of milk powder can be manufactured. The type of heat treatment that the milk has been subjected to and the drying process will have an effect on the properties of the finished powder. A powder that performs well in bakery goods may be unstable when added to hot coffee. Roller-dried milk is generally purchased in bulk packs and used for cooking. Spray-dried whole or skimmed milk is relatively versatile as it is a good emulsifier and has good water-binding properties. It also has a good 'dairy' flavour, but can be expensive.

Safe, fat-free egg powder is a fairly new product. It can be reconstituted with water or skimmed milk and used in baking or for scambled eggs and omelettes. It is free from salmonella and has no cholesterol.

Dried goods, like milk and egg powders, should be stored carefully. They can be easily contaminated by airborne bacteria, particularly in a humid atmosphere. Keep packs sealed.

Dried foods are convenient to store and generally easy-to-use. Portion packing is rare, but most products are easy to measure.

Bottling, the method of preserving whole and portions of fruits in syrup, although still available for the domestic market, is less applicable to the catering industry. Jams and marmalades may now be purchased in portion packs for the customer and A10 tins (see Table 8.1 on page 137) for use in cooking. Pickles and sauces are now the main application of bottled foods for the caterer.

Canning, although a relatively old method of preservation, is still widely-used. The principle of canning is to put food into a sealed container so that no bacteria or other micro-organisms can get in, and then to heat it sufficiently to destroy any micro-organisms which may have already been present. It is also necessary to remove any air (create a vacuum) to restrict bacterial growth. Liquids (brines and syrups) are used with loose items, vegetables and fruits, to help exclude the air.

The sterlising process results in cooking which can

affect the flavour, texture and colour of products. Additives may be used to restore or replace natural characteristics which have been lost during preservation. For items such as fruit juices, the process of aseptic canning is used to avoid the heat process and retain a natural, fresh character.

Aseptic canning
This involves preparing and packing the produce under completely sterile conditions, thus avoiding the need for sterilsation. The process has enabled the wider application of fresh produce, not just stored in the traditional 'tin' can, but also in waxed cartons.

Although, in theory, canned goods may keep for many years, it is not good practice to encourage prolonged storage.

One possible exception is high-grade canned sardines which, in order to meet the demands of connoisseurs, were once laid down like wine. During years of storage the cans were turned at regular intervals to ensure uniform penetration of oil.

Although food may not be contaminated by bacteria there may be changes in colour, texture and/or flavour that result from prolonged storage. Stock turnover, depending on the type of operation, should range between two and six months. Both on delivery and during storage cans should be examined. Any blown, damaged, leaking or rusty cans should be returned to the supplier (if discovered on delivery) or destroyed. In an effort to ensure good stock rotation, attempts should be made to identify any date coding marks which appear on the label or on the can itself.

Canned foods are ready-to-serve or require heating only. They are most convenient from a preparation standpoint. Little labour is needed and the speed of preparation permits fast response to variations in demand. Canned foods have a long shelf life and can therefore be bought infrequently and in large amounts, if space permits.

Careful choice of optimum can size (see Table 8.1) is important as the largest cans are not always the most cost-effective. Consideration must be given to volume, turnover and wastage. The difference in contents, both quality and quantity, of canned produce from different producers makes sample testing essential. It is not safe to assume that the best producer of canned peaches will also produce the best canned apples.

Freezing is seen by many people as the ultimate convenience. Some have even argued that most frozen food is fresher than fresh (which may be market-stale). It is generally true that most frozen foods are harvested when they are in peak condition and processed immediately whereas fresh produce may take several days to get to the kitchen. Processing will result in some nutritional loss, but so too will delay between harvest and cooking of fresh produce.

Speed of processing is the essence of good freezing, not just in relation to speed from field to freezer, but also the actual time taken to freeze the product. During the freezing process, ice particles form in the food. The faster the process the smaller the ice particles. If the ice particles are large they will break the cell walls of the food resulting in the collapse of the product once defrosted. Most freezing processes involve temperatures of approximately $-18°C$. Cryogenic freezing (the use of liquid nitrogen) results in the use of a process temperature of approximately $-196°C$ and very rapid freezing. Although expensive it is worthwhile for the finest products, especially those where collapse is likely, for example, strawberries.

Temperature control throughout processing, purchase, receipt and storage is critical. Check the temperature of frozen foods on delivery. If the

Table 8.1 Buying canned goods

| Can size | Approximate weight/volume | | | | Typical commodity contents | Approx. portions |
	Metric	Imperial	Metric	Imperial		
A10	3.0 kg	6.6 lb	2.6 l	110 fl oz	Fruit, vegetables	24
A 6	2.6 kg	4.6 lb	1.8 l	76 fl oz	Fruit (solid pack) Jams Meat (tongue)	24 120 24
A 5	1.4 kg	3.0 lb	1.2 l	50 fl oz	Fruit juices Meat roll	10 16
A 2/	820 g	1.8 lb	850 ml	30 fl oz	Fruit, vegetables Soup	6 5
A 2	475 g	1.2 lb	568 ml	20 fl oz	Fruit, vegetables Soup	4 3
Flat	450 g	1.0 lb			Meat, fish	5
A 1/	410 g	14 oz	454 ml	16 fl oz	Fruit, vegetables	3
A 1	320 g	10 oz	312 ml	11 fl oz	Baked beans Pilchards Soup	3 3 2
Picnic	225 g	8 oz	227 ml	8 fl oz	Fruit salad Baked beans	2 2
	140 g	5 oz	170 ml	6 fl oz	Baked beans, peas	1

temperature is above −10°C the delivery should be rejected. Date coding should be identified and checked. Good storage procedures, stock rotation and temperature checks should be maintained.

Frozen foods generally require more costly storage facilities. Shelf life is shorter than that of canned goods so deliveries would need to be fairly frequent.

Chilling is becoming a more widely-applied form of convenience, especially in relation to ready-to-serve products. In some cases, the chilling process is allied to vacuum packing and gas flushing. Modified atmosphere packing (MAP) involves the use of inert gases, under controlled conditions, to replace the air in a pack rather than removing it. The absence of oxygen, further restricts bacterial growth.

Perhaps the greatest convenience is to be found in ready-to use foods. Many butchers are responding effectively to demand by supplying value-added products, such as kebabs, paupiettes, marinated meats and breaded poultry. Ready-to-serve dishes usually have the added advantage of being portion-controlled. However, shelf life is often short and deliveries must be frequent.

Irradiation (the exposure of food to limited doses of ionising radiation) results in a form of pasteurisation. Growth of salmonella and listeria is inhibited, but the product is not sterile. The process inhibits sprouting and food spoilage. It is not suitable for all foods; fatty foods in particular do not benefit from the process. It has been found suitable for some fruits and vegetables (fresh and dried), seafood and poultry, pulses, grains and spices. There is some loss of vitamin C (up to 70 per cent in some fruits). The process is, apparently, impossible to detect and it may be possible for food which might have been unfit for human consumption to pass current food tests after being irradiated.

There is evidence that at least one company has used the process of irradiation to treat food which had originally failed its own minimum standards.

Irradiation, under licence, became legal in January 1991. Irradiated food must be accompanied by appropriate documentation during transportation and storage. Food or dishes that contain irradiated products, must be declared, as irradiated produce, on menus. The only exception is where an ingredient is only a minor part of the dish, for example, a spice.

To the caterer, convenience food can mean a saving of labour and space, quicker preparation, an extended shelf life or ease of portioning. Processed foods are generally free of waste, compact and easy to store, simple to prepare and provide consistent quality, menu continuity, stock, cost and portion controls. For many caterers, portion packing will be the single most important convenience. Caterers differ in their views about the degree of convenience of various foods. There is no universally-acceptable system of convenience measurement enabling any one type to be accurately ranked.

How the caterer will incorporate convenience products into kitchen routines depends on the nature of the catering establishment and the facilities, staff and equipment available. Basically, the aim must be to eliminate from the kitchen all work which can more advantageously be carried out under factory conditions where modern manufacturing techniques can be employed, as long as the standard of cuisine does not suffer and customer acceptance is maintained. To determine the relevant advantages, the chef or manager must examine the operational cycle, identify problems and decide whether they can be overcome, bearing in mind the following:

- Labour – the cost and availability of kitchen labour must be assessed.
- Time – the speed of preparation must be considered in relation to service standards.
- Quality and variety – the possibility of achieving higher quality food standards must be examined as well as the opportunity of providing dishes not otherwise available. The absence of alternatives may be due to lack of time or skill, or to the effects of season or locality.
- Space – less storage and handling space may be required when handling processed foods; the residual space may be put to better, more profitable use.
- Hygiene – ready-to-use foods have most, if not all, of their waste removed. The elimination of such waste before food reaches the kitchen reduces

food handling and avoids or eases waste disposal and cleaning problems. Properly stored tinned, frozen and dried foods do not allow the growth of bacteria.

- Cost – frequently, cost is the deciding factor. Whilst saving of labour is usually the most apparent economy, the ability to control food quality, yield, portion size and waste are aspects which enable the caterer to regulate final operational costs more accurately.

Experience of convenience food usage varies between systems that are totally dependent on convenience products to those using none, with most caterers falling somewhere between the two. Ideal usage levels are dependent on operational style, brand image, menu, price and customer acceptance.

GROCERY ITEMS

Familiarity with the complete range of grocery commodities requires a vast knowledge on the part of the food purchaser. Few would attempt to carry this knowledge in their heads and the wise caterer will not hesitate to make full use of reference material regarding grades, type, pack and quality marks of various produce.

When examining suppliers' catalogues it immediately becomes apparent that there is a wide variety of packaging styles and unit and package sizes for most products. It will, therefore, be necessary to:

- Reduce all quotations to a single unit size for comparison. Price per portion provides the most useful comparison so long as all costs are identified.
- Relate price to quality (tested samples).
- Identify the relative advantages and disadvantages of large and small unit/pack sizes. For example, small packs are usually more expensive but are more controllable (easier to measure), sealed packs retain flavour and prevent contamination, and the handling, measuring and weighing of stock is reduced.

Caterers should purchase those products that offer most benefits at the best price.

Detailed discussion of each commodity is beyond the scope of this book. However, some discussion of selected examples, by way of highlighting significant points, will be useful.

CEREALS AND CEREAL PRODUCTS

Food value

Cereals perform an important function in the Western diet and are a major source of starch and dietary fibre. Caterers have long been aware of increased demand from customers for wholemeal products (not only breadflour but other cereal products) and of the general public's knowledge of fibre's nutritional significance.

Flour
Wholemeal has 8.5 per cent fibre;
Brown has 5.1 per cent fibre;
White has 2.7 per cent fibre.

Additionally, cereals contain some protein and are a good source of vitamin B. The wheatgerm contains protein, oils and vitamins.

Calcium carbonate, vitamin B1, nicotinic acid and iron are all added (by law) to white flour to replace the nutrients that are extracted with the bran and germ.

Source

Cereals are defined as the seed heads of cultivated grasses and include the following varieties:

- wheat;
- oats;
- maize (corn);
- barley;
- rye;
- rice.

Although they are not actually cereals, for culinary purposes the following are usually associated with cereals;

- arrowroot – high-grade starch from the maranta plant;
- fecule – potato flour;
- sago – from the pith of the sago palm (pure starch);
- tapioca – from the root of the cassava plant.

Quality

This is determined during processing and in the case of flour is based on the extraction rate. The best flour is 'extracted' during the early stages of the milling process. Patents grade is the finest flour, using only the best 25–40 per cent of the grain taken from early rollings. Bakers grade is a 70 per cent extraction and 'straight run' has no patents grade removed.

The quality of flour is also related to its catering use and in this respect two particular measures apply, relative to the protein (gluten) content. Gluten is formed when the flour is mixed with water. Strong (high-protein) flour is high in gluten (17 per cent) and therefore more suited to the production of doughs, yeast goods and puff pastry. Soft (low-protein) flour is relatively low in gluten (8 per cent) and is best suited to cakes, biscuits, pastries and general kitchen use. Self-raising flour has a medium-level gluten content (12 per cent) with baking powder added.

Processing

Although all cereals can be ground to produce flour, some (oats and barley in particular) are less adaptable than others, although oatmeal and barleymeal do have their uses.

Rice flour may be used as a thickening but is more commonly used in the preparation of pastry items.

Maize is ground into a flour (cornflour) which is almost exclusively used as a thickening.

Wheat is by far the most versatile and widely-used of all cereals. Ground coarsely it produces semolina which may be used in the preparation of milk puddings or in the manufacture of pasta.

Finely-ground flour may be purchased in a variety of forms: white, using 75 per cent of the grain; brown using 85 per cent; or wholemeal using 100 per cent including the bran. Varieties with added wheatgerm or added bran may also be purchased.

Most cereals are manufactured into one or more varieties of breakfast cereals.

Function in cookery

Whether in natural, crushed, rolled or ground form, or as a processed product, cereals (particularly wheat) are one of the principal kitchen ingredients.

It may not be until asked to provide for a coeliac diet, where even the minutest trace of wheat will prevent further absorption of nutrients, that a chef might truly appreciate the extent to which starch permeates the modern menu.

Starch, in one form or another, is responsible for providing bulk and form in many recipes. Made into a malleable batter or dough, the protein will set when cooked, providing rigid structure and/or crisp texture. Cereals may be used as a basic ingredient or as a coating. When heated in liquid they will thicken and bind. Each starch has unique characteristics, such that cornflour may give an opaque, waxy appearance to a thickened sauce whilst arrowroot will achieve the same thickening effect but the pure clarity of the original liquid will still be retained.

Purchasing specifications

Flour should be specified by strength and/or extraction, according to recipe requirements.

A wide range of rices are available – basmati, brown, arborio, patna, carolina (pudding rice) – each having particular attributes of colour, texture and shape. They are often divided simply into long and short (round) grain although this belies the wealth of interest and variety that is available to enhance dishes and menus. Wild rice is not a true rice as such.

Pasta is available in over 80 varieties, allowing for differences in shape, size and method of convenience, and is available fresh as well as tinned and dried. A combination of a dozen pastas, three basic sauces and some additional ingredients would produce a relatively extensive menu.

Noodles, both Chinese and Italian, are also obtainable in many forms, including flour, rice and egg recipes. As with rice and pasta the wealth of varieties may be used simply to add interest to the menu or specific selection may be considered essential to dish authenticity.

Storage, hygiene and health

All cereals should be stored in a cool, dry, well-ventilated area. If flour and cereals are stored loose, empty and clean storage bins frequently. Do not mix new stock with old. Flour and cereal products are subject to infestation by weevils so use tight-fitting lids.

Plain flour may keep for up to six months, self-raising for between two and three months, and wholemeal, because of the fat content and subsequent risk of rancidity, for between one and two months.

Profitable usage

Depending on kitchen and recipe requirements there may be some advantage in purchasing cereals, rice and pasta in small units rather than bulk. Small packs, although more expensive, are cleaner and easier to use and may have benefits with regard to stock and cost control.

Table 8.2 Nutritional content of nuts

	Water (%)	Protein (%)	Fat (%)	Carbohydrate (%)
Almond	5	19	54	20
Brazil	5	14	67	11
Cashew	5	17	46	29
Chestnut	52	3	2	42
Coconut	51	4	35	9
Hazelnut	6	13	62	17
Pecan	3	9	71	15
Peanut	6	26	48	19
Pine kernel	6	31	47	12
Pistachio	5	20	54	19
Walnut	4	15	64	16

NUTS

Food value

Nuts are generally high in protein, B vitamins and fat (see Table 8.2). They are a good source of carbohydrate, mineral salts and fibre, but may be difficult to digest. They are an important element in the vegetarian diet.

Source

Nuts are defined as the reproductive seed (kernel) of a plant or tree, the most common varieties of which are almond, brazil, cashew, chestnut, coconut, hazelnut, pecan, peanut, pistachio, pine kernel and walnut.

Quality

Quality is normally identified by good size and relative weight. There should be no signs of mildew or mustiness.

Processing

Dessert nuts are those that are sold with their shell on, the only processing required is the removal of any fibrous 'flesh' that may have surrounded the nut, cleaning, drying and grading.

For kitchen use, most nuts will be shelled. Further processing may include halving, slicing, chopping, grinding, roasting and/or salting (see Figure 8.1).

Function in cookery

Nuts are used throughout the menu to add contrast of colour, flavour and texture to dishes both sweet and savoury. They may be used in a variety of forms from whole to ground. When ground they may substitute, or partially substitute, for flour as a basic recipe ingredient. Compared to flour, nuts have a high fat content which will increase the richness of a recipe.

Purchasing specifications

Nuts may be purchased in a variety of pack forms and weight ranges, from individual, foil-wrapped snacks to large sacks. They may also be purchased in a wide variety of specifications (see Figure 8.1).

	Shell on	Skin on	Whole skinned	Roasted	Salted	Halved (split)	Sliced (flaked)	Chopped (nib)	Ground	Other
Almond	√	√	√			√	√	√	√	Sugard almonds Almond paste (marzipan)
Brazil	√	√	√				√			Choclolate covered
Cashew	√			√	√					
Chestnut	√		√					√		Glacé (in syrup) Pureé/paste (may be sweetened)
Coconut	√						√	√		Desiccated – various sizes
Hazelnut	√	√	√					√		Chocolate covered Paste
Pecan	√		√							
Peanut	√	√	√	√	√			√		Paste (buttor)
Pine kernel			√							
Pistachio	√	√	√	√	√			√		
Walnut	√		√			√		√		

Figure 8.1 *Nuts – methods of processing (purchase specification)*

Storage, hygiene and health

Nuts are highly-perishable and subject to insect infestation. A relatively high fat content makes them susceptible to rancidity. Shelled nuts (halves, flakes, nib or ground) should be kept in airtight containers.

Dessert nuts (shell on) should be kept in a cool, dry, well-ventilated store. Avoid nuts which appear damp or mouldy.

Profitable usage

Nuts are an expensive commodity, they should, therefore, be purchased in small quantities and used with care. Although they are attractive as an ingredient or garnish to a wide variety of savoury as well as sweet dishes, it is all too easy to be over-generous. Cost dishes carefully and make sure that measurements are accurately controlled.

DRIED FRUITS

Food value

Dried fruit is a good source of most vitamins and minerals, although the absence of vitamin C should be noted. Dried fruit is also an important source of natural sugars and fibre.

Source

Most fruits can be dried either naturally or mechanically. Although available throughout the world, dried fruit tends to be associated with the Mediterranean.

Quality

Quality is dependent to a large extent on method of processing. Most fruits are now sold ready-for-use and they require no further cleaning as stalks and stones have been removed.

Processing

In the traditional method, the fruit was spread out in the sun, with larger fruits halved or sliced. Some fruits were treated with sulphur to prevent enzymic browning. Traditional methods have now largely been superseded by mechanical methods, particularly forced air drying. The mechanical process provides for a more predictable/controllable end product.

Function in cookery

The prime purpose of dried fruits, other than substituting for the fresh alternative, is to add moistness and natural sweetness to dishes. Although they may be used with meats and savoury dishes they are most commonly associated with the production of cakes and pastries. When poached (compôte) they may be used as a luncheon sweet or breakfast dish.

Purchasing specifications

Although dried vine fruit is generally associated with baking, for example, currants and sultanas, a wide variety of other fruits are available for cooking and serving as dishes in their own right, for example, a compôte of prunes or figs. Various fruits may also be used in other dishes, for example, muesli or loin of pork with apricots.

Almost all dried fruit is available in sealed polythene bags. Some may be purchased in vacuum packs. These fruits normally require less reconstitution (soaking) and in many cases may be used without soaking.

Various fruits, for example, apricots, are available as organically grown and additionally, or alternatively, may have been processed without the use of sulphur.

Storage, hygiene and health

Dried fruit is best left in its sealed packaging. Once opened it should be transferred into airtight containers.

Profitable usage

Dried fruit is not normally identified as a profitable item, although it is an important ingredient in profitable bakery and pastry items. Some dried fruits can be used to advantage as a garnish or accompaniment to more expensive sweet and savoury dishes, and the association with health food can be used to advantage when promoting menu items.

HERBS AND SPICES

Food value

Most herbs and spices have little nutritional value but are considered an indispensable kitchen aid, adding colour and flavour.
Herbs are obtained from the leaves and/or stems of plants. Most originate from either the carrot family (for example, parsley, fennel, dill and coriander) or from the mint family (for example, sage, thyme and

oregano). Although generally considered best when fresh, most herbs are widely-used in the dried form.

Spices are obtained from dried seeds, pods, berries, roots, stems, buds and bark. Spices have great historical significance being the prime cause for developments in trading and the discovery, through the spice routes, of new continents. Commonly-used in dried and/or powdered form, they are often expensive and some, like saffron, are extremely expensive. Therefore, they are usually purchased in small quantities.

Their volatile oils, which provide the aroma and flavour, are lost over time, particularly if a spice is in powdered form and stored incorrectly. Dried herbs and spices should be stored in airtight containers.

Flavourings

- Extracts – entirely pure and very expensive.
- Essential oils – a form of extract, mainly from citrus fruits and spices.
- Essences – natural flavourings.

CONDIMENTS

Salt

Salt (sodium chloride) is essential to health, stabilising body fluids and preventing muscle cramps, although for some people salt will be restricted on medical grounds. Salt is considered essential in the kitchen as a flavour enhancer and provides one of the oldest forms of preservation.

Salt may be extracted from the sea (sea salt) by the process of evaporation or it may be mined (rock salt). There are three grades of rock salt – superfine, fine and medium crystal. Sea salt is available as either fine or large crystal. Salt used to be susceptible to dampness and clogging, but most salts are now treated to ensure a free flow.

Other salts include low-sodium salt, iodized salt and flavoured salts (for example, celery salt or garlic salt).

There is an historical association between spices and currency. For example:

- a 'peppercorn rent' now means a nominal sum, but originally a half pound of peppercorns was the equivalent of a week's wages;
- salary comes from the Roman 'salt ration';
- 'not worth his salt' is an Old English expression used to describe someone who does not earn his pay.

In fact the English language is now 'peppered' with nouns and adjectives derived from spices and condiments.

Pepper

Pepper is obtainable as black or white whole corns or ground. Non-dried, green peppercorns are available tinned or bottled in brine. Both black and white peppercorns originate from the berries of the same plant. Black pepper is obtained from green fruit, fermented with the skin on and allowed to dry. For white pepper, the berries are allowed to ripen, then soaked in water to remove the skins and dried. White pepper is less pungent than black.

Mustard

There are various national preferences; English, French, German and American being the most common. The French, in particular, have a wide variety of regional mustards. Flavours range from mild to strong; some are sharp others sweet. Textures range from the smooth, such as the standard English and Dijon, to the coarse varieties which include mustard and other seeds. Customer preference also varies and for this reason many caterers will consider it necessary to carry a range of mustards.

Consideration must also be given to the benefits of purchasing prepared mustard as against the traditional, powdered mustard. Although English mustard is preferred by many customers its preparation and use will require particular attention. It has a tendency to dry out so causing waste. However, powdered mustard remains an important ingredient in the kitchen.

It has long been rumoured that the fortunes of mustard producers are derived more from the mustard that is left on the side of the plate or dried out in the pot, than from what is actually consumed.

Vinegar

Originally vinegar (vin aigre), as the name suggests, was produced from sour wine. Wine vinegar remains popular in wine-producing countries. In Britain, where surplus wine is less easy to come by, malt vinegar is more popular, although cider vinegar and distilled vinegar are also widely-used. Malt vinegar is produced from sour, unhopped, beer; cider vinegar from sour cider. Distilled vinegar involves the removal of natural colour and flavour, and results in a higher acid content, more suited to the preservation of watery vegetables.

Other varieties of vinegar include herb and fruit vinegars. Herb vinegar is produced by infusion where fresh herbs, such as tarragon, are placed into a bottle of vinegar and left so the flavour of the herb is drawn into the vinegar. Obviously light vinegars, with little natural flavour of their own, are most suited to this purpose. Fruit, for example, raspberries, may also be infused in vinegar. Once strained the fruit vinegar is then normally boiled.

Other varieties of vinegar include balsamic, sherry, rice and many combinations such as cider and herb or honey and caper.

The use of these various vinegars, together with with mustards herbs and oils (mentioned below), as dressings on salads and as ingredients in recipes make for an infinite variety of flavour combinations to enhance all manner of dishes.

Oils

Oil can be obtained from a wide variety of sources (see Chapter 5). When used as a condiment it is always of plant origin, with olive being the most popular. Although blends may be used, single flavours offer more interest. Almond, avocado, grapeseed, hazelnut, pine seed, sesame seed and walnut oils each have unique and delicate flavours. All of these oils are expensive and should therefore be used with care.

Olive oil may be defined as virgin when the product results from an extraction without heating or refining. Additional terms identifying the acidity level are: extra (less than 1 per cent acidity), fine and semi-fine. Plain virgin oil normally has an acidity level in excess of 4 per cent.

Quality

Good-quality condiments are generally expensive, but (as with many other commodities) good quality used sparingly is often more beneficial and cost-effective than cheaper alternatives. Their expense also serves to highlight the care and control that should be observed in selection, purchase and storage.

Profitable usage

The profitability of condiments is difficult to determine. They are essential ingredients in most dishes and a necessary addition to the table. Because of the small quantities used it is often difficult to determine what portion cost to include when costing a recipe. For this reason, many caterers will make a percentage addition, 5–10 per cent, to all recipes to allow for all elements, such as herbs and spices, which are too small to cost directly.

The availability of good quality table condiments may influence a customer's choice of restaurant and may be one more factor that make customers willing to pay that little bit more.

SUGAR

Food value

As a basic food, sugar provides an essential source of energy, although many would argue that there is sufficient natural sugar available in the foods we eat to make the use of refined sugar unnecessary. Excess sugar is converted into fat.

There is hardly any nutritional difference between brown and white sugars, neither contain any colouring, flavouring or preservative. The natural flavour and colour of brown sugar derives from molasses.

Plants manufacture sugar, as an energy store, by the process of photosynthesis, converting energy from sunlight.

> The sugar cycle is essential to life on earth. Humans transfer blood sugar into energy and release carbon dioxide, by breathing out, into the air. Carbon dioxide is required by plants for photosynthesis and as a result plants release oxygen, which is required by humans, into the air.

Source

Although all plants contain sugar in some form, two plants in particular are the source of refined sugar: sugar cane (a gigantic grass resembling bamboo) and sugar beet (a root vegetable). There is no difference between the two once they have been refined.

Quality

Quality values in relation to sugar are dependent on the view of the user and the purpose the sugar serves. On the one hand the refining process may improve quality, if purity is a major concern, whilst on the other hand if naturalness, colour and flavour are sought then the refining process will detract from quality. It is necesssary to determine the function sugar is to serve before specifying quality requirements. Some types of catering may require the purchase of several types.

Processing

A sweet liquid is extracted from the cane by crushing and from beet by soaking. The liquid is then heated and crystals are allowed to form. Raw, brown sugar crystals are removed from the remaining syrup (molasses). The raw brown sugar is further refined to produce white crystals. The white crystals are then sieved and graded as granulated or castor. Icing sugar requires further milling and cube sugar is moistened and pressed into shape.

Function in cookery

Apart from its obvious role as a sweetener sugar serves a variety of functions. If caramelised it can be used to colour and flavour both sweet and savoury dishes. When used in baking, it functions as an activator for yeast products, as a tenderiser to disperse protein through gluten and keep the gluten soft, and as a lightener when creaming/aerating with fat. It also acts as an anti-coagulant, helping to delay the coagulation of egg dishes, for example, custards. Sugar provides adhesive strength, together with the protein (egg white) in meringue. It helps retain moisture in cakes and, as has already been mentioned, serves as an important preservative.

Purchasing specifications

Sugar may be purchased in a variety of forms for different purposes, for example:

- castor;
- granulated;
- preserving sugar;
- icing;
- cube;
- coffee crystals;
- demerara;
- barbados;
- syrup;
- fondant;
- molasses;
- treacle.

Price may be related to sugar type, therefore consider carefully how sugar is to be used and control its use once purchased. Ask, for example, whether castor sugar is essential; would granulated sugar suffice?

Storage, hygiene and health

Keep sugar in sealed containers in a cool, dry, well-ventilated store.

Profitable usage

Although it is difficult to assess sugar alone as a profit-generating item, it is obviously an important contributor to two of the menu's most profitable areas, namely sweets and beverages. For this reason, it is worth selecting and using sugars and sweeteners with care. Pay particular attention to the effect of sugar on the finished product (i.e. the difference between the use of castor and granulated sugar in a fine pastry product) and to the merchandising value of special sugars (including coloured crystals) to enhance coffee sales.

TEA

In the mid-1980s tea declined in sales, but since then there has been an upsurge due mainly to a revival of interest in the variety of quality, speciality blends. Tea bags have now become an accepted medium (85 per cent of caterers now use tea bags). Once considered to contain only the poorest quality brew, tea bags can now include the best blends, with consistent quality and, above all, affording easy and accurate portion control.

Source

India, China, Ceylon (Sri Lanka), Indonesia, Kenya and East Africa are all tea-exporting countries.

Tea is produced from the leaves of a bush, Camellia sinensis, which was originally native to China and was imported into India. India now produces the bulk (30 per cent) of the world's tea. Pruning, for ease of picking, gives the tree a bush-like appearance.

Quality

The flavour and quality of tea depends on the variety, soil and climate conditions, and is also influenced by the method of processing. The best tea is obtained from the buds and new leaf growth.

Although the wide variety of strengths, blends and flavours can make the selection of the ideal tea difficult, there is a grading system for quality promoted by the Tea Council (see Figure 8.2).

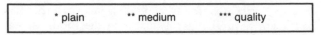

* plain	** medium	*** quality

Figure 8.2   *The Tea Council star system*

Orange pekoe is the largest leaf and dust the very smallest (see Figure 8.3). Large leaves brew slowly; small leaves brew quickly and are often used in tea bags.

The quality of the final brew is also affected by the water (hard or soft) and the type, condition and cleanliness of boiling and brewing equipment (china, aluminium or stainless steel).

Processing

Tea leaves may be green (dried immediately), oolong (half-fermented) or black (fully-fermented and oxidised). The leaves may then be sold as a specific variety or, more commonly, various leaves are carefully mixed to produce a particular blend.

Purchasing units and specifications

Loose tea may be purchased in anything from 14 g ½ oz) packs up to 45 kg (100 lb) foil-lined chests. Tea bags may be purchased in a wide variety of unit/pack sizes including 20, 50, 100 and 250 portion packs.

Tea may be purchased by reference to:

- country of origin;
- region/variety;
- colour – green, oolong or black;
- blend;
- brand.

Tea may also be flavoured with flowers or essential oils, for example, jasmine, mint, cinnamon, camomile and lime.

Leaf	Broken leaf	Smaller leaf
Orange pekoe	Broken orange pekoe	Orange fannings
Pekoe	Broken pekoe	Fannings
Souchong		Dust

Figure 8.3   *Quality of tea as indicated by leaf size*

Storage, hygiene and health

Tea must be stored in a clean, dry, airtight container in a well-ventilated, dry store away from excess moisture and strong-smelling foods.

Profitable usage

Tea, carefully produced and controlled, has to be just about the most profitable item that can appear on any caterer's menu, although not all caterers offer tea. Even at modest prices a gross profit of 75 per cent should be achievable and for many operations it should be over 90 per cent.

COFFEE

Most customers consider coffee to be of significant importance in their enjoyment of a meal. The trend is towards offering a wider variety of blends and methods. Even the best coffee is potentially a highly-profitable item on any menu. There is no need to serve cheap alternatives.

To meet growing demand, the caterer is faced with a wide variety of blends to choose from. Choice of blend is dependent on individual taste, influenced by the customer.

An understanding of the range of beans, blends and various preparation processes involved may make the purchase decision easier.

Source

Brazil and Columbia produce the bulk of the world's coffee, but other important sources include Indonesia, Kenya, Jamaica and East Africa.

Coffee is obtained from a tree (bush) bearing cherry-like fruit containing two seeds (beans). There are two specific types of bean, arabica (native to Ethiopia, but now grown in various parts of the world) and robusta. Arabica beans grow best in highland regions; robusta are more suited to tropical lowlands.

Quality

Coffee quality is related to a number of factors including plant species, soil condition, climate and processing method. In particular, the degree of roasting influences the final flavour of the coffee. Light-roast results in a mild flavour which is popular as a breakfast blend; dark-roast develops a more substantial, bitter flavour which is more suited to dinner.

Coffee will lose flavour during storage. Once roasted and ground it should be used as quickly as possible, certainly within ten days. Similarly, coffee starts to lose its flavour soon after it has been brewed and can turn bitter if kept hot for more than 20 minutes.

Processing

The flesh is removed from the fruit revealing two beans which are cleaned, dried and graded. The 'green' beans may then be:

- roasted;
- ground (fresh or vacuum packed);
- brewed and dried as powder or freeze-dried granules;
- brewed and reduced to an essence (often flavoured with chicory).

Purchasing specifications

- By bean – arabica or robusta;
- By roast – low, medium, full (high), continental;
- By blend – French (chicory), Viennese (figs), breakfast (mild), dinner (strong);
- By process – instant powder, AFD granules, whole beans, ground beans, vending packs;
- By method – jug, cafetiere/plunger, filter, French drip pot/Neopolitan pot, espresso, percolator, cona.

Fresh coffee may be coarse or fine-ground to suit the particular needs of the brewing method, for example:
- course-ground – jug;
- medium-ground – plunger, cona or cafetiere;
- fine-ground – filter, drip or espresso;
- pulverised – Turkish.

Storage

Once purchased, coffee should be stored in an airtight container in a well-ventilated, dry store.

Profitable usage

Beverages are important because, for most caterers, they account for a small proportion of purchase expenditure, but a large proportion of sales. Even using the finest ingredients, served in generous portions and at a reasonable price, should result in a gross profit of between 70–80 per cent. In many instances, gross profit margins will be even higher.

Bulk brewing used to be the norm, but the current trend is towards a fresh, individual brew in individual pots with correct brewing techniques.

The trend towards espresso and cappuccino coffees can mean a high capital investment in machinery, but this is often recovered through the premium price that customers will pay for these products.

For both the caterer and the customer the multi-portion 'pour over' filter coffee, remains one of the more popular methods. When offering a selection of coffees, individual cafetiere and portion 'lid' filters can be very cost-effective. Although they are more expensive (cafetiere being up to twice the cost of pour over and individual filters as much as three times), they have the advantage of reducing waste and giving a fresh brew and greater choice for each customer.

Whatever the method of brewing, the caterer may be tempted with offers of 'free', on-loan brewing equipment which is most commonly tied to the purchase of a particular brand of coffee. Such offers can prove to be very beneficial to the caterer, but careful consideration of the terms and conditions is necessary before making any commitment. If the caterer's purchases are restricted to the one particular supplier then the opportunity to respond to other offers is lost. Also to be considered are the price (of the coffee), quality and service offered by such a supplier. The caterer will undoubtedly pay above the odds for the coffee, but in doing so may achieve consistent quality, and reliable deliveries and servicing of equipment.

Caterers should consider the promotion of their most profitable menu item, beverages. Sales and profits may be further improved by offering a coffee/tea menu, describing the characteristics of each blend on offer.

LEGISLATION

The following is a list of the relevant acts and regulations:

The Food (Control of Irradiation) Regulations 1990;
The Food Safety Act 1990;
The Food Labelling (Amendment) Regulations 1990;
The Food and Environmental Protection Act 1985;
The Food Act 1984;
The Food Labelling Regulations 1984;
The Bread and Flour Regulations 1984;
The Imported Foods Regulations 1984;
The Meat Products and Spreadable Fish Products Regulations 1984;
The Sweeteners in Food Regulations 1983;
The Emulsifiers and Stabilisers in Food Regulations 1980;
The Miscellaneous Additives in Food Regulations 1980;
The Preservatives in Food Regulations 1979;
The Coffee and Coffee Products Regulations 1978;
The Condensed Milk and Dried Milk Regulations 1977;
The Cocoa and Chocolate Regulations 1976;
The Food (Control of Irradiation) Regulations 1967;
The Ice Cream Regulations 1967;
The Liquid Egg (Pasteurisation) Regulations 1963;
The Ice Cream (Heat Treatment, etc) Regulations 1959;
The Food Standards (General Provisions) Order 1944.

Summary

It is now recognised that in many types of catering, new problems, especially those of increased labour cost, may be countered by the greater use of products packed in ready-to-use form. Increasing food cost engenders ever-increasing concern with tight specifications, portion control and use of convenience alternatives.

Consideration of convenience and grocery purchases may be influenced by the type of supply channel (as discussed in Chapter 4). Canned goods are primarily distributed by wholesalers; frozen and fully prepared foods by manufacturers; and dry foods are predominantly wholesale, but a growing proportion are obtained direct from the manufacturer. The greatest level of convenience may derive from the one-drop supply, where a range of products can be ordered and delivered together, thus making smaller purchase quantities of some products more viable.

No doubt the debate about the relative merits of fresh and convenience foods will continue. How fresh is fresh? Most frozen produce is now packed and in the deep freeze within two to three hours. Fresh food may be several days old by the time it gets to the kitchen. Some nutrients are lost during processing, but appearance and texture may be of greater importance than nutritional content for some caterers. The caterer should not forget to consider customers' perceptions – would they recognise or accept fresh peas. Whether we like it or not our customers' palates have become attuned to such items as frozen peas.

The specification of grocery and convenience products can be difficult. Unit sizes vary considerably, making cost comparisons difficult. Inspection on delivery is restricted to examining packaging and packet labels; the testing of actual product quality before accepting delivery becomes impossible. Products are often identified by brand name and assumptions are made about quality. Constant vigilance is required in order to maintain standards and ensure that brand-name products continue to meet requirements. Grocery and convenience products may often be purchased by fixed-term contract. Contract periods should be limited (six to 12 months) and products need to be re-tested before renewal of the contract.

Despite the problems that exist, the proportion of convenience foods used by most caterers is likely to continue increasing. However, as demand for convenience products increases so should competition among food manufacturers, leading to increasing product quality.

Control, Procedure and Documentation

> The basic function of control is to protect the operation's assets through:
> - physical security of raw materials;
> - documentation of transactions and movement of materials;
> - accurate costing and pricing.

Control is ensuring that what was intended to happen actually happens.

Raw materials are purchased with the express intention of providing a return on investment (profit). Control systems are concerned with the provision of suitable facilities, equipment and manpower to prevent loss and minimise investment, thus ensuring optimum profit.

OBJECTIVES OF CONTROL

There are four main objectives:
- to prevent spoilage;
- to deter pilferage;
- to prevent fraud or theft;
- to avoid duplication or excessive stock holding.

Spoilage

This can occur for a variety of reasons. For example, stock is held too long due to over-ordering, the stock is not rotated, i.e. old stock is used before fresh or the correct environmental conditions are not being maintained.

Pilferage

In some catering establishments losses due to staff eating or drinking on duty are regarded as inevitable or a perk of the job. This should not be the case. Other industries, notably the retail industry, have been successful in implementing policies to reduce pilferage. The catering industry can also introduce similarly effective controls so long as conditions of employment, including entitlement to meals, are clearly defined.

Fraud and theft

This refers to the physical removal of funds or goods from the premises by anyone not permitted to do so. This need not be due to the premises being broken into. The thief may be someone employed by the establishment or a tradesperson making deliveries. Desirability of cash and/or raw materials, transferability and ease of disposal only serve to increase the risk of fraud or theft.

> Wastage or loss of raw materials can occur in any or all of the following ways:
> - careless buying or ordering;
> - lack of honest supervision on receipt of the goods;
> - unsuitable storage facilities;
> - unauthorised issues from stores;
> - inappropriate methods of production;
> - over-production, resulting from poor forecasting;
> - lack of portion control;
> - inefficient utilisation of surplus requirements;
> - theft.

Efficiency and effectiveness of control is dependent on three main elements:

- facilities and equipment;
- personnel – responsibility, skill, training and honesty;
- handling procedures and documentation (see Figure 9.1 overleaf).

FACILITIES AND EQUIPMENT

All the care and attention paid to purchasing will be to no avail if goods are stored incorrectly. In this respect, the caterer must clearly identify the objectives of storage and ensure that these are met.

Planning and layout of the stores should be influenced by the flow of materials: receiving and checking deliveries, storage of goods, disposal of waste, control of issues and method of recording and documentation.

> Ideally, the stores area should be on the same level as the delivery area and the food production area. Where possible, stores should be close to the main user. Windows provide access for both sunlight and intruders, so should be avoided. Air conditioning (filtered), temperature and humidity controls help to provide a clean, dry and well-ventilated environment. The size and type of store depend on the particular style of operation and the size and frequency of deliveries.

In general, storage space for a restaurant should be about 0.5 m² (5 ft²) per cover and for a hotel 1.5 m² (15 ft²) per room. This will vary from sector to sector. Fast-food operators, for instance, typically have a small storage area for the volume of trade they are doing. They rely on frequent delivery of a limited range of goods in order to reduce stock levels and improve controlability.

There should be adequate space within the stores for making up orders and issues to the various departments. Similar materials should be grouped together and the most frequently-used items should be stored in the most convenient positions.

Space is also taken up by waste, particularly empty boxes, paper and so on. Many catering establishments have waste compactors to solve this problem. Compacting waste has two additional advantages:

- preventing theft by crushing up waste materials that could otherwise be used for hiding goods;
- if waste is sorted (paper, glass) it may be sold, thus providing additional income to offset sorting and compacting costs.

Ventilation

Adequate ventilation helps to maintain temperature levels, and reduce humidity and odours that might taint foodstuffs.

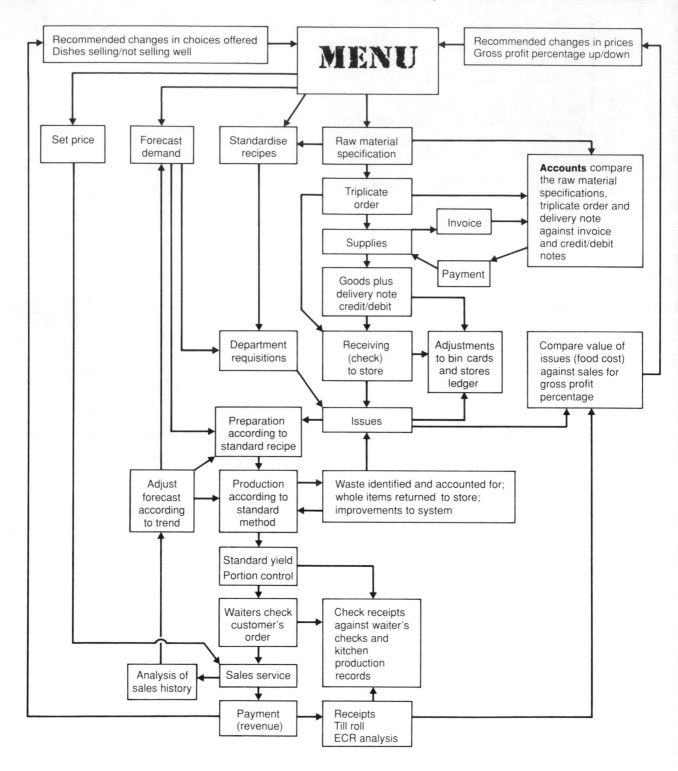

Figure 9.1 *Stock and cash control – handling procedure and documentation*

Lighting

Although direct sunlight should be avoided, the area should be well-lit. The multitude of racks and shelves inherent in a storage facility frequently create dark corners which can cause accidents and could provide the opportunity for theft.

Shelving

Access to shelves should ideally be from both sides and shelves should not touch walls. Adjustable shelf heights provide flexibility, but the bottom shelf should be at least 20 cm from the floor and the top shelf should not be above eye level unless proper steps are available.

The best storage facilities are flexible, that is they use strong, mobile shelving which is easy to dismantle for cleaning. Racks which provide for the circulation of air are preferable for perishables (fruit and vegetables). If bins are used for cereals and pulses, they should be on wheels. Sufficient surplus containers should be available to ensure regular, frequent, cleaning and to avoid the temptation to tip new stock on top of old.

Insulation

Stores should not be located near heat sources or hot areas such as boiler rooms or extraction ducting from the kitchen. All hot pipes, if they run through storage areas, should be insulated. Measures should be taken to reduce damp and condensation.

Safety

Shelves should be secure and good practices employed. These include not storing heavy items on high shelves, limiting the top shelf height to 1.8 m, providing suitable equipment for the movement of stock (trolleys), having adequate aisle widths and keeping the stores clean and tidy.

Hygiene

Good hygiene practice begins with the use of well-designed, easy-to-clean materials for shelving, floors and walls, which greatly assist the cleaning and hygiene of the stores area. The hygienic handling of raw material resources is further aided by a sound understanding of the causes of food deterioration and food poisoning.

Insects and vermin

Rats, mice, cockroaches, flies, ants, wasps and bees all conspire to transfer bacteria. The ever-vigilant storeperson will look for signs of damage, gnawing and droppings. The catering manager must ensure that sufficient funds are provided to maintain the fabric of the building and to prevent access to vermin.

Low-temperature storage

Refrigeration and deep-freeze facilities are generally used for the storage of wet products, meat, fish and dairy produce. There should be adequate refrigeration and deep-freezer space to ensure emptying and cleaning according to planned schedules. Where possible, use commodity-specific chilled and refrigerated cabinets and freezers, i.e. a fish fridge, a cooked meat cabinet and an ice cream deep-freeze. It is imperative that raw and cooked foods are separated.

Refrigeration and low temperature storage should conform to the following criteria in order to ensure correct storage conditions. Refrigerators or coolers hold the temperature at between 3–4°C with a minimum of 0°C. Fresh meat, fish and dairy products should be held at this temperature. For long-term storage, fresh fruit and vegetables can be held in coolers at a slightly higher temperature of about 8°C (although care should be taken with some items, for example, bananas and avocados, where chilling may speed discolouration).

Freezer units should maintain a temperature between −23°C to −17°C. If frozen food is allowed to reach a temperature of −5°C, even though it has not thawed, as such, its storage life may be reduced. Food, particularly protein items, should be well-protected if damage through freezer-burn is to be prevented. Once damage or loss of quality has occurred it cannot be restored or reversed. An equipment breakdown or even a thermostat malfunction could result in several hundred pounds worth of spoiled goods. Equipment should be serviced regularly by experts, and in the case of refrigeration regular and properly conducted defrosting should take place.

Hard-surfaced, easily-cleaned, non-porous fixtures, floors and walls are essential. Walk-in fridges and freezers should have smooth floors, be well-lit and have an interior door lock release.

PERSONNEL

Experts would argue that physical security of stock is little use if staff are dishonest. Management should try to ensure that only honest staff are employed. As well as being honest, the personnel responsible for receiving, storing and issuing goods must be competent. In smaller units it is often the chef who carries out these functions. It is in the chef's own interest to effectively control commodities as performance is usually measured by ability to achieve the desired level of gross profit.

One of the most important aspects of control is to separate the functions of ordering and receiving in order to prevent any possible fraud.

In larger operations there will be stores personnel with responsibility for these functions. In these circumstances it is common to have rigid rules concerning access to stores areas, requisitions for goods (all of which should be in writing on the correct form) and set times for the issue of goods. Specifically, the storekeeper should be conscientious, sharp-witted and knowledgeable, both in relation to the raw materials handled and the principles and procedures of control and book-keeping.

The duties and responsibilities of a storekeeper are to:

- check deliveries against copy order and delivery note;
- transfer goods to stores and amend the bin cards;
- write up the goods received book;
- on receipt of invoice, check against delivery note and copy order, check prices and calculations, and enter onto stock record cards;
- pass invoice, if correct, to accounts for payment and entry into purchases day book;
- issue goods to departments only on receipt of an authorised requisition and amend the bin cards accordingly;
- prepare issues analysis from the requisitions and pass to the kitchen manager for statistical reports and analysis, and comparison with income (sales).

A manager and the kitchen staff, once aware of the purpose of kitchen records and control, can apply them more effectively. Far from being hostile to staff interests, control tends to reassure staff by creating confidence in management, increasing staff awareness of costs and improving their morale. Most staff like to do a good job. Effective management made manifest through businesslike control engenders confidence, a readiness to accept responsibility and discourages the weaker staff from malpractices.

HANDLING AND DOCUMENTATION

Kitchen records and control procedures are designed for practical purposes. Keeping accounts is a practical activity, registering business progress and helping to adjust it. So a chef must attach importance to records,

albeit simple ones, which are necessary within the department.

In summary, within kitchens and food stores, the purpose of records is to:

- ensure incoming goods accord in quantity and quality with what was actually ordered;
- record the receipt of such goods to ensure their safe custody;
- control the movement of goods both from stores to sections requisitioning them, and from kitchen to other outlets;
- enable the cost of goods consumed (food cost) to be compared with the corresponding food sales figure;
- prevent or limit losses through deterioration, carelessness and pilferage.

Procedures may vary but the following basic steps are usual in keeping a record of goods received and issued (see also Chapter 4).

Ordering goods

Order from suppliers on a printed, serially-numbered, triplicate order form (see Figure 9.2):

- the top copy is for the tradesperson;
- a second copy goes to the stores to authorise subsequent reception of goods and to provide for checks on weight and quality on arrival;
- the third copy is usually sent to control or accounts office for comparison with the supplier's invoice (when that arrives) to ensure that payment is made only for goods actually ordered and received.

Ordering of goods by telephone is fairly common practice, especially in regard to fresh produce delivered daily. An order form must be made out immediately and sent as confirmation of the order, a facsimile (fax) machine would provide the most immediate response.

Receipt of goods

The importance of the goods-receiving procedure is easily under-estimated. The difficulty of making good sales from bad purchase is well-known. Commodities which do not match specification make kitchen production, quality control and profit maintenance harder. Other forms of loss also have to be prevented and as soon as goods are received and checked they should be stored correctly and away from risk of loss, damage or pilferage. In small operations, receiving can be done by owners or managers. In larger units, responsibility may be delegated, usually to a stores or control clerk. Many operations leave the checking of stores to anyone who happens to be available. Deliveries are frequently unchecked even when the delivery note (see Figure 9.3) is signed, usually as a result of pressure of work or to get the deliveryperson out of the way.

Deliverypeople are busy, they will want to dump and run. They and their employer, the supplier, must

Specimen order form

(Name and address of establishment)

Order Form

Serial number: .... Date: ....

To: (Name of supplier)
Please supply on (insert date and time delivery required) the following:

Description	Quantity	£	p

Signed: ....
Chef de Cuisine
or Authorised Deputy

Note: The quantity column is always provided; a money column is often useful.

Figure 9.2 *Order form*

Reference number ....

Delivery Note

Name and address of supplier

Delivered to:

As per order number .... Date: ....

Quantity unit/case	Item description	Unit price	Total value

Delivered by .... Total ______

Received by ....

Figure 9.3 *Delivery note*

> Suspicion of malpractice:
> - the driver in a rush;
> - the driver who always arrives at your busiest period.

be reminded that a certain level of service is expected and that no responsibility for goods will be accepted until the delivery has been thoroughly checked and the delivery note duly signed. Staff checking deliveries should be trained to do so quickly and efficiently, without being pressurised by the deliveryperson. All unsealed items should be checked and weighed.

> Check deliveries using the following details (match copy of order to delivery note):
> - quantity – numerical measurement of units, weight or volume;
> - unit – the trade pack, single container, case, unit of weight or unit of volume;
> - description – qualification of the nature and quality of the goods, such as trade or brand name;
> - price – the unit cost value at which it was desired to purchase the commodity.

Supervision during receipt of deliveries should ensure that:

- the receiver is competent and authorised, (normally only one person should be authorised to receive deliveries).
- the receiver is familiar with the purchase specifications.
- the receiving area is large enough and properly equipped, for example, there are a set of scales, a sink (to remove ice from fish, etc.) and a hand basin.

- goods are inspected, weighed and counted to ensure against – commodities not matching specifications, excess fat on meat, excess dirt in potato sacks, colour and crispness of vegetables, salads and fruits; short weight or count (possible pilferage); damage or deterioration, blown cans, broken packs, pests or contamination.
- goods are promptly brought into the store in order to deter pilferage and prevent deterioration.

If, for any reason, goods cannot be unpacked on arrival, the delivery note should be annotated 'contents unknown' before signing.

> **Blind receiving**
> Blind receiving can be a useful system. The stores receiving clerk is issued with a list showing only what goods are expected. The receiver therefore has to check (weigh/count) every item in order to be able to enter the delivery into the goods received book. The system has been shown to improve the quality of the checking procedure.

Loss or damage of delivery

If on checking, goods are missing or damaged, then the supplier and carrier must be notified immediately. In most cases, supplier and carrier are one and the same person, and the situation can be easily remedied. If a separate carrier is involved then a claim will have to be raised against the carrier concerned, usually within three days, in order that liability can be assessed. The Sale of Goods Act 1893, includes provision regarding transfer of ownership. This is important in determining who bears any loss. Most contracts in catering specify the supplier as responsible for delivery of goods to the buyer's premises, but once on the latter's premises ownership and responsibility is transferred to the buyer.

To avoid deliveries at the wrong time and when no one is on duty for checking, insert time and place of delivery onto the order. This then becomes a condition of the contract with which the supplier must conform. The supplier would suffer subsequently any loss if goods are left in the wrong place or at the wrong time (i.e .when stores are shut or staff are not on duty). Lack of control in goods receiving is quickly noted by any potential thief.

It is helpful to caterers if a supplier prices all delivery notes. The goods received book can then be used as a check against the invoice which usually arrives after the goods.

Chargeable containers

Containers such as casks, cases and bottles are often chargeable. Money can be lost if chargeable containers are not properly controlled. A return and empties book should be kept for this purpose. Containers may be returned via regular carriers, a suitable comment being added to the delivery note, and a credit note raised by the supplier.

Invoices

Once the goods have been delivered the supplier will send an invoice, which is the document that asks for payment.

The main difference between a delivery note and an invoice (see Figures 9.3 and 9.4) is that the invoice shows the amount due. Some suppliers, in order to reduce paperwork and overhead costs, use only one document which is a combined delivery note and invoice, and is given to the purchaser at the time of delivery. In certain cases, the delivery note will

Reference number ....

Invoice

Name and address of supplier

____

____

Account to: ________________

____

____

Previous Balance ________

Delivery note ref.	Date	Quantity unit/case	Item description	Unit price	Total value

Total ________

Discount ________

Less payment received ________

Balance due ________

Figure 9.4 *Invoice*

contain prices, but the invoice will not be sent out until the month end. This is most common in the case of daily deliveries of fresh foods where there will be daily changes to market prices. The manager, through the storekeeper, will need to keep an accurate account.

Invoices when received should be sent directly to accounts or the control office. Occasionally, an invoice may arrive before the goods. Care must be taken not to process this document until the goods are received and checked. In the accounts or control office, invoices will be married to the office copy of the original order and matched against the certified delivery note. Prices can then be checked as well as the calculations on the invoice. Normally invoices are summarised (see Figure 9.5 overleaf) on a daily basis by the accounts office and when checked are entered into the account of the respective supplier. Payment is usually made on a monthly basis.

Invoices Summary

Date	Supplier	Invoice serial no.	Amount £	Amount p	Order no.	Remarks

Figure 9.5   *Invoices summary*

Credit/debit notes

In cases where the purchaser returns goods to the supplier, the supplier may well send out a credit note (see Figure 9.6). Credit notes are checked against goods return notes to see that they agree with regard

Credit Note

Reference number . . . .

Name and address of supplier
_____
_____

Delivered to: _____
_____
_____

Date . . . .

Quantity unit/case	Item description	Unit price	Total value

Authorised by . . . .   Credit value _____

Figure 9.6   *Credit note*

Debit Note

Reference number . . . .

Name and address of supplier
_____

To the account of: _____
_____
_____

Date . . . .

Detail	Value

Total _____

Authorised by . . . .

Figure 9.7   *Debit note*

to both quantity and price. If, for any reason, the caterer accepts additional goods, not shown on the delivery note, then a debit note (see Figure 9.7) should be raised by the supplier or representative, the deliveryperson.

Payment

The caterer will pay the supplier according to mutually-agreed terms. This may be upon receipt of the invoice, once per month or upon receipt of a regular statement of account. Such statements should be checked against invoices, delivery notes and credit/debit notes.

Documentation must be accompanied by supervision, for even after careful receipt procedures, goods may still sustain losses through:

- theft from stores;
- deterioration owing to poor physical conditions;
- depredation by pests (rodents and insects);
- faulty control and issues without requisitions.

The storekeeper's paperwork

- Bin cards – to show quantities in stock (Figure 9.8);
- Stores ledger – quantities plus prices (Figure 9.9);
- Stores requisitions – record authorised issues (Figure 9.10);
- Stock transfer notes – record authorised movement;
- Stock return notes – record unused items;
- Triplicate order – request to purchase goods (Figure 9.2);
- Supplier delivery note – details of items delivered (Figure 9.3);
- Credit/debit note – details of items credited/debited (Figures 9.6 and 9.7);
- Container record – identify movement of chargeable containers;
- Purchase invoice – payment due (Figure 9.4).

Goods received and stock records

As well as dealing with documentation sent by suppliers, the storekeeper is also required to maintain stock records. This varies from unit to unit and there is a growing trend for all stores records to be computerised. Nonetheless, a simple system traditionally used in the catering industry is to record daily supplies in a goods received book, maintain bin cards of all stock items, and issue goods to departments only on receipt of a written requisition. Records of movements of stock in and out of stores will be recorded in a stores ledger.

A goods received record may be loose-leaf sheets or a bound book with duplicate copies. The purpose of this record is to identify what actual goods were received on any given day. This can assist in establishing the shelf life of goods, turnover of stock, stock levels and so on. Although we have assumed that the storekeeper deals with all documentation mentioned so far, it is not unusual for the control office to handle all invoices, credit notes and statements. The storekeeper would forward to this office all delivery notes and goods return notes. The goods received book and the stores ledger, together with bin cards, may be the only documentation held and maintained by the storekeeper.

Where bin cards (see Figure 9.8) are maintained and entries are made as goods are issued or received, the bin card should, at any given time, show the running (current) balance. Originally the bin cards were kept with the 'bin' which was the place of storage for an item, such as a wine rack, a shelf or a container. Now it is more common for bin cards to be found in a loose-leaf folder or as a file held on computer record. This, to a certain extent, defeats the purpose of a bin card which was to provide a quick, visual check between recorded stock movement and actual stock held. For this reason, many traditionalists still retain the old system (often in tandem with modern developments).

Bin Card

Commodity:

Date	Receipt or issue voucher no.	Received	Issued	Balance

Minimum/maximum stocks ....

Figure 9.8 *Bin card*

Where stock cards are used, balancing of individual cards may be done at the end of each day.

Generally, both bin cards and stock cards are concerned with, and show, quantities only. Calculating the value of receipts and issues is, as a rule, done in the control or accounts office. The chef's and/or storekeeper's first duty is to account for the quantities entrusted to them.

A stock book (stores ledger) recording both quantities and values helps in calculating the value of

Stores Ledger

Item . . . .

Unit size . . . .

Maximum stock level   . . . .

Minimum stock level   . . . .

Re-order level   . . . .

Date	Supplier	Delivery reference	Department	Requisition number	Quantity			Unit price	Value
					Received	Issued	Balance		

Note: This type of information may now be stored, by many caterers, on a computer running a spreadsheet program.

Figure 9.9   *Stores ledger*

goods issued and in calculating the gross profit percentage, either on a daily or a weekly basis (see Figure 9.9).

A storekeeper, on completing work on the bin/stock cards, can pass requisitions to the accounts office to be priced in order to control the value of goods transferred to the kitchen. An alternative method is the triplicate system of requisition – one copy to go to the accounts office, one copy to remain in stores and the third to be returned, with the goods issued, to the requisitioning department. There is then no delay in passing requisitions from stores to accounts. A system may also regulate the return of goods from kitchen to stores which would involve the use of a stores returned form to record both quantities and values. This practice should be discouraged in favour of more accurate ordering, based on reliable forecasts. The risk of malpractice will be in proportion to the frequency of movement of goods.

If an operation's size is sufficient to justify it, a kitchen clerk can control goods received into the kitchen, both by direct delivery and through the stores, as well as transfers of finished products to the restaurant/banqueting departments. Details of the daily value of goods issued to the kitchen from stores can be passed to the clerk from the accounts office.

Details on a requisition include:

- requisition number (sequence);
- date;
- department requisitioning;
- quantity;
- description (accurate);
- authorised signature (legible);
- receiver's signature.

Space may also be included for stock codes and bin numbers, and calculations of unit and total values.

Issuing goods to departments

Usually on a daily basis, at a specified time of the day, goods will be issued from the stores to the various departments. To order goods from stores each department will be required to complete a requisition (see Figure 9.10). Every requisition must be signed by an authorised person, such as the Head Chef or Restaurant Manager. Such orders are usually written in duplicate, one copy going to stores and one being retained by the department.

Requisitions should be specific in detail, especially where there may be variations in size and type of product. For example, canned peaches can come in A1, A2.5, or A10 tins; be whole, in halves, sliced, diced or pulp; and be in syrup, in water, in fruit juice or in a solid pack.

Within the total control system, issued goods have to be valued or costed. The relatively simple records kept in the kitchen or kitchen stores are a base for evaluation and further control. Strict control is kept over the issue of requisition books. Pages should be numbered sequentially and a record kept as to which department has been issued with which range of numbers. No unauthorised issues should be made from the storeroom and only authorised staff should have access to it. Responsibility for a storeroom must be assigned to a storekeeper or a named person. If unauthorised access to stores is allowed, then it is unrealistic to expect any one person to accept responsibility as a storekeeper.

Specimen internal requisition form (duplicate pad)

Serial No: 43881

[Name of establishment]

Internal Requisition

From section ...... (e.g., Saucier) Date: ....

Please supply:

Stock code	Item	Quantity required	Value
0004	Butter (unsalted)	2 kg	
0001	Milk	1 l	
0007	Eggs	30	
		Total value	

Signed ....

Section ....

Received by ....

Note: Always Z a requisition to prevent fradulent insertion of additional items.

Figure 9.10 *Internal requisition*

EFFECTIVE CONTROL

The best method of control is often the simplest. A good stock-control system will provide for control over the movement of materials, and over the level of stock holding and stock records from which information can be easily extracted.

Design and implementation of a suitable system is unique to each operation but the most successful systems are based on the identification and understanding of critical control points (CCPs).

Critical control points (CCPs) and the production cycle

- Purchasing – accurate forecasts and specifications.
- Receiving – observation and documentation.
- Issuing – standard recipes and requisitions.
- Preparation – standard recipes and accurate scales.
- Cooking – standard methods, recipes and yields.
- Holding – temperature control and batch cooking.
- Service – standard procedures and portion control.
- Payment (revenue) – analysis.

COST CONTROL

In its simplest form, cost control involves the calculation of totals for each requisition and the summation of daily/weekly totals in a stores ledger. This assists in identifying where and how the financial resources of the operation have been spent and whether or not they have been spent wisely. It can be useful to break down expenditure under various headings, for example, meat, fish, fruit and vegetables, and record headings as percentages of the total cost for comparison purposes (see Figure 9.11).

Stock levels are an important factor in the cost control and profitability of an organisation. If the stock level is too high the organisation is likely to be wasteful, capital will be tied up unnecessarily and probably with a loan at a high interest rate. There is more likely to be deterioration, particularly of perishables.

	Opening stock	Add (net) purchases	Total	Less closing stock	Consumption	% total consumption	Budget	+ Variance	− Variance
Consumption of Provisions									
– – – – – ended – – – – –									
Meat									
Poulty									
Fish									
Ham/bacon									
Vegetables									
Fruit									
Groceries									
Tea									
Coffee									
Ice cream									
Cheese									

Food sales
Consumption _____
Gross profit _____

Gross profit percentage _____

Figure 9.11   *Consumption record*

Space will be allocated for storage that might well be more profitably used for other activities. Extra stock-taking will be required and the risk of pilferage will be high.

On the other hand, if stock levels are too low there are more likely to be unnecessary changes in routine. It may be necessary to pay more for extra deliveries. Management of the organisation is likely to be determined by crisis rather than by objectives. Consequently, there will be a greater proportion of dissatisfied customers.

The remedy is simple. Be aware of the changes in taste and eating habits, identify the demand for each commodity and assess the availability of raw materials. Calculate the lead time and speed of delivery, and fix minimum and maximum stock levels in order to calculate the ideal re-order levels based on product shelf-life for each commodity. The minimum/maximum stock and re-order levels should be recorded on the bin card. The whole of this activity could be computerised. Both ordering and holding stock costs money; a balance must be achieved between frequent orders of small deliveries and the cost of holding large stores over long periods.

Stocktaking

Stocktaking is a time-consuming and expensive task. In complex businesses, stock will be found in several different locations – stores, stillroom, larder and kitchen – and this complicates the stocktaking task. The large number of locations where stocks are kept may result in clerical stocktaking errors.

The stocktaker's main objectives are:

- To establish, for each item – total purchase; average price (for purchase period); cost increase/decrease on previous period; opening stock, purchases and closing stock.
- To identify slow-moving items.
- To compare usage with sales.
- To deter loss, waste and fraud.
- To determine stock turnover for each group of items. The cost of stock consumed divided by average (cost) value of the stock equals the rate of stock turnover for the period.

Stocktaking discourages fraud as do random checks of stock, cash, deliveries, sales and personnel.

Correct stocktaking and accurate inventories are important, for faults may lead to under- or over-ordering. Stocktaking must take place at regular intervals and on a continuous basis. Normally a section of the stores is checked each week or month depending on the operation's size.

It is unwise to keep rigidly to a pattern of checking, the ability to predict how and when any particular stock item is to be checked might encourage dishonesty. Random spot checks are advisable. Discrepancies revealed in actual, as well as book, stock must be pursued to identify the date, approximate time and location of the fault's occurence, and a reason for the discrepancy sought.

Kitchen commodities are so numerous that a recording system can become cumbersome by having to provide for a multitude of entries. Grouping items into a logical and orderly manner is desirable both for stock-keeping purposes and also for physical storage on shelves, bins, fridges and freezers. Such arrangements may not obviate the need to record individual items but aid simplicity if there are defined commodity groups, such as fruit dried, fruit tinned and fruit frozen.

> Stock-care and stocktaking effectiveness may be aided by:
>
> - the layout of stores (design stock-sheets to match);
> - re-checking each count;
> - clear and accurate recording;
> - consistency in the use of units (avoid confusion between cans/cases/ kilos/pounds/dozens);
> - a logical (tidy) grouping of commodities;
> - reference to previous records.

Stocktaking helps reveal losses from store due to pilferage, deterioration or negligence. It is only necessary to compare the total value of issues from stores with the value of goods received, adjusted for opening and closing stocks. In other words, the value of issues should be equal to commencing stock plus stores received less final stock.

Reducing waste

So far, no attempt has been made to separate waste. It is important that waste is identified and accurately recorded for cost-control purposes.

Waste control

Several chapters in this book refer to the advantages of short menus. Shortness is an aid to control, for the fewer items there are the easier they are to track and check. This is especially so when using standard recipes which should always give the same yields. Even so, vigilance against excessive loss in preparation must never be relaxed. Convenience commodities, though apparently costing more, may be found more economical in being waste-free. Even where economies are not obtained as a result of using convenience products they are often chosen because they are easier to control.

Leaks and losses may be tracked through the number of portions prepared, served and left over. As previously observed, left-overs are undesirable. Apart from dishes unsold, plate waste should also be monitored and reasons sought for what is rejected. Excessive plate waste can usually be tracked to either poor standards of cookery and presentation or over-large portions. Within these two broad categories there are also specific faults of cookery, portioning and service to identify.

The food swill average is calculated to be about 200 g

(8 oz) for every three customers, although this may vary between different types of operation. So, occasional check-weighing of swill can be useful. Goods misappropriated and taken away from restaurants and hotels may be 'spirited' away via the swill or garbage bin. Food of apparently good quality may be found in the swill. This demands further investigation, especially if such items are found to be well-protected in double polythene bags. Supervised spot checks on swill will act as a deterrent in many cases.

As to food loss through dishonesty, the screening of staff carrying goods out and management's freedom to stop and search may nowadays be written into contracts of employment. Otherwise a personal search may be regarded as an infringement of staff rights. Screening is most easily facilitated by having all staff entering and leaving by the same door, for example, the time-keeper's office or back door. It is wise to insist that bags and carriers are not brought into the catering department, but deposited at the entry point. Over-large handbags and hold-alls are unnecessary, especially if the employer provides suitable washing and changing facilities and secure lockers.

Control of waste starts with the positive action of careful selection of menu items, menu monitoring and the elimination of unpopular items. Unsold food may be due to many causes – over-production, too wide a choice, vagaries of the weather and failure to note competing local events and attractions.

The reality of most kitchen operations is that waste occurs through over-production or poor portion control after stock has been written off by traditional, consumption-based systems. There is a movement from consumption-based stock control, with its high level of investment in an extensive range of stock items to cover any eventuality, towards purchase-control systems based on forecast demand and production levels. This development is aided by the use

Control Sheet (Larder)

Week: . . . .

| Item* | Weight or measure | | Day of the week | | | | | | | Totals | Balance |
			Sun.	Mon.	Tue.	Wed.	Thur.	Fri.	Sat.		
Lobster	Each	Received	—	12	—	17	—	—	—	29	
		Issued	—	4	5	3	4	—	—	16	13
Sole	kg (lb)	Received	—	—	—	—	40	24	—	64	
		Issued [continue, for each item required]	—	—	—	—	16	20	22	58	6

Note: * Fish, poultry, game, fruit, etc.

Figure 9.12   *Larder control sheet*

of computers which speed the analysis of figures, providing daily predictions.

Transition from consumption-based to production and purchase control systems is happening because expenditure has to be controlled through more efficient management information systems (computers) which allow for the input of raw data (supplies, stock levels, recipes and yield) and the output of production control, scheduling, purchasing and pricing information.

Management in large establishments commonly require control of costly items, even after their actual issue to the kitchen, particularly in the case of more expensive perishable foodstuffs handled in the larder and cold-rooms (see Figure 9.12).

If these basic records are kept accurately then it is possible for remaining kitchen records and calculations to be done outside the kitchen department. In certain operations, management policy may be to confine kitchen recording to such limits. Certainly, commodity control or safeguarding of stock is of over-riding importance in a catering operation and it is essential to support the control of input with an equally efficient control of output (sales and transfers). It is therefore necessary to consider further aspects, such as portion control and the control of issues to food service staff.

Care should be taken over documentary evidence and accounting records should be kept for several years. Entries into the goods received book and stores ledger provide a historical record and the totals required in analysis, such as the issues analysis sheet and the weekly invoice analysis sheet.

PHYSICAL CONTROL

As was discussed in Chapter 3, standardised recipes, yield and portion control form the basis for dish costing and pricing. Control is not possible without strict adherence to standardised recipes and accurate portioning. Accurate portioning cannot be maintained by paperwork and forms. It demands physical controls, which include:

- workable standard recipes, costed and re-costed, and rigorously applied;

- visual guides to plate and dish layouts;

- suitably-sized implements, ladles, serving spoons and serving dishes (see Table 9.1 overleaf);

- meat cuts, steaks, chops, escalopes and chicken portions, accurately weighed in the larder or purchased to preportioned specifications;

- skill, and effective training, in carving or in using slicing machines with demonstration servings arranged to cover a dinner plate;

- a clear distinction between table d'hôte and à la carte portions, where applicable. It may be useful to use different presentation styles to avoid confusion;

- regular, frequent control checks and feedback.

Table 9.1 Portion control equipment

Item	Application	Approximate
Baking dishes	Baked dishes	Sizes up to 40 cm (16 in.)
Butchers' knives	Raw meats	20 cm, 25 cm, 30 cm, 35 cm (8 in., 10 in., 12 in., 14 in.)
Butter pat machines	Butter pats	6 g (¼ oz) upwards
Casserole dishes	Stews and casseroles	225 g (8 oz)
Cheese cutters	Slicing cheese	Up to 30 slices per 450 g (1 lb)
Cooks' knives	Slicing meats etc.	20 cm, 25 cm, 30 cm, 35 cm (8 in., 10 in., 12 in., 14 in.)
Custard cups	Custards, trifles and fools	150 g, 175 g, 200 g (5 oz, 6 oz, 7 oz)
Disposables: foil cases	Entrée and pie dishes	Various
paper cups	Tea and coffee	200 ml, 225 ml (7 oz, 8 oz)
paper soufflé cases	Jams, sauces	14 ml to 142 ml (½ oz to 5 oz)
Extendable trellis cutter	Multi-cutting sweets	
Fruit and vegetables juice glasses	Appetisers	71 ml, 142 ml (2½ oz, 5 oz)
Hand and power slicers	Meats, bread and butter	Various
Individual creamers	Cream	28 ml, 71 ml (1 oz, 2½ oz)
Individual pie dishes	Meat and fruit pies	11 cm, 13 cm (4½ in. 5 in.)
Iron spoons	Stews, etc.	25 cm, 30 cm, 35 cm (10 in., 12 in., 14 in.)
Ladles	Sauces, soups	28 ml to 284 ml (1 oz to 10 oz)
Milk dispensers	For tea and coffee	21 ml and 284 ml (¾ oz and 10 oz measure)
Pastry markers	Pie-cut marking	6, 7, 8 cuts per pie
Perforated spoons	Vegetables (e.g. beans, peas)	33 cm (13 in.)
Pie tins	Baking pies	7.5 cm to 23 cm (3 in. to 9 in.)
Pudding basins	Puddings, meat and sweet	100 g to 1.35 kg (4 oz to 3 lb)
Pudding roll tins	Puddings	30 cm, 35 cm (12 in., 14 in.)
Ramekins	Ramekins and soufflés	54 g, 113 g (2¾ oz, 4½ oz)
Scoops	Ice cream, solid purées	12, 16, 20, 24, 30, 40, 60, scoop measures per 1½ litre (1 quart)
Small-weight scales	Portion weighing	12 g to 1.8 kg (½ oz to 4 lb)
Soup bowls	Soup	18 cm, 20 cm, 21 cm, 23 cm (7 in., 8 in., 8½ in., 9 in.)
Soup, fish, meat and entrée plates	Soup, fish, meat and entrées	18 cm, 20 cm, 21 cm, 23 cm (7 in., 8 in., 8½ in., 9 in.)
Steak moulds	Minced beef, hamburgers, etc.	100/125 g (4 oz) upwards
Sundae dishes	Composite ice cream dishes	50 g, 100 g, 175 g, 225 g (2 oz, 4 oz, 6 oz, 8 oz)
Sweet, cheese and bread and butter plates	Sweet, cheese and bread and butter	15 cm, 16 cm, 18 cm (6 in., 6½ in., 7 in.)
Tea and coffee cups	Tea and coffee	142 ml, 198 ml, 227 ml, 255 ml (5 oz, 7 oz, 8 oz, 9 oz)
Tea measuring machine	Tea for pot service	450 g, 0.9 kg (1 lb, 2 lb)
Woven wire vegetable servers	Peas, sprouts, etc	50 g, 75 g, 100 g (2 oz, 3 oz, 4 oz)

Note: The foregoing list is again indicative rather than exhaustive: many other utensils and containers, such as tureens, tea pots, sauceboats, coupes and cocottes have portioning application.

Those responsible for purchasing and portion control must understand fully the effects of cooking, cooking loss and shrinkage (see Chapter 3).

In whatever way portions are determined, kitchen equipment and utensils should be exploited to control them. Scales are essential for determining the weight

A sales record may show 18 portions of a dish sold, but when asked how many were issued the chef may reply 24. If that many were prepared and now all are gone, somewhere along the line six portions have been lost. The fate of lost portions must be ascertained. Were some lost in cooking (excess shrinkage of roast meat) or portioning (over-large portions served) or perhaps used as staff meals? In short, even when a required number has been prepared and sales recorded, questioning, checks and continuous supervision are required.

of expensive protein items (for example, meat and fish). After weighing several portions, eye judgement may suffice, but should not be encouraged particularly in the inexperienced. In any case, further checks must be made by comparing the number of weighed portions plus waste and trimming against the weight of the original joint or fish. Portion-serving utensils should be clearly marked and used intelligently. The value of spoons, scoops and ladles in control is that it is often easier to guide staff in level servings of one or two scoops than 50 g (2 oz) or 100 g (4 oz) portions.

Serving dishes and plates must be selected to conform to portion size. Too large a dish or plate increases the tendency to serve over-large portions. The use of multi-portion trays must be guided by ease of portioning rather than ease of accounting. It is easier to divide a large rectangle into nine, 12 or 16 than it is into ten.

As is the case in so much kitchen activity, the best basis for an effective system of portion control is simplicity, staff co-operation and training. A dining-room checking system must be supported by effective control in kitchen service. Management supervision of portions served is required to prevent collusion between waiting and kitchen staff with a view to a waiter earning enhanced tips.

Portion control is not a negative procedure, but rather ensures that the price of a dish is neither more nor less than it should be.

KITCHEN PERCENTAGES

Percentages, particularly food cost and gross profit, were discussed in Chapter 3. However their significance in regard to the control function cannot be ignored.

To recap, the difference between food cost and selling price may be expressed as a percentage. Percentage targets may be applied to each commodity, to a course, to a whole meal or to a menu. Management issues directives setting percentage guidelines to ensure the desired margin of gross profit on sales. This ensures:

- kitchen compliance with cost constraints;
- catering staff relate food costs to allowances;
- consumption and usage of food is controlled;
- commodity costs are calculated and accounted for;
- purchasing prices are constantly monitored to ensure efficient use of financial resources.

In the percentage method, the chef or kitchen manager is responsible for attaining the percentage target. Any differences noted are investigated and the cause ascertained. A consumption sheet aids control and shows the variances when items are expressed as a percentage of total consumption. On any costing system a check must be kept on labour and overheads, as well as raw material costs. If costs increase without adjustment to prices, target profit will not be maintained despite efficient physical controls.

Food cost percentages remain a valuable guide to spotting defects and losses in food operations. If they are too high then check for:

- unwise purchasing;
- faulty receiving;
- commodity wastage;
- pilferage;
- poor hygiene;
- spoilage as a result of excess purchases or poor storage;
- over-production;
- poor methods of preparation, cookery or service;
- poor menu planning;
- inadequate control.

However, if they are too low, check for poor food quality. Too low a food cost is not the obvious benefit it may seem, it must result from poor quality or smaller-than-calculated portions being sold. Either way, customers are bound to notice and although they may not complain they are unlikely to return.

Summary

A chef or caterer may rely on the accountant's department or a similar office for ultimate calculations of percentage and profitability. Such calculations depend on adequate and reliable information in the form of records, checks and requisitions, from kitchen and all associated food-service areas. The kitchen management team must remain responsible for conscientious and accurate record-keeping within the catering department.

In a well-run business, supplies of food and other materials must be available when they are needed. Having too much stock on hand can be as harmful as having too little. The level of stock-holding and the system of control must be compatible, and both must be suited to the operation concerned.

Staff at all levels must be aware of their responsibilities with regard to efficient recording and control of the movement of food and food products.

Kitchen operations are governed by percentages and food costs. Identifying the movement of materials by their monetary value will highlight deficiencies of purchase or storage and losses through waste or pilferage, as well as clearly indicating the achievement of profit. Food control should, therefore, be based on careful recording and accuracy of calculations.

Any calculations based on forecasted activity must be compared with actual costs and any variance identified and accounted for. Although the kitchen is often considered to be an area of cost control it should also be governed by profit incentives. The accounting system of a catering establishment will be designed to reveal the ultimate profitability or otherwise of the food operation. However, historical records and accounting systems can do little more than measure performance and reveal where action is needed. In addition to these warning signs there are also signals of a more practical kind that the caterer must heed. Such signs are to be found in larder left-overs, accumulation of stocks in the dry-goods store, plate waste and dishes which do not sell. The study of these points must support the control and profitability of a kitchen operation.

Possible causes of unsatisfactory results are:

- human weakness – pilferage, negligence or insufficient training;
- documentary weakness – inadequate accounting procedure, input/output errors;
- physical weakness – insufficient provision of deterrents and inadequate physical checks;
- poor supervision – poor portion control, failure to use standardised recipes, carelessness in receiving, storing, handling, cooking and serving, spoilage, over-purchasing, not claiming credits, and billing errors.

To practical people, kitchen records and calculations can seem irksome. It is just as well that simplicity is the essence of a good control system. Caterers and chefs seek methods that do not involve too much time and where errors of calculations are reduced to the minimum. A system which is too elaborate can cost more than the materials saved. Thus, records and control must be adapted to suit the operation not the reverse. Whatever system is adopted it must be properly pursued for any relaxation can quickly be exploited by lazy or dishonest staff.

Record and control activity, important though it is, is but one of the activities that the kitchen manager is called upon to undertake and supervise. Respect and enthusiasm for this task, together with all other aspects of meal production and merchandising that are undertaken, may add complexity, but also adds to the fascination of this rewarding and important duty.

Check list

1. Match duplicate order with delivery note, make a note of discrepancies and check quantity and quality of goods against specification. Transfer goods to stores with a goods received note (GRN). Dispatch copy of goods received note to buyer and another copy to invoice department.

2. Match duplicate order with goods received and supplier's delivery note (invoice), note discrepancies and pass to check 3.

3. Check for 'date payable', discounts, debit or credit notes, produce remittance advice and cheque. Pass to check 4.

4. Counter-sign cheque for payment to supplier (preferably done by personnel independent from checks 1, 2 and 3 above).

5. Goods issued to production kitchen on receipt of a requisition. Requisition priced and copy returned with goods to manufacturer.

6. Product specification checked against raw materials required. Product costed against price of goods issued from stores.

7. Kitchen informed of wages and overheads attributable to production. Gross profit target identified.

8. Check for waste loss and fraud; unused items (raw materials) accounted for.

9. Cost (wastage) as a result of quality control accounted for.

10. Usable material saved, documented and allowances made.

11. Finished goods identified at full cost plus (including materials, labour, overheads and net profit).

12. Restaurant check (customer order) raised.

13. Check goods leaving service area against restaurant check.

14. Cash received reconciled against restaurant check.

15. Comparison made between cash received (sales), cost of raw materials and anticipated revenue. Any variance identified and explained.

Menu Analysis and Profitability

Most of the emphasis thus far has been in relation to management before the event (menu planning, dish development, costing/pricing, purchasing, raw materials and stock control). However, it is important to recognise the significance of management after the event when the opportunity arises to minitor and improve performance.

Many caterers would appear to have adopted a 'let sleeping dogs lie' philosophy. They seem reluctant to interfere with what, at first observation, is apparently a successful operation. Menus are renewed annually and prices changed every six months, because 'that is the way it has always been done'. To some extent there may be good reason for not changing an apparently successful formula. Certainly there is no value in change for the sake of change, and no change should take place without a sound reason.

Menu analysis enables customer preference to be identified, profitability and performance to be assessed, and gives reason for change. Menu analysis allows for the opportunity to predetermine levels of profitability and enables gross profit and net profit targets to be set. It provides budget information for performance to be measured against. But most of all it enables real evaluation of precisely how successful the operation is and/or could be.

Decisions will be influenced by assessment of what is possible and how it may be achieved. Broadly speaking, such assessment can be developed on two levels:

- Operational (control activity) – more detailed analysis of menus and profitability, control of receipts and revenue.
- Financial (policy decisions) – the interpretation of

financial reports, ratio analysis, break-even analysis and budgeting.

MENU ANALYSIS

The value of a well-planned menu cannot be overstated. Ensuring customer satisfaction is, after all, the prime concern of the caterer. However, the need to satisfy the customer has to be balanced against the need to produce a return on investment for the owner/shareholders/investors. The ultimate objective of any commercial business must be to achieve a return on investment above current bank or building society investment rates.

As has been discussed in earlier chapters, the key to profitability is to respond to consumer demand which may be identified through the process of market research. Menu analysis is the means by which caterers can contribute to assessment of market opportunities by examining their own internal records. The aim being to identify the progress and performance of every item on the menu.

What is happening? What is possible? The quality of response to these questions will be influenced by the quality of recording and reporting that exists within the operation. Caterers have frequently used the excuse that 'they are too busy making money to be bothered with paperwork'. Whilst it may be possible to cite examples of 'successful' operations that exist with little or no paperwork, it is certainly not possible to determine precisely how successful they are. Catering is a low-cost, high-volume industry and as such time, resources and energy can be easily wasted.

Whilst some paperwork will be required by law (evidence of transactions, revenue, expenditure and profit for taxation purposes) this and other similar information provide the means by which the efficiency and effectiveness of the operation can be measured for purely business purposes. Efficiency and effectiveness may be defined as the most economical use of resources, time and money in order to produce the most profitable sales mix.

Menu analysis is the means by which the most profitable sales mix can be determined, by assessing the menu in light of the contribution made by each dish to the overall success of the operation. In the absence of effective menu analysis, poor performance may be incorrectly attributed to other causes, for example, purchasing. Successful analysis depends on the availability of accurate data regarding each dish.

SALES HISTORY

Menu analysis begins with sales history. What have we sold and why?

Buyers in other trades, such as retailing in department stores, only determine what merchandise to buy and levels of stock to maintain after careful analysis of existing sales reports, charts and other research material. Despite the possibility that variables in catering may be greater than other kinds of business, menu makers should similarly rely on sales information.

Menu sales history records the proportions in which the various items sell. It is concerned with popularity, selling price, portion cost and gross profit contribution.

Caterers should record sales, even if only by annotating the menu itself. Frequency and consistency of recording ensure the accuracy and reliability of any conclusions that may be drawn. Ideally a suitably simple record chart should be drawn, following the menu format and sequence of the dishes. The number of each item sold should be extracted from the sales checks, itemiser tills, electronic cash registers (ECRs), electronic point of sale systems (EPOSs) or computer records, by the cashier or kitchen clerk. This will enable dishes to be identified by popularity (see Table 10.1). See also Chapter 3 where forecasting is covered in detail.

MENU POPULARITY INDEX

Menu popularity analysis will provide detail not just on the mix of sales, but also on individual customer choices. The information resulting from menu analysis can be dealt with in quite simple terms by producing a popularity index, which if presented in percentage form can be useful for comparison over time, for identifying trends and to produce a weekly/monthly review of the hit parade (of menu items), identifying the climbers, the firm favourites, the falling stars and the no hopers. Simple menu analysis highlights potential sales opportunities and identifies possible problems. More detailed analysis will provide detailed statistics regarding gross profit contribution by dish or groups of items (starters, main dishes, sweets).

This form of activity enables the caterer to make decisions about where/when to change the selection of dishes offered, adjust prices or move items to a more prominent position on the menu.

Table 10.1 Menu popularity

Item	Cost (£)	Selling price (£)	Number sold	Popularity index (%)	
Soup	0.20	0.80	110	23.9	*Starters*
Prawn coctail	0.45	1.20	20	4.4	
Lasagne	0.40	1.30	80	17.4	
Shepherd's pie	0.35	1.30	30	6.5	
Steak pie	1.40	1.80	180	39.1	
Chicken curry	0.50	1.80	80	17.4	
Ham salad	0.60	1.75	60	13.0	
Ploughman's	0.40	1.60	20	4.4	
Salmon salad	0.80	1.20	10	2.2	*Main course*
Chips	0.12	0.80	250	54.4	*Accompaniment*

Note: Percentage calculations are based on the assumption that all customers (460) took a main course.

Menu sales history and the popularity index help to establish forecasts of future sales and enable tighter production controls. Not only are they a guide to menu adjustment and future purchasing, but they also aid the calculation of what menu costs/prices should be.

Management also rely on sales history and profit and loss records to pinpoint where the operation is losing money. This may, in turn, suggest where investigation and analysis may be required into other aspects, such as kitchen layout, equipment, staffing or other procedures, in order to improve efficiency and effectiveness.

SALES MIX

Sales mix may be seen as the comparison between departments, for example, between food and drink. The mix between food and drink might differ daily, i.e. there may be more drink sold at the week-end. This information can be useful in the allocation of staff and resources. It is also useful from a promotional aspect, for it would not be a good idea to offer a free glass of wine with a meal at the week-end, should this only result in a reduction in drink sales. However, a glass of wine offered mid-week may not only encourage sales of additional meals, but might also cause the customer to purchase an additional glass of wine or some other beverage.

The most useful application of sales mix is in making a comparison between menu items (starters/main course/sweets). It is an important influence on profitability, especially where each item or group of items carries a different gross profit margin.

Menu analysis allows sales mix to be assessed in the light of each item's contribution to overall profit.

Contribution may be measured by selling capacity, cost price, gross profit performance or even preparation nuisance value as compared to cost benefit. How difficult is a dish to produce? How essential is it to the success of the operation? It may be possible to argue that a difficult dish, although less profitable than other items, is essential because it has become the signature dish of the business, i.e. the dish that most customers associate with the business (although do not necessarily purchase).

The aim of menu analysis is to identify and correct poor performance which may be caused by poor purchasing, poor portion control, rising costs, waste,

fraud and/or loss. But it may also result from a poor sales mix, for example, some items being sold aggressively while others are ignored, food service staff selling low-priced items resulting in high activity producing a low revenue.

PROFITABILITY

For most caterers, efficiency is measured in terms of profitability. All caterers, even so-called, non-profit operations, measure efficiency using profit terminology as expressed by the relationship between food cost, gross profit and selling price.

One measure of efficiency is the ideal (potential) food cost percentage; the cost of food under ideal conditions as measured against the actual food cost percentage achieved. Any variance should be identified and explained.

An alternative method would be to compare achievable gross profit with actual gross profit. Achievable gross profit is calculated from sales realised during normal business as compared against costed recipes for the dishes sold. This is then compared against actual gross profit calculated at the end of the trading period, based on the actual cost of goods sold as shown on the balance sheet.

In order that such comparisons are reliable and effective, accurate figures (forecast demand, pricing/costing, raw material specifications, standardised recipes/yield) must be produced. The caterer must make sure that:

- up-to-date costings are available for all the items on the menu;
- the selling prices are up-to-date and accurate;
- standardised recipes, methods and yields are adhered to;
- accurate detail regarding the number of any and all items sold is available.

In calculating sales, income and profitability, figures must *not* include VAT since this element is collected on behalf of the Treasury and as such cannot be counted as contributing to operational income and most certainly does not contribute to profit. Staff meals are an expense of employing staff, not of directly feeding the customer, and should therefore be included in gross profit (labour cost) not food cost. Staff meals should be identified at sales price in order to identify all costs, including production, as a labour cost (see Figure 10.1).

Food cost	Sales	VAT	Staff meals	GP%
1000	3450	450	50	
1000	3450	X	X	70.01
1000	3000	✓	X	66.66
950	3450	X	✓	72.86
950	3000	✓	✓	68.85 the *true* figure

Note: In this example there are over six points' difference between the lowest and highest gross profit percentage figure. Clearly this could critically affect the performance of the operation and in particular lead to incorrect assumptions being made about net profit.

Figure 10.1   *Effect of staff meals and VAT on gross profit*

IMPROVING PROFITABILITY

The information gathered for menu analysis can be extended to include gross profit (GP) and gross profit percentage (GP%). The resulting data can be tabulated (see Table 10.2).

This information can then be extended to include calculatious of the various contributions made by each item on the basis of:

- monetary value of the item's contribution to total sales, i.e. selling price × number sold;
- the percentage of the total that this figure represents;
- the weighted average gross profit, i.e. weighting the gross profit figure in terms of its popularity (GP% × percentage total).

The total weighted average divided by 100 indicates the achievable gross profit. In this case the gross profit works out at 59.35 per cent (see Table 10.3).

Table 10.2   Tabulation of GP and GP%

Item	Cost (£)	Selling price (£)	Number sold	GP (£)	GP (%)
Soup	0.20	0.80	110	0.60	75.0
Prawn cocktail	0.45	1.20	20	0.75	62.5
Lasagne	0.40	1.30	80	0.90	69.2
Shepherd's pie	0.35	1.30	30	0.95	73.1
Steak pie	1.40	1.80	180	0.40	22.2
Chicken curry	0.50	1.80	80	1.30	72.2
Ham salad	0.60	1.75	60	1.15	65.7
Ploughman's	0.40	1.60	20	1.20	75.0
Salmon salad	0.80	1.20	10	0.40	33.3
Chips	0.12	0.80	250	0.62	77.5

Table 10.3   Tabulation of weighted average

Item	Cost (£)	Selling price (£)	Number sold	GP (£)	GP (%)	Value (£)	Percentage total (%)	Weighted average
Soup	0.20	0.80	110	0.60	75.0	88	8.8	660
Prawn cocktail	0.45	1.20	20	0.75	62.5	24	2.4	150
Lasagne	0.40	1.30	80	0.90	69.2	104	10.4	720
Shepherd's pie	0.35	1.30	30	0.95	73.1	39	3.9	285
Steak pie	1.40	1.80	180	0.40	22.2	252	25.2	560
Chicken curry	0.50	1.80	80	1.30	72.2	144	14.4	1040
Ham salad	0.60	1.75	60	1.15	65.7	105	10.5	690
Ploughman's	0.40	1.60	20	1.20	75.0	32	3.2	240
Salmon salad	0.80	1.20	10	0.40	33.3	12	1.2	40
Chips	0.12	0.80	250	0.62	77.5	200	20.0	1550
Totals						1000		5935

> **Menu analysis (sales mix) profitability – method**
> - List the items/dishes.
> - Count the items.
> - Provide the total number of each item sold.
> - Multiply that total by the sales price to give sales value.
> - Sum the values of each item and express each item's value as a percentage of the sum of those values.
> - Multiply each of those percentages by the GP of each item.
> - Sum the weighted averages and divide by 100; this will then give the achievable gross profit for those items.
>
> This kind of analysis shows: popularity of items (i.e. number sold); revenue earned from each item; total sales; and achievable gross profit.

With the information now available it is easy to predict the effect of:

- eliminating items or adding items to the menu;
- reducing the food cost of an item;
- increasing/decreasing the emphasis on the menu for an item;
- selective price increases/decreases.

For example, if we were to remove the salmon salad from the menu, the achievable gross profit is improved to 59.66 per cent (see Table 10.4).

If the cost of the steak pie were reduced through more efficient purchasing procedures, for example by 20p, then the achievable gross profit is improved to 62.15 per cent (see Table 10.5).

Obviously, if both adjustments considered above are made, the achievable gross profit is improved even further.

This, in essence, is the basis for menu engineering or manipulation of the gross profit. Computers, running a simple speadsheet program, are ideally suited to this type of 'What if?' analysis.

Considerable care should be taken in drawing conclusions from the above analysis. Remember that customers are idiosyncratic and cannot be programmed to respond in a predetermined way to changes.

As shown above, the removal of an item assumes no change to the remaining items. What would happen if removing the cheap salmon salad led to customers missing the soup (because the alternative main course was more expensive)?

The example shown in Table 10.6 assumes that by removing the salmon salad, ten soup sales are lost and ten additional portions of steak pie are sold. In this case at least, removing an item does not necessarily improve profitability. Obviously, it might have been

Table 10.4   Effect on GP% by removing one item from the menu

Item	Cost (£)	Selling price (£)	Number sold	GP (£)	GP (%)	Value (£)	Percentage total (%)	Weighted average
Soup	0.20	0.80	110	0.60	75.0	88	8.9	667.5
Prawn cocktail	0.45	1.20	20	0.75	62.5	24	2.4	150.0
Lasagne	0.40	1.30	80	0.90	69.2	104	10.5	726.6
Shepherd's pie	0.35	1.30	30	0.95	73.1	39	4.0	292.4
Steak pie	1.40	1.80	180	0.40	22.2	252	25.5	566.1
Chicken curry	0.50	1.80	80	1.30	72.2	144	14.6	1054.1
Ham salad	0.60	1.75	60	1.15	65.7	105	10.6	696.4
Ploughman's	0.40	1.60	20	1.20	75.0	32	3.3	247.5
Salmon salad	–	–	–	–	–	–	–	–
Chips	0.12	0.80	250	0.62	77.5	200	20.2	1565.5
Totals						988		5966.1

a different story if customer allegiance had switched to prawn cocktail and chicken curry.

A further criticism of this approach is its concen-tration on percentage rather than cash comparisons. This is especially true if only the food cost percentage is identified (see Table 10.7).

Table 10.5 Effect on GP% by reducing the food cost of one item on the menu

Item	Cost (£)	Selling price (£)	Number sold	GP (£)	GP (%)	Value (£)	Percentage total (%)	Weighted average
Soup	0.20	0.80	110	0.60	75.0	88	8.8	660
Prawn cocktail	0.45	1.20	20	0.75	62.5	24	2.4	150
Lasagne	0.40	1.30	80	0.90	69.2	104	10.4	720
Shepherd's pie	0.35	1.30	30	0.95	73.1	39	3.9	285
Steak pie	1.20	1.80	180	0.60	33.3	252	25.2	839
Chicken curry	0.50	1.80	80	1.30	72.2	144	14.4	1040
Ham salad	0.60	1.75	60	1.15	65.7	105	10.5	690
Ploughman's	0.40	1.60	20	1.20	75.0	32	3.2	240
Salmon salad	0.80	1.20	10	0.40	33.3	12	1.2	40
Chips	0.12	0.80	250	0.62	77.5	200	20.0	1550
Totals						1000		6215

Table 10.6 Effect of changes in sales to some menu items

Item	Cost (£)	Selling price (£)	Number sold	GP (£)	GP (%)	Value (£)	Percentage total (%)	Weighted average
Soup	0.20	0.80	100	0.60	75.0	80	7.5	562.5
Prawn cocktail	0.45	1.20	20	0.75	62.5	24	2.3	143.8
Lasagne	0.40	1.30	80	0.90	69.2	104	9.7	671.2
Shepherd's pie	0.35	1.30	30	0.95	73.1	39	3.7	270.5
Steak pie	1.40	1.80	190	0.40	22.2	342	31.9	708.2
Chicken curry	0.50	1.80	80	1.30	72.2	144	13.4	967.5
Ham salad	0.60	1.75	60	1.15	65.7	105	9.8	643.9
Ploughman's	0.40	1.60	20	1.20	75.0	32	3.0	225.0
Salmon salad	–	–	–	–	–	–	–	–
Chips	0.12	0.80	250	0.62	77.5	200	18.7	1449.3
Totals						1072		5641.9

Table 10.7 Effect of introducing labour costs

Item	Cost (£)	Selling price (£)	Number sold	Food cost (%)	GP (after food) (£)	Labour cost (£)	Labour cost (%)	Profit after food and labour (£)	Total cash value (£)
Soup	0.20	0.80	110	25.0	0.60	40	50.0	0.20	22.0
Prawn cocktail	0.45	1.20	20	37.5	0.75	30	25.0	0.45	9.0
Lasagne	0.40	1.30	80	30.8	0.90	50	38.5	0.40	32.0
Shepherd's pie	0.35	1.30	30	26.9	0.95	50	38.5	0.45	13.5
Steak pie	1.40	1.80	180	77.8	0.40	50	27.8	(0.10)	(18.0)
Chicken curry	0.50	1.80	80	27.8	1.30	50	27.8	0.80	64.0
Ham salad	0.60	1.75	60	34.3	1.15	20	11.4	0.95	57.0
Ploughman's	0.40	1.60	20	25.0	1.20	20	12.5	1.00	20.0
Salmon salad	0.80	1.20	10	66.6	0.40	20	16.7	0.20	2.0
Chips	0.12	0.80	250	22.5	0.68	10	12.5	0.58	145.0

Note: Numbers in brackets are negative values.

Introducing labour costs into the calculation shows that it is actually chips, chicken curry and ham salad that are our major earners, with lasagne, soup and ploughman's also making an important contribution. The steak pie actually loses money, but this may be acceptable. It may earn its way if it is a signature dish, the product that most customers identify with and if it attracts customers who try other things. If, as is likely, it is linked to the purchase of chips then the meal as a whole generates a 48p contribution toward overheads and net profit.

Removing an item from the menu may increase percentage profit whilst reducing the actual cash in the till. For this reason, all changes must be closely monitored. Menu engineering should be a continuous process. Do it and do it again.

Cash gross profit per cover is considered by many to be the best indicator of profitability.

PROFIT SENSITIVITY

If an increase in profit is desirable, possible responses might be to increase turnover, increase prices and/or reduce costs. It is possible to produce suitable mathematical formulae which in theory are capable of being used. But even if these solutions are mathematically correct there is no guarantee that they will actually have the desired effect.

Profit sensitivity analysis is concerned with identifying which element of revenue has the greatest influence on profit and what effect, if any, a price change will have.

In regard to the effect of price changes, the generally accepted rule of economics suggests that as price increases so volume purchased will decrease. However, some products respond more readily to changes in price; a phenomenon known as elasticity. A product's price is described as elastic when an increase or decrease in price results in a marked change to volume purchased. A product may be described as inelastic, where a change in price results in little or no change in volume, for example, bread, milk and petrol are all inelastic. We generally buy whatever is essential regardless of the price; luxury goods and especially eating out are more elastic. We go without if the price is too high or shop around for cheaper alternatives.

There is often no way of predicting our customers' responses to a price change. Therefore, price changes have to be monitored carefully in order to identify resulting trends. It will be useful to know how responsive (elastic) each of the menu items is to price change.

The profit multiplier may be used as an indication of profit sensitivity and price elasticity.

Profit sensitivity analysis – method
- Identify key factors likely to affect net profit.
- Assume a change in each factor and, holding other things constant, calculate the effect on net profit.
- Calculate the profit multiplier by dividing the change in net profit by the change in key factor. For example, if the number of covers is increased by 10 per cent and, as a result, the net profit increases by 40 per cent then the profit multiplier is 4.
- Rank the profit multiplier for each menu item and draw appropriate conclusions.

PROFIT MAXIMISATION

As discussed in earlier chapters, selling price is dependent on quality, cost (materials, wages, overheads) and the required amount of profit. If customers are to return, it is folly to make them spend more than they intended so consider, from the customer's point of view:

- the selection of items;

- the price (in total and by group).

Most customers check prices, so there should not be too much difference between the cheapest and most expensive dishes in each group.

Many caterers confuse popularity (the volume of sales for any item) and profitability. Menu items may be arranged in a grid (see Figure 10.2) ranking performance both in terms of volume (popularity) and cash contribution.

Cash cow (high sales and high profit contribution) – This produces a bountiful supply of cash, if cared for, serviced and fed regularly. It may be used to nurture less-profitable items.

Plough horse (high sales and low profit contribution) – Works hard, but benefits are not always immediately apparent. It needs a tight rein if it is to be kept on track.

Cuddly panda (low sales but high profit contribution) – Loveable but elusive, needs careful study and plenty of attention if it is to be fruitful.

Dodo (low sales and low profit) – Probably extinct, in which case bury it. If it is not then swift and probably drastic action is needed to revive it before it does expire.

As inspired by the Boston Matrix, developed by the Boston Consulting Group, using expressive animal analogies.

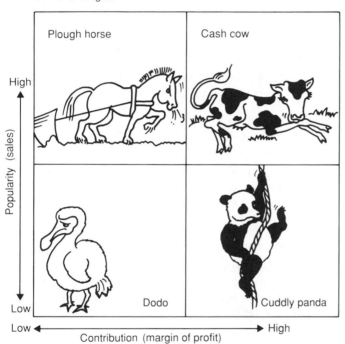

Low price; good value	Sought after item and price does not matter
Low price but uninteresting	Tempting but over-priced

Possible customer perception

Figure 10.2   *Performance – popularity and contribution*

PROFIT STRATEGY

Generally the idea is to try to manoeuvre menu items toward the top-right of the grid shown in Figure 10.2.

Cash cow

The most profitable (high volume, high cash contribution) item and warrants further promotion and merchandising, with prime menu positioning. Care should be taken to maintain quality. Price increases may be possible but should be approached with caution.

Plough horse

Maintain value, review costs and portion sizes. Careful price increases through enhanced benefits and added value, extra garnish and/or choice of sauces. Try re-packaging or linking sales to other items.

Cuddly panda

Reappraise, research and try a variety of options; plan and monitor development; increase promotion. Re-styling the product or adding value may help to improve sales. Decreasing price is less likely to revive an old favourite, but may help to promote a new item.

Dodo

Is this an old product in decline? Can it be revamped? Is it a new product which has not yet gained attention? In the latter case try differing promotion styles. Where both volume and cash contribution are low it may be wisest to eliminate or replace the item.

CUSTOMER SPENDING

Careful examination of customer spending can prove to be one of the more useful aspects of analysis.

There are two approaches to average spend, either per item or per customer. Comparing the two can indicate opportunities for change. If the average spend on the main course was £12 and the average spend per customer £15, then it is safe to assume that starters and/or sweets will not sell if the customer orders a drink. If starters and sweets carry a high gross profit then the caterer should consider reducing the price (and cost) of main courses and promoting starters and sweets. For example, if a 170 g (6 oz) steak normally sells at £10 try selling a 112 g (4 oz) steak at £8 to see if a sweet or starter is also taken.

Other useful information may be provided by examining:

- Rate of occupancy (seat turnover) – calculated as the number of customers divided by the number of available seats. Are people sitting too long? Is the service too slow?
- Sales per seat – calculated as the sales (revenue) divided by the number of available seats.

This can be a useful comparison between two units offering the same menu, all other factors being the same.

Consider also, average gross profit (total cash gross profit divided by the number of customers), for example:

Number of covers	Average spend (£)	Total sales	Total food cost (£)	Total GP (£)	%GP	Food cost per cover (£)	GP per cover (£)
500	£4.00	£2000	£800	£1200	60	£1.60	£2.40
400	£4.50	£1800	£720	£1080	60	£1.80	£2.70

If, by spending a little more (20p) per cover on raw materials, an increase in average spend (50p) were achieved; then although total takings and £GP were reduced, GP% would remain the same (60 per cent) but £GP per cover would be improved. Although it might be argued that more cash in the till was preferable, if this could only be achieved under stress, then it would be more sensible to go for lower turnover in order to maintain quality. The example, relating as it does to examination of the gross profit, does not take into account staffing. So that although serving 500 covers puts more money in the till, it may indeed be necessary to use some of that increased revenue to pay increased labour costs resulting from the increase in business.

In this example at least, comparing number of covers and £GP per cover, it would seem that 'less is more'.

PRODUCT LIFE CYCLE AND MENU FATIGUE

In terms of profit sensitivity and customer spending we cannot exclude the popularity of an item. Popularity is usually subject to change, in fashion or trend.

It is generally agreed that all products go through what is defined as a life cycle (see Figure 10.3). This process of growth, maturity and eventual decline in sales applies equally to menu items. Too many items in the decline phase will result in menu fatigue – a tired, uninteresting menu.

The product life cycle may be influenced by management decisions, particularly the way in which the product is promoted. Three methods are worthy of consideration:

- Association of product, menu items, with complementary items, for example, the association of food with drink (curry and lager).
- Merchandising or displaying products in such a way as to attract attention and emphasise the particular benefits of the product. This can be achieved by: displaying the food itself on buffets, hot counters or trolleys; the use of special notices, blackboards or tent cards on the table; or through menu presentation, position on the menu or graphical representation, for example, photographs.
- Adding value, which may be perceived as:
  real value – change in portion size and/or additional items;
  implied value – descriptions (trendy items), presentation and menu design;

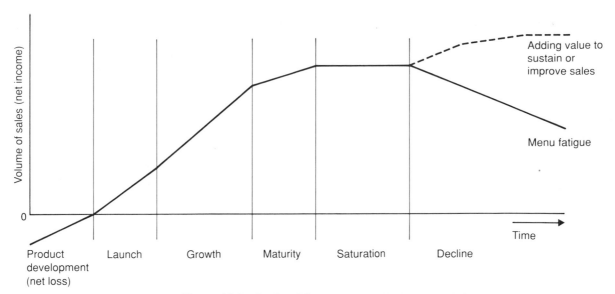

Figure 10.3   *Product life cycle and menu fatigue*

association – atmosphere/surroundings, staff attitude/motivation, hygiene (food/presentation/surroundings), quality of food and service.

ANALYSIS OF RECEIPTS AND REVENUE

Although primarily the function of senior management, supervisors at departmental level should be able to draw some conclusions from a financial report. In particular, they should be able to identify how the activity of their department has influenced the overall figures.

The analysis of receipts and revenue is dependent on the quality of control procedures which may be seen as having two interdependent objectives – physical and documentary control.

Physical control

This includes security of assets, such as cash, resources and information, installing locks and night safes, instilling correct procedures and employing honest personnel.

Documentary control

This includes evidence of transactions, cash book and till rolls. These documents provide the material that will be the source for further analysis and financial reports.

The prime aim must be to identify the actual profit which will not always be the same as cash surplus at the end of the trading period.

The legal constraints relevant to control, analysis and reporting cannot be ignored. The collection and handling of money, identifying cost, revenue and profit imposes on the caterer the responsibility of reporting to government departments (taxation) and investors (dividend). The accuracy of such reports is reliant on the quality of data collection and recording.

There are various approaches to the collection of data, including:

- intuition/gut reaction;
- manual/mechanical methods where the till roll may be the only record;
- electronic means (for example, EPOS) which electronically store and report sales data and FTEPOS which extends EPOS to automatic transfer of funds through the use of plastic cards;
- computers which are capable of being linked to stock control and purchasing systems, as well as interpreting the data into management reports.

In addition to detailed pricing of a customer's check/bill a good system should also analyse sales by dish, staff, department and method of payment.

Daily sales and production analysis

Analysis and control are often stated in relation to sales. Control by the selling price has the advantage that all activity is measured against potential income.

The catering industry is generally subject to fluctuations in business activity. Relating costs and profits to sales is relevant because of the instability of volume of sales.

The method is easy to apply where materials are purchased in saleable units, for example, bar stock, bottles and packets. It is less easy to apply where recipes are involved (the selling price of a range of ingredients would be variable according to the dishes capable of being produced from them). But once the ingredients are assembled we can attribute a selling price according to the completed dish and all further calculations, including loss, waste and fraud, can be based on this notional price.

The analysis of sales and revenue is primarily concerned with identifying the flow of funds through the operation. Measuring cash flow is important, cash is a resource and as such should be as productive as any other asset.

Making cash work

Speed in and out – the value of money does not depreciate with use, the more it is used the better. For example:

- Stock turnover and stock levels – do not waste cash holding stock.
- Make suppliers wait for cash – so long as there is no penalty.
- Encourage customers to pay quickly – send invoices promptly, offer incentives for early payment and/or pre-payment.
- Limit the amount of credit given – be selective and state credit terms.

Optimise debt by making the maximum use of suppliers' money to run the business. However, there is a risk as being in debt could weaken the caterer's bargaining position; there may be difficulties in maintaining raw material specifications/quality and standards.

IMPROVING PROFITABILITY THROUGH WASTE REDUCTION

In the pursuit of increased profitability through improvements to sales revenue, volume and margin, it is easy to neglect the opportunities that may arise through good housekeeping and the prevention of waste. A simple productivity check-list may be used to identify leakages.

RATIO ANALYSIS

Ratio analysis is a useful control tool; it meausres the degree of efficiency, levels of activity and use of resources (raw materials, labour and cash). At a financial, policy level, ratio analysis is used to make comparisons between assets, liabilities, capital and debts.

At an operational level, ratio analysis is frequently used to compare labour and material costs or performance between departments, for example, food and drink. It is particularly important that food expenses and profit or loss should be separated from those of beverages, so that one does not subsidise or disguise the losses of the other. At a departmental level, ratio analysis may be used to compare the elements within the menu, for example, starters versus sweets, in order to identify trends.

Productivity check-list
- Constantly seek to improve purchasing, receiving, storage, preparation and cooking to minimise food cost.
- Exploit any ability to buy in bulk to gain volume discount (beware of the risks, as identified in Chapter 4).
- Ensure that control measures are reviewed, through consultation with supervisors and other management staff.
- Make the best use of staff, their skills and their working hours (consider the use of part-time staff or job shares). Part-time staff can be utilised at peak periods, saving on the overall labour costs.
- Evaluate external training and use on-the-job training to improve staff morale and effectiveness, and give customer satisfaction and value for money.
- Keep food preparation and kitchen output efficient through a maintenance and equipment check programme.
- Be aware of energy conservation and constantly measure usage and procedures.
- Consider the application of computer control wherever feasible in the operation.

VARIANCE ANALYSIS

Variance analysis is used for the identification of errors, waste, loss or fraud by comparing expected and actual results.

Variance
This is defined as the difference between expected (forecast/budget) and actual figures, and involves:
- setting standards/product specifications;
- performance evaluation;
- comparison of budget with actual;
- analysis of costs and revenue;
- determination of cause;
- identification of responsibility;
- corrective action.

The approach is to break down the error into its two main causal parts, usage and price (see Table 10.8 overleaf). Obviously, if expenditure has been more than anticipated, it could have been caused by either more of an item being used than was necessary, by a higher than anticipated price being paid or possibly by a combination of both usage and price. Identifying and attributing cause requires strict adherence to standard recipes and methods, and accurate recording of purchases and production.

Causes of variance
- Change in price of input – bad estimating; bad buying.
- Change in quality – poor specification; poor selection; poor receiving.
- Change in personnel – vague personnel specification.
- Change in method – inaccurate job descriptions.
- Efficiency of use – bad workmanship; poor production system.
- Theft or fraud – poor control procedures.

Table 10.8   Variance – dish example

Steak pie

Standard recipe	Planned quantity	Planned price	Actual quantity	Actual price	Usage	Price
Chuck steak	3 oz	1.30 per lb	2 oz	1.50	+	−
Lamb kidney	1 oz	0.90 per lb	1 oz	1.00	−	
Onion	1 oz	0.60 per lb	1 oz	0.52		+
Parsley	pinch	0.01	pinch	0.01		
Beef stock	0.2 pt	0.20 per pt	0.4 pt	0.15	−	+
Flour	0.5 oz	0.40 per lb	1 oz	0.38	−	+
Margarine/lard	1 oz	1.20 per lb	1 oz	1.20		
Flour	2 oz	0.40 per lb	3 oz	0.38	−	+
Seasoning	pinch	0.01	pinch	0.01		

(+: favourable   −: unfavourable)

Note: Both recipes work out at 53.5p per portion to produce. This begs the question 'Why calculate the variance?' The trained observer will have identified that although the cost of production is the same, the quality is unlikely to be comparable. Also, forecasting and purchasing will have been based on standardised recipes; using more or less of a product will cause confusion at a later date.

Variance may be expressed as being favourable or unfavourable.

1. Price variance (purchasing function):
   unfavourable – paying more for food items than expected using higher quality than specified and neglecting discounts;
   favourable – paying less for food than budgeted (inferior goods may be being used).

2. Usage variance (production function):
   unfavourable – non-adherence to standardise recipes, waste, spoilage, poor portion control and pilferage;
   favourable – customers getting smaller portions, increased efficiency and improved kitchen practices.

Variance analysis – method
Look for variance and/or trends and explain reasons for change. Note and investigate any difference and ascertain the cause. A consumption sheet (see Chapter 9) aids control and shows variances when items are expressed as a percentage of consumption. Percentages are easier to chart and compare than cash figures. On any costing system, keep a check on labour and overhead costs. If these increase without adjustments being made to the selling price, the target profit will not be maintained, despite efficient control over the food cost percentage.

Centralising the production of food is seen by many caterers as being the ideal reason to reduce the opportunity for variance to occur. Systems like cook-freeze, cook-chill and sous-vide may be used to achieve greater efficiency and reduce waste.

Clearly variance can be reduced through stricter operational control in purchasing, receiving, storing, issuing, production and selling.

Confusion can be caused when trying to identify variance between three elements: budgeted, potential and actual costs. These are defined as follows:

- Budgeted cost – what was intended at the planning stage.
- Potential cost – expectations based on current prices, standard recipes and yield, during production.
- Actual cost – final real cost, from the trading accounts, after sales.

Variance between budgeted and potential costs may be seen as a policy problem requiring a change in prices, recipes, portion size or sales mix. Variance between potential and actual costs is an operational control problem related to the identification of waste, loss and/or fraud.

Variance analysis can be applied to any aspect of the operation. It is a control procedure, ensuring that what was intended to happen actually happens. Variance analysis will provide only signals for a manager to respond to. The various elements are frequently dependent on one another; a favourable price variance may often result in an unfavourable usage variance.

BREAK-EVEN ANALYSIS

Reference was made at the beginning of this chapter to management after the event. Analysis also provides the opportunity to make predictions about future events. In particular, the caterer might be concerned with the break-even position and whether or not profitability can be improved through economies of scale.

Break-even analysis charts the relationship between costs and sales as volume increases. Based on the identification of costs as either fixed or variable (semi-variable or managed cost must be attributed to one or the other), total cost (expenditure) is equal to fixed cost plus variable cost. Break even is that point where total expenditure is equal to total income (sales). It provides the opportunity to compare potential income against expenditure in order to make judgements about the viability of a business, i.e. a 40-seater restaurant with a break-even point of 60 covers is not viable, unless more than one sitting is possible.

Break-even analysis is best represented on a graph (see Figure 10.4). More precise information may be gathered from the break-even formula:

$$\text{Break even} = \frac{\text{Fixed cost}}{\text{Selling price} - \text{Variable cost}}$$

expressed in units (number of covers or portions sold).

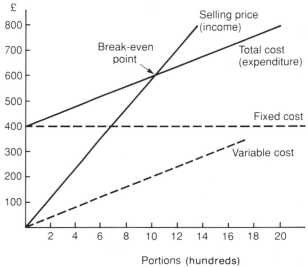

Figure 10.4 *Break-even analysis*

- Fixed costs – remain the same no matter how many portions are produced, for example, rent and rates.
- Variable costs – vary with the number of portions produced, usually in direct proportion, for example, raw materials.
- Total costs – are equal to fixed costs plus variable costs (including managed costs).
- Break-even point – is that point at which income exactly equals expenditure.

Figure 10.4, fixed costs are shown as £400. Variable costs are 20p per portion (200 portions = £40, 1000 portions = £200, etc.). The total cost of the first portion would therefore be £400.20 and we would have to sell it at that price in order to break even.

However, assuming a more reasonable selling price of 60p we can see, from the graph, that 1000 portions would need to be sold in order to break even. This can also be proved mathematically:

1000 portions @ 60p	£600 income
Fixed cost	£400
Variable cost (1000 @ 20p)	£200
	£600 expenditure

A computer, running a spreadsheet (break-even analysis) program, provides the opportunity to feed in a variety of different scenario and 'What if?' questions.

ECONOMIES OF SCALE

The theory recognises that, because fixed costs remain the same regardless of the number of units produced, as production volume increases the cost of producing each additional unit gets less.

As fixed costs are divided equally between all of the units produced, at some point the amount of fixed cost allocated to each unit would be so small that by comparison with variable (raw material) costs it becomes less significant. The change is most dramatic in the early stages, but becomes less significant as output increases. Note the shape of the curve in Figure 10.5.

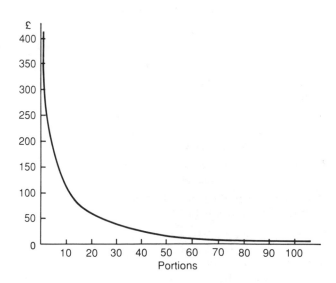

Figure 10.5 *Economies of scale*

Using the previous example (fixed cost = £400): if only one portion is sold it should bear the whole burden of the fixed cost; if two are sold then they share the burden 400/2 = £200 per portion; if 200 are sold then the cost is further reduced 400/2000 = £2 per portion; and so on. Following this example to its logical conclusion, if 1000 portions are sold then fixed cost per portion will be 40p (400/1000). If the variable cost (20p) is added we arrive at the suggested selling price of 60p to break even.

If output (and sales) were doubled then the fixed cost per portion would be halved (400/2000 = 20p) giving a new total cost of 40p which would provide a profit of 20p and/or offer the opportunity to reduce price in order to further increase sales.

Break-even analysis and economies of scale may be used together to examine pricing strategy. Take for instance the information presented in Figures 10.4 and 10.5. Bearing in mind the basic principle of economics, that sales are likely to increase as price decreases, then if sales/production are increased there is a greater margin of profit, therefore more opportunity to reduce price. The question remains as to whether any additional costs are incurred in improving the profit margin by selling more? This, indeed, highlights the flaw in both break-even analysis and economies of scale. Both methods are based on the comparison and analysis of fixed costs and variable costs; both ignore managed (semi-variable) costs.

What has not been considered are those semi-variable costs which are in the manager's control. Reducing price and increasing volume would only be worthwhile if any changes in managed cost (heat, light, fuel and/or labour) were kept within the assumed increase in profitability.

Of course, economies of scale and break-even analysis are only theories; assumptions about the future are subject to change, trend and fashion. Therefore, actual performance must be continuously monitored, measured and recorded.

BUDGETS

Finally, after analysis and predictions have been made, a budget may be set. A budget provides the catalyst between planning and control. It enables cost and profit control centres to be identified, authority and responsibility delegated, and objectives (price/cost/profit standards) to be set.

Formulation of budgets – necessary information
- Full detail of past performance.
- Assessment of current trends.
- Customer detail; disposable income.
- Staffing detail.
- Raw material detail.
- Other expenses.
- Planned level of service.
- Proposed price.

The advantage of budgeting is that once standards of performance have been set, they can be monitored and measured, thus providing the basis by which the progress of a business can be regulated. From an operational point of view, clear lines of responsibility can be identified and unit managers provided with the authority to optimise the use of resources, keep expenditure within income and co-ordinate all activities.

Budgets may be set for:

- sales (target revenue for period);
- purchases (food cost percentage);
- expenses (incremental or percentage);
- labour (incremental based on inflation and wage rises);
- maintenance (fixed, planned schedules).

Budgets may be used to set sales or turnover targets, but they are most often seen as determining cost limits, often on an annual basis with an incremental (percentage) increase each year.

Zero budgeting requires the manager to prepare a forecast for expenditure based on estimated business activity for each budget period. Each budget period allows for irregular expenditure and is considered separately. The starting point, or base, for each budget is zero. No account is taken of previous budgets or previous expenditure.

The efficiency and effectiveness of budgets may be influenced by the choice of budget periods; 12 calendar months or 13 equal months (four-week periods) per year.

Calendar months are useful for seasonal operations where it is useful to compare one year's performance against the next. Where business is consistent throughout the year the use of 13 equal months (four-week periods) may be more viable. Choice will be dependent on company policy and operational need.

Methods of assessing performance are as follows:
- Measure against the same period last month (only relevant if turnover is consistent, not seasonal).
- Measure against the same period last year (or several years ago) (relevant for seasonal activity if inflation is built in).
- Measure against forecast budget (useful if operation is in a period of growth or change).
- Use all three or permutations of any two.

FINANCIAL REPORTS

Although information may be gathered for a variety of specific reasons and the results of analysis presented in a variety of different forms, all may be brought together in the presentation of financial reports, internal policy statements and the company annual report, all of which attempt to summarise the company's position.

Examination of the financial reports may provide suggestions for future activity and objective setting, for example:

- number of meals served – increase volume;
- stock turnover – reduce capital investment;
- gross profit – maximise potential;
- productivity – improve efficiency/effectiveness;
- assets – security, reduce waste/loss/fraud.

Summary

Successful, profitable enterprises are scarcely ever beyond improvement. Efficient control is only achieved through scrutiny of each aspect of production and service.

The main objective of menu analysis is to ensure optimum profit from the food operation. This is done by keeping costs in line with management policy and at the same time maintaining quality and quantity of food commensurate with customer expectations.

Try to eliminate items that do not pay their way. Concentrate on high-profit/high-volume items. Consider product life-cycle and menu fatigue.

Profitability can be improved through menu engineering, but always bear in mind the contribution of staff, equipment/facilities, merchandising and product quality. *All* employees should be cost conscious. All resources (raw materials, equipment) should be cost-effective.

Profit maximisation is dependent on knowledge of customer, product, competitors and, as a result of careful analysis, thorough knowledge of your own operation.

If the amount of choice on a menu is excessive, profitability may be reduced because customers do not read through the whole menu. Large choice is also wasteful in storage space, money tied up in stock, deterioration rate and customer time/loss of revenue. When endeavouring to identify profit every element has a cost and should therefore be charged.

Each department should be fully credited for its contribution. A good system relies on efficient and effective recording and reporting of stock control and daily percentages.

Mechanised billing aids speed, efficiency and effectiveness.

Simple things are important, like ensuring that every customer is bound to be charged.

Computerisation, the further development of management reporting and forecasting, can substantially improve speed, efficiency and effectiveness. Computers can be used to simulate proposed functions/projects as hypothetical figures can be fed in and comparisons made. Therefore, optimum potential profit can be determined before a project is started.

Menu analysis linked to profit planning has the advantage that all the activities of the operation are related to a specific objective. Although founded on historical evidence it does ensure that management thought is directed toward the future. It is pro-active rather than reactive and is a continuous process.

Check list

Poor performance may result from:

- human weakness – bad arithmetic and paperwork, inefficiency and fraud;
- operational weakness – in receiving, storing, production and service, failure to maintain standards and poor documentation;
- menu weakness – no market orientation, no sales analysis and no regular update;
- financial weakness – in purchasing, pricing, budgeting and forecasting.

1. Analyse sales, identify sales history, menu popularity and sales mix.
2. Assess profitability, profit sensitivity and identify areas of opportunity for profit maximisation.
3. Apply menu engineering techniques.
4. Consider customer spending, product life cycle and menu fatigue.
5. Apply profit strategies.
6. Analyse receipts and revenue.
7. Examine ratio and variance analysis.
8. Look to the future, through break-even analysis.
9. Optimise economies of scale.
10. Use budgets to identify cost and control centres.
11. Examine financial reports to identify new opportunities.
12. Repeat the above process.

Bibliography and recommended further reading

Bissell, F., *Sainsbury's Book of Food*, Websters International, 1989.

Cameron, A., *The Science of Food and Cooking*, Arnold, 1978.

The Caterer's Guide to Dairy Products, Dairy Produce Advisory Service, 1990.

Contemporary Cuisine from New Zealand Lamb, a Caterer's Guide, New Zealand Lamb Catering Advisory Service, 1990.

Cracknell, H. L., Kaufmann, R. J. and Nobis, G., *Practical, Professional Catering*, MacMillan, 1987.

Cracknell, H. L. and Nobis, G., *Practical Professional Gastronomy*, MacMillan 1985.

Croner's Catering, Croner Publication Ltd, 1991.

Davis, B., *Commodities*, Heinemann, 1988.

Davis, B. and Stone, S., *Food and Beverage Management*, Heinemann, 1987.

Dowell, P. and Bailey, A., *The Book of Ingredients*, Michael Joseph

Fearn, D. A., *Food and Beverage Management*, Butterworths, 1985.

Field, D., *Hotel and Catering Law in Britain*, Sweet and Maxwell, 1982.

Fuller, J., *Modern Restaurant Service*, Stanley Thornes, 1983.

Fuller, J. and Kirk, D., *Kitchen Planning and Management*, Butterworth Heinemann, 1991.

Godowski, S., *Microcomputers in the Hotel and Catering Industry*, Heinemann, 1986.

Gullen, H. and Rhodes, G., *Management in the Hotel and Catering Industry*, Batsford Technical, 1983.

Jones, P., *Food Service Operations*, Cassell, 1983.

Jones, P. (Ed.), *Management in Service Industries*, Pitman, 1989.

Kotas, R. and Davis, B. *Food and Beverage Control*, International Textbook Co., 1986.

Kotler, P., *Marketing Management*, Prentice Hall, 1984.

MAFF, *Manual of Nutrition*, HMSO.

MacCarthy, D., *Food Focus*, Food from Britain, 1989.

McDonald, M., *Marketing Plans*, Heinemann, 1985.

McGee, H., *On Food and Cooking*, Allen and Unwin, 1986.

Merrick, P. and Jones, P., *The Management of Catering Operations*, Holt, Rhinehart and Winston, 1986.

Miller, J. E., *Menu Pricing and Strategy*, Van Nostrand Reinhold, 1980.

Montagne, P., *Larouse Gastronomique*, Hamlyn Publishing Group, 1979.

Moore, R., Stone, J. and Tattersall, H., *The Meat Buyer's Guide for Caterers*, International Thomson Publishing Ltd., 1985.

Odgers, P., *Purchasing, Costing and Control*, Stanley Thornes, 1991.

Ryan, D. A., *Business Aspects of Catering*, Pitman, 1989.

Shepherd, J. W., *Marketing Practice in the Hotel and Catering Industry*, Batsford Technical, 1985.

Specifications for the Purchase of Fish, The Sea Fish Industry Authority, 1990.

Sprenger, R. A., *Hygiene for Management*, Highfield Publications, 1988.

Stobart, T., *The Cook's Encyclopaedia*, MacMillan, 1982.

Sumner, J., *Improve Your Marketing Technique*, Northwood Books.

Tannahill, R., *Food in History*, Penguin, 1988.

Index